How to Do *Everything* with Your

Digital Video Camcorder

W9-BAZ-645

How to Do *Everything* with Your Digital Video Camcorder

Dave Johnson
Todd Stauffer
Rick Broida

McGraw-Hill/Osborne

New York Chicago San Francisco Lisbon
London Madrid Mexico City Milan New Delhi
San Juan Seoul Singapore Sydney Toronto

McGraw-Hill/Osborne
2100 Powell Street, 10th Floor
Emeryville, California 94608
U.S.A.

To arrange bulk purchase discounts for sales promotions, premiums, or fund-raisers, please contact **McGraw-Hill**/Osborne at the above address. For information on translations or book distributors outside the U.S.A., please see the International Contact Information page immediately following the index of this book.

How to Do Everything with Your Digital Video Camcorder

1234567890 CUS CUS 019876543

ISBN 0-07-223069-x

Publisher:	Brandon A. Nordin
Vice President &	
Associate Publisher	Scott Rogers
Executive Editor	Jane Brownlow
Acquisitions Editor	Katie Conley
Project Editor	Jenn Tust
Acquisitions Coordinator	Athena Honore
Technical Editor	Gene Hirsch
Copy Editors	Ann Fothergill-Brown
Proofreader	Debby Schryer
Indexer	Debby Schryer
Composition	Anzai! Inc.
Illustrators	Bert Schopf
Series Design	Mickey Galicia
Cover Series Design	Dodie Shoemaker

This book was composed with Corel VENTURA™ Publisher.

Dedication

I dedicate my one-third of this book to everyone
that Rick and Todd exclude in their dedications.
—Dave

I dedicate my portion of this book to Dave's
family. Grant them strength.
—Todd

I dedicate three-fifths of my one-third of this
book to the fine people at Fifth Third Bank, and
the remaining two-fifths to Dave's one-third.
—Rick

About the Authors

Dave Johnson writes about technology from his home in Colorado Springs, Colorado. He's Editor of *Mobility Magazine* and writes a weekly electronic newsletter on digital imaging for *PC World* magazine. In addition, he's the author of nearly three dozen books, including *Robot Invasion: 7 Cool and Easy Robot Projects, How to Do Everything with Your Digital Camera,* and *How to Do Everything with Your Palm Handheld* (the latter with Rick Broida). His short story for early readers, *The Wild Cookie*, has been transformed into an interactive storybook on CD-ROM. In his spare time, Dave photographs wildlife—particularly wolves, tigers, and sharks—and works as a scuba instructor.

Todd Stauffer is the author or co-author of more than thirty books about computing and the Internet including, *Get Creative: Digital Video Ideas* with Nina Parikh and *How to Do Everything with your iMac*, both from Osborne/McGraw-Hill. He's the originator of the How to Do Everything series. Todd is the publisher of numerous web sites and of the *Jackson Free Press*, a news and culture tabloid in Jackson, Miss., where he lives with Donna Ladd, his cat, her cat, and another cat that will have very little to do with the first two.

Rick Broida has written about computers and technology for more than 15 years. A regular contributor to CNET and *Computer Shopper*, he specializes in mobile technology. In 1997, recognizing the unparalleled popularity of the Palm PDA and the need for a printed resource covering the platform, Rick founded *Handheld Computing* (formerly *Tap Magazine*). He currently serves as editor of that magazine, which now covers all handheld platforms and devices. Rick is the author of *How to Do Everything with Your GPS* and the "Tech Savvy" column for Michigan's *Observer & Eccentric* newspapers. He lives in Michigan with his wife and two children.

Contents at a Glance

Contents

Acknowledgments

Thanks to all the great folks at Osborne who are always fun to work with—especially folks like Jane Brownlow, Katie Conley, Jenn Tust, and editor-extraordinaire Ann Fothergill-Brown. If it weren't for all of you, then we, the authors, would have had to seriously "wing it" through tons of stuff that we're not qualified to do. Heck, we don't even have the phone number for the guy at the printer, so the book may never have even gotten done. So, we thank you.

We'd also like to thank our respective friends, families, caseworkers, parole officers, and therapists for having the patience to see us through yet another book. They all have names, but they know them, and that's what's important. Particularly when you're trying to cash a check.

Introduction

Welcome to *How to Do Everything with Your Digital Video Camcorder*. This is not your typical book on digital video—we wrote it to answer all the questions we had about digital video when we were first starting out. Between the three of us, we have a few decades of experience with digital video, and all that knowledge was leaking out all over the floor, making a mess. It was time to get it into a book before we had to shampoo the carpets yet again.

With that vaguely disturbing imagery over with, let us add that we know what it feels like to have a new digital video camcorder and to search fruitlessly for answers to seemingly obvious questions. We've read books that make passing references to "control your depth of field" without explaining what either the aperture or depth of field actually is. Or mention that you need B-roll footage in the alternate video track without really ever saying what B roll is. Some sort of breakfast treat?

So we mapped out all of the things you might need to know. We start right at the beginning and cover the basics of handling your camcorder. We also explain how to prepare your PC or Mac for video. And we go into detail about getting all that footage onto your computer for editing. Speaking of which, you'll find Mac and PC coverage throughout this book, because the world is neither just Windows nor just Mac OS. We cover it all.

Keep in mind that we wrote this book so that you could sit down and read it through like a novel if you want to—but we realize few people will actually do that. If you're looking for specific information, we've organized the book so topics should be easy to find. The book follows the flow of video production: specific chapters on working with audio, titles, and still images follow the chapters on basic video editing, and DVD and videotape production at the very end of the book.

As you read, these special elements will help you to get the most out of the book:

- **How To** These special boxes explain, in a nutshell, how to accomplish key tasks throughout the book. You can read the How To box for a summary of what the chapter at-large is explaining.

- **Notes** The extra information provided in the notes is handy for digital video trivia contests (you know you want to have one) but isn't essential to understanding the current topic.

- **Tips** These tell you how to do something in a better, faster, or smarter way.

- **Sidebars** These talk about related topics that are pretty darned interesting, but that you can skip if you prefer.

Within the text, you'll also find specially formatted words. New terms are in italics, and specific phrases that you will see on the screen or need to type yourself appear in bold.

Want to contact us? You can send PC-related questions and comments to Dave or Rick:

dvquestions@bydavejohnson.com
rickbroidal@excite.com

Send your Mac-specific questions and comments to Todd:
questions@mac-upgrade.com

Can't get enough of us? You can stay in touch with Dave through his free weekly e-mail newsletter about digital photography and digital video for *PC World* magazine. You can subscribe to *Digital Focus* by visiting pcworld.com and clicking on the newsletters link. Rick and Todd are too classy to include such shameless plugs for their own endeavors, which include *Handheld Computing* and the *Jackson Free Press*, respectively.

Thanks, and enjoy reading the book!

Part I

Introduction to Digital Video

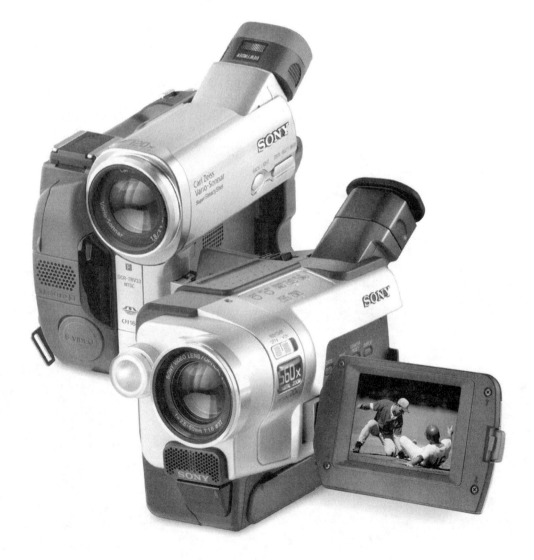

Chapter 1

Getting Started in Digital Video

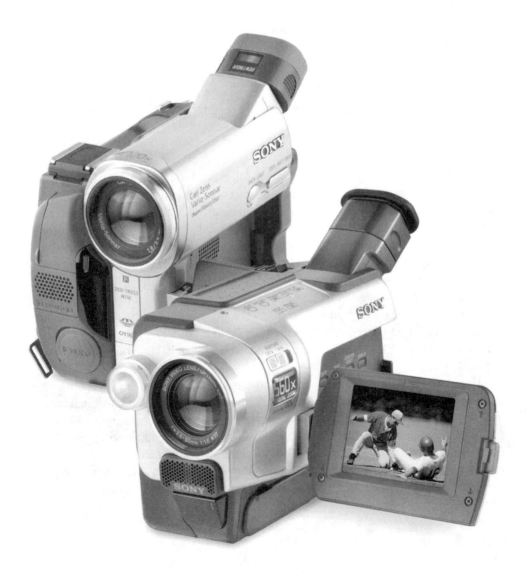

How to...

- Identify your digital video goals
- Do cool things with digital video
- Understand the video production process
- Shop for a digital camcorder
- Identify the most important camcorder features
- Decide on a video format
- Choose the right video editing software for PC
- Choose the right video editing software for Macintosh
- Make sense of video file formats

Admit it. Every year at Oscar time, you indulge in a little fantasy. You hear your name in the list of nominees for best director—or perhaps best screenplay. You see the glitterati leap to their feet when you're announced as the winner. You picture yourself cartwheeling to the podium, grasping that gold statue, and planting a big wet one on Halle Berry (or Brad Pitt, if you prefer). The next day, offers pour in from all the big studios. Tom Hanks wants to do lunch. Someone leaves a big bag of cash outside your hotel room door.

And to think: It all started with your camcorder.

Whether you aspire to produce Academy Award–winning documentaries, shoot a commercial for your car dealership, capture the kids for all eternity, or just whittle your Hawaiian-vacation video into something watchable, you've come to the right book.

Thanks to the advent of affordable digital camcorders and amazingly capable desktop video editing software, you can perform remarkable feats of moviemaking. You don't need a *Titanic*-sized budget, a degree in film production, or even a lot of technical know-how. You just need a decent camcorder, a reasonably powerful computer, the right software, and this book. Assuming that you already own this book and that you're not just standing around Barnes & Noble trying to decide if it's worth the money (it is, trust us), you're already one-quarter of the way there.

What Is Digital Video?

First things first. Let's talk about digital video: what it is, what you can do with it, and why all the fuss. Boiled down to basics, we're talking about video that you shoot with a digital camcorder—a device that records images and audio as a series of numbers rather than as magnetic patterns. A traditional film camera exposes twenty-four frames of film per second, the result of which is essentially a series of still photographs captured quickly enough that they pass for moving images. A traditional video camera, or camcorder, dispenses with film in favor of magnetic tape, and combines a *charge-coupled device* (CCD)—the electronic sensor that captures images—with the equivalent of a tiny VCR. It also records at thirty frames per second, because that's the standard for television viewing.

Digital camcorders are more remarkable still, because they convert images and audio into bits of data: 0's and 1's. Those 0's and 1's can easily be copied to a computer for editing and other purposes, without the loss of quality that occurs when analog tape is copied. Perhaps you've heard people talk about "second-generation" or "third-generation" copies of a tape. Those terms refer to copies of copies. Every time you copy an analog tape to another analog tape, you lose detail. Not so with digital media, because your video is just raw data—0s and 1s—and so there's no quality or clarity or fidelity to lose.

As a result, the material that winds up on your PC or Macintosh looks as pristine as it did when you captured it. And that, in a nutshell, is the power of digital camcorders. (They also record at a higher resolution than analog camcorders do, resulting in sharper-looking images…but that's another discussion entirely.)

When you edit your video on a PC, and then output the finished product to a computer file, blank DVD, or even another tape, you're still dealing with the same perfect data—no quality is lost in the transfer. That, in a nutshell, is the power of digital video.

If the Data Is Digital, Why Are There Tapes?

If a digital camcorder records information as 0's and 1's, why does it still rely on tapes? Why can't you just insert one of those little memory cards, the same kind used in digital cameras and MP3 players? In a word: volume. Not volume as in audio level, but volume as in the amount of data that needs to be recorded. Digital video requires a lot of storage space. Just a few minutes' worth can burn through even a high-capacity memory card. Tape may be annoyingly analog—you still have to rewind and fast-forward it, an affront to the digital age—but you can store upwards of ninety minutes of video on a single cassette. Plus, it's cheap.

That said, the digital camcorders of the future will likely record directly to a CD or DVD (some models already do), which you can then pop into your home player for instant viewing or into your computer for easy copying. Why not record to a built-in hard drive? Because then you'd have a fixed amount of storage space and no way to swap in another hard drive when the first one filled.

NOTE *If you already own an analog camcorder, don't despair. You can still transfer video to your PC or Mac for editing and enjoy good results. See Chapter 4 for more information. That said, we didn't call this book How to Do Everything with Your Analog Camcorder. If you want to capture the best video possible, digital is the way to go.*

Cool Things to Do with Digital Video

Armed with a digital camcorder and desktop video editing software, you might be wondering exactly what you can accomplish. Truth be told, the sky's the limit. You probably have some specific goals in mind, such as recording the kids' school play, but with a little time and creativity you can do a lot more. Some examples:

- Create a music video starring yourself, the kids, or the whole family.

- Gather footage of the baby and assemble it into a memorable montage of his or her first year.

- Record a friend's wedding, then deliver an edited mini-movie as a gift.

- Celebrate someone's important birthday or anniversary by interviewing friends and family for a faux documentary.

- Trim your vacation video from a four-hour snoozefest to a fifteen-minute adventure.

- Record a spoof of your favorite movie, television show, or commercial.

- Make a promotional video for your business or special interest group.

- Produce an actual television commercial for your business.

- Create a documentary about a subject that interests you, then sell it for big bucks.

The Cool Tools at Your Disposal

Part of identifying your digital video (hereafter known as *DV*) goals is recognizing the tools that you have at your disposal. We're not talking about slapping together a few disparate video clips and calling it a movie. Digital camcorders and desktop editing software offer a surprising wealth of functions for both the budding filmmaker and the everyday video enthusiast who wants to do it better—functions that, when used properly, can produce high-caliber, professional-looking results. For instance, you can

- Present video in black-and-white—even if it was shot in color.

- Add slow- and fast-motion effects.

- Incorporate Hollywood-quality transitions between scenes.

- Add sound effects and soundtracks.

- Edit scenes down to the millisecond.

- Add film-style letterboxes to your video.

- Shoot at night or in total darkness.

In other words, you're going to have some amazing tools at your disposal. In the pages and chapters to come, we'll show you not only when and how to work with those tools, but also how to use them in creative and effective ways.

Video Production from A to Z

On the face of it, video production is a fairly straightforward process. You shoot your movies, transfer the material to your computer, edit the parts into a cohesive package, and output a finished product. Of course, when you break those four steps down and look at what's involved in each one, things get a little more complicated. Let's take a closer look.

- **Shooting Your Movies** Shooting movies sounds simple enough—just point the camera and start recording—but obviously there's a bit more to it. For starters, there's the small matter of the camcorder. If you're in the market for one, check out "Shopping for a Camcorder" later in this chapter. Then there's knowing what to do with it. For that you'll need Chapter 3, which covers topics such as storyboards, shot composition, lighting, and other crucial aspects of successful videomaking.

- **Transferring the Material** Once you've got the raw footage in your camera, you need to copy it to your PC or Mac for editing. Chapter 4 reveals everything you need to know about that, including specifying video quality and managing the space on your hard disk (which can get used up in a hurry, believe us).

- **Editing the Movie** If shooting the movie is fifty percent of the process, editing the movie is definitely the other fifty percent. Editing (known in the biz as *post-production*) involves more than just splicing clips together. (Actually, "splicing" is a film term—you're not actually going to be cutting and taping together pieces of film. You'll be pointing and clicking with a mouse.) Chapters 5 and 6 delve into the nitty-gritty of video editing (on a PC and Mac, respectively): everything from adding scenes from outside sources to figuring out which transitions to use. (Hint: Just because you can make a frame explode like fireworks doesn't mean you should.) Chapters 7, 8, 9, and 10 focus on other aspects of the production process, including sound and titles. That stuff can be time-consuming, but it's also the fun part.

- **Creating a Finished Product** Now that your movie is made, what are you going to do with it? Copy it to a VHS tape? Burn it to a CD or DVD? Share it on the Web? Chapters 12 and 13 give you the full scoop on moving your masterpiece from your PC or Mac to...wherever!

Did you know?

Steven Soderbergh Shot an Entire Movie on a Digital Camcorder

Steven Soderbergh is one of Rick's favorite directors, having produced such movie gems as *Out of Sight* and *Erin Brockovich*. The man is a true filmmaker—which makes all the more intriguing his decision to use a digital camcorder to shoot *Full Frontal* in 2002. Specifically, Soderbergh used a Canon XL1S, a decidedly high-end model (it sells for around $4,000), but certainly far less expensive than a film camera (and the film to go with it). The editing of *Full Frontal* was particularly inexpensive, as it was handled on Power Mac G4 systems running Final Cut Pro software.

The moral of the story? If you think you can't make a Hollywood-caliber movie with a digital camcorder and desktop computer, think again. And *Full Frontal*, though hardly first-rate cinema, is like a complete course in shoestring filmmaking.

Shopping for a Camcorder

If you think it's tough choosing a desktop computer, digital camera, or PDA, just wait till you try to pick a digital camcorder. At last count, there were roughly six trillion different models (five trillion of them from Sony), each packed with a dizzying array of features. We pity the uneducated consumer who strolls into a Best Buy or clicks into the Amazon.com Electronics section, because settling on a model will seem downright impossible.

TIP   *If you visit your local newsstand, you can probably have your pick of half a dozen magazines offering camcorder buying guides. Those are good resources. We also recommend perusing the user-supplied ratings for specific models at sites such as Amazon.com and Epinions.com, which provide information and opinions from real-world users.*

Fortunately, it's not impossible to choose the right camcorder, once you know what to look for. Obviously your budget is going to be a key factor. If you have just $400 or so to work with, that's going to limit your choices much more than, say, an $800 budget. But you should also consider your motivation for buying the camcorder. Do you want it primarily for shooting around the house (kids, parties, and so on) and capturing vacation memories? Is it something that you need for business purposes? Are you thinking seriously about making movies or documentaries? Certainly, camcorders that can be used for all of those tasks are available, but identifying your goals in advance can help save you time and money when you're ready to plunk down the plastic.

NOTE   *For the purposes of this book, we're focusing primarily on consumer camcorders: those priced under $1,500. You can spend thousands for a so-called prosumer model, which you may want to consider if you have serious videomaking aspirations. But we think that most users will be satisfied with camcorders in the $400 to $1,000 range.*

What We Bought: The Authors' Camcorder Picks

Totally by accident, this book's three authors represent the full spectrum of camcorder buyers. Rick owns an entry-level model; Dave, a mid-range model; and Todd, a "prosumer" model. We thought it would be helpful to describe what we bought, why we bought it, and what we think of it.

Rick   I bought my JVC GR-DVF21 in late 1999, just a month before my daughter was born. She was my sole reason for purchasing it, and my sole use for it for the next year or two. The MiniDV format was relatively new at that time, and the GR-DVF21 was one of the least-expensive MiniDV camcorders I could find. I'm happy to report that it has been an ideal camera for family moviemaking, although it lacks two features I wish it had: image stabilization and a microphone input. The latter would allow me to plug in a wireless microphone for the faux documentaries I've been making lately. Audio is half the battle in successful videomaking (lighting is the other half), and so I'm going to make sure that my next camcorder has superior sound features.

Dave   I've been through many camcorders over the years. My dream model would be something like the Canon XL1, with three independent CCDs, great optical image stabilization, and professional-caliber design. But it's too big for my main application—underwater video while scuba diving. Consequently, I chose my current model, the Sony DCR-PC110, for its small size and ability to fit into the Light & Motion Mako underwater housing. I use it above water as well, and overall I'm thrilled with its performance and small size. My next purchase? I'm thinking about getting a high definition television

(HDTV) camcorder. The first consumer-priced models were just starting to arrive on store shelves as we wrote this chapter.

Todd   I bought the Canon GL1 in late 2000, thanks to its reputation as an affordable three-chip camcorder that could be used in a professional setting. While I would have loved a Canon XL1, which is Canon's high-end, professional MiniDV camcorder, the GL1 offered the same image quality without some of the pricey features such as interchangeable lenses and built-in XLR audio inputs. Still, the GL1 can be used "in the field" for professional-level DV filming, including documentary- and film-festival-quality work, with the added advantage that it's unobtrusive enough so that people who are being filmed with the GL1 don't feel as if they're "on television" the way they do when they're filmed with higher-end professional camcorders. The result is sometimes a more relaxed interviewee. The GL1 is respected enough in the industry that you can buy impressive sound-gathering, image-filtering, and other accessories for it. In fact, my GL1 has done more video work than I have, because I occasionally rent it out to film crews and small productions that don't have enough in-house equipment!

What to Look For in a Camcorder

Ready to shop? No you're not. You need information first, credit card second. In the subsections that follow, we've spotlighted certain features we think are important to consider—or at least to understand. You're about to make a fairly sizable investment, and so it pays to do some research. You don't want to discover after the fact that you've bought the wrong camcorder for your needs.

Batteries

Batteries play a huge role in the effectiveness and enjoyment of a digital camcorder, but few buyers take the time to do the necessary battery homework. That means pricing (and perhaps buying, upfront) spare batteries, and paying close attention to how the camcorder charges them. Ideally, your new camcorder will come with an external charger so that you can keep one battery charging while the other is in use. Without an external charger, you have to charge the battery while it's in the camcorder—not exactly convenient.

> TIP   *You can extend battery life considerably by closing the LCD window and using the viewfinder (if the camcorder has one)—especially if the camcorder is on a tripod, and you plan to just leave it running.*

Digital Camera Capability

One of the hot new trends in digital camcorders is, ironically, still photography. Many models now offer the option to snap digital photos, so you don't have to carry both a camera and a camcorder when you travel. For the moment, however, this feature requires compromise. Camcorder optics—lens, image sensor, and so on—are different from those of digital cameras, and so photo quality won't be quite as good. What's more, resolution tends to be fairly limited—no more than one megapixel in most models.

> TIP   *Even low-resolution photos snapped by a camcorder can be an asset, so long as they're intended for use in your movies, not for prints. Pictures that don't look that great when printed will probably still look fine on a television screen, which is relatively low-res anyway.*

The good news is that progress is being made in this convergence of camera and camcorder. At press time, Sony was on the verge of shipping the DCR-PC330, a MiniDV model that can capture three-megapixel stills.

Most camcorders with digital-camera capability rely on removable flash-memory cards to store photos, just as standalone cameras do. If you already own a camera, PDA, or MP3 player that uses a certain variety of memory card (such as CompactFlash, Memory Stick, or Secure Digital), it makes sense to choose a camcorder that uses the same flavor. That way, you get more bang for the buck from the cards you buy.

On the other hand, memory cards are so ridiculously cheap these days that it's silly to slant your buying decision largely toward trying to double-use a $40 memory card. If you come down to two pretty evenly matched camcorders, and one of them uses the same kind of storage as your existing MP3 player, you know what to do. Otherwise, choose the camcorder based on features, capabilities, and ease of use—and simply buy an extra memory card if the "right" camcorder ends up using some format you don't already own.

Digital Effects

Many camcorders include special-effects modes that can spruce up or improve your movies. One of the most popular is night-shot mode, which enables you to shoot when little ambient light is available. Other common effects include black-and-white recording, sepia mode (which adds an antique, brownish-looking tint to the images), and fades.

Some camcorders even allow you to do rudimentary titling, allowing you to overlay text such as "Sarah's 3rd Birthday." However, we don't place much value on this feature, because your desktop editing software will offer a far greater variety of titling options—with better-looking results, too.

Indeed, many of the special effects built into digital camcorders are better left alone, because you can accomplish much more in the post-production process. The one exception is night-shot mode. You should definitely look for a camcorder that offers this feature if you expect to shoot in low light settings.

Image Stabilization

If there's one feature you should insist on, it's image stabilization. Through no minor feat of digital magic, stabilization helps to compensate for the inevitable shakiness and movement that occur when a camcorder isn't on a tripod. Of course, there may be times when you *want* shakiness and movement, in which case you can just switch image stabilization off. Fortunately, this feature can be found even in lower-end camcorders.

One important distinction: Better digital camcorders come with a feature called *optical image stabilization,* and that's always far superior to the *digital image stabilization* found in most consumer-priced digital camcorders. If you have a choice, go optical. Not only is the image stabilization more effective, the image itself remains sharp and clear. Digital image stabilization may soften the image in its attempt to reduce camera shake.

Megapixels Demystified

What does this talk about megapixels mean?

A megapixel is a million pixels. (Imagine a picture made up of a grid of 1000 horizontal pixels by 1000 vertical pixels.) The more, the merrier. If your camera can capture three-megapixel images, you can safely make 8×10-inch prints with the images it captures. The image from a one-megapixel camera, on the other hand, would be a blurry mess at any print size larger than about three inches across.

Microphone Input

All camcorders have built-in microphones, which are fine for shooting in close quarters or where audio isn't a major concern. However, if your project requires top-notch audio, you'll want the option of plugging in a microphone, be it one that clips to your subject's lapel or something like a shotgun microphone for minimizing noise from your surroundings.

> **TIP**   *A headphone jack is another major perk, because you can use it to monitor the audio that's being recorded, preventing surprises later.*

Size and Style

Saying that digital camcorders come in all shapes and sizes is like saying that Dave has weird taste in music. Some camcorders are big, some are small. Some are shaped vertically (they're taller than they are wide), some are horizontal. Some models qualify as compact, others as ultra-compact.

Size is obviously something of a personal issue. If you travel a lot and want the smallest possible camcorder—one that fits easily into a carry-on bag, or even a pocket or a purse—you'll want an ultra-compact model. The Sony DCR-IP5 is one of the smallest camcorders on the planet: it measures just four inches high by two inches wide, and weighs a mere eleven ounces. But some compromises are associated with getting that small, as you'll learn in "Video Format," next.

Video Format

Video format is perhaps the most crucial decision you'll make in choosing a camcorder—but it's also an easy one. Format refers to the type of media used for storing video. In most cases, "storage" means one of a few different varieties of tape, but you might also want to consider optical media. Let's take a look at the "Big Four" of camcorder video formats:

- ■ **Digital8**   Although Digital8 is, natch, a digital format, it has the advantage of being backward-compatible with 8 mm and Hi8 tapes, which were used in many analog camcorders. If you have a significant tape collection in those formats and want to be able to view those tapes on your new camcorder (or copy them more easily to your PC), consider a Digital8 model. Otherwise, steer clear. Digital8 camcorders tend to be bulky as compared with the latest MiniDV models.

- ■ **MiniDV**   MiniDV is the current DV champ, because it's the most popular and versatile digital format. Unless you have a specific reason for choosing something else—say, the backward-compatibility of Digital8 or the ultra-compact nature of MicroMV—MiniDV is the way to go.

- ■ **MicroMV**   MicroMV is a proprietary video format used exclusively in Sony camcorders. MicroMV tapes have the advantage of being about seventy percent smaller than MiniDV tapes, which is how Sony can engineer such teeny camcorders as the DCR-IP5. However, you have to consider an important limitation: software compatibility. Unlike other formats, MicroMV uses MPEG-2 for recording compression, and many desktop video editing programs don't support MPEG-2. Fortunately, Pinnacle Studio, the Windows program that this book focuses on, does include support for MicroMV. (At the time of writing, no Mac applications were compatible with MicroMV, and so the format isn't recommended for Mac users.)

■ **DVD**   For many videomakers, DVD is the end goal for their productions, so why not record directly to it in the first place? A handful of camcorders now do exactly that, allowing you to pop discs out of your camcorder and into your home DVD player. However, Dave has tried several of the first-generation DVD camcorders, and his opinion of them is not good. They're bulky, they offer limited recording time on each three-inch disc (less than an hour in high-quality mode), and they pose issues similar to those encountered with MicroMV when it comes to editing video on a computer. DVD camcorders may improve with time, but for now we highly recommend sticking with MiniDV.

Zoom

Finally, we come to zoom, a feature that camcorder manufacturers love to crow about. You'll see specs that tout, say, a 10× optical zoom and *120× digital zoom!* Before you get too excited, make sure that you understand the difference between the two. As in digital cameras, "optical zoom" refers to the magnification capabilities of the lens—and that's the only spec that really matters. Digital zoom simply enlarges the center pixels of the image, the result of which is usually very grainy video. Considering a camcorder's optical zoom capabilities in your purchase decision is definitely good, but the rule of thumb here is the same as for photography: the best zooming is done with your feet.

Choosing the Right DV Software

Many DV camcorders come bundled with video editing software, as do some computers. Heck, Windows XP includes Windows Movie Maker 2, and most new Macs come with iMovie 3—one of the key Mac programs on which this book focuses.

Dozens of video editing packages are available for both platforms, each with different features, learning curves, and price tags. For PC users, we think that the winning product is Pinnacle Studio 8 (see Figure 1-1), which offers a wealth of advanced features, a very easy interface, and a list price of just $99.99. That's the Windows program that is the focus of our chapters about editing, titling, and so on. That said, many of the concepts and techniques that we teach are applicable to any video editing software. If you plan to choose another product or you want to stick with something else that you already have, feel free.

FIGURE 1-1   Pinnacle Studio 8 is the undisputed champ among Windows video editing programs. We highly recommend it for all amateur videomakers.

TIP   *Don't pay list price for Studio 8. After visiting the price-comparison site PriceGrabber.com, we found the software selling for as little as $53 online (not including shipping). That's an amazingly good deal for this program.*

Mac users can take either of two really different approaches, depending on needs and interest. (And, although the two products may offer different sides of the video editing coin, both products are from Apple itself.) iMovie 3 (see Figure 1-2), which comes with all new Macs, is a wonderful application for home and small-business use. It's easy to grasp and as fully featured as you could possibly expect (and then some), including some great titles, scene transitions, special effects, and a few tools to deal with audio and music. iMovie is also integrated very closely with Apple's iDVD software, which can be used to create and burn DVD movies if your Mac is equipped to handle that.

FIGURE 1-2   iMovie 3 comes bundled with new Macintosh systems and offers a wide range of editing tools for home-movie makers.

For "prosumer" users, Apple offers Final Cut Express, which approaches the high end, but is still reasonably affordable. (List price is $299. You *can* get it cheaper. At the time of writing, it was $99 with the purchase of a Mac or trade-in of a competitive program.) Final Cut Express is powerful enough for editing a documentary, a business sales video, or even a film-festival submission. It's not quite as easy to use as iMovie, but its power resembles that of software costing a great deal more, particularly in how it works with multiple tracks of video and audio. It also works well with iDVD from Apple (or its professional-level cousin, DVD Pro), and other Apple offerings such as the SoundTrack music editor. iMovie and Final Cut are both covered in the Mac-specific editing sections; but, again, the lessons are applicable to pretty much any editing suite.

Video File Formats and Codecs

1

While we're on the subject of digital video files, it's worth pointing out that there isn't just one video file format used by everyone from Moscow to Miami. If there were just one, we'd all live simpler, more stress-free lives—and software developers can't have that, can they?

In fact, there are a handful of common video file formats you should know about:

- ■ **AVI**   The AVI (short for Audio Video Interleaved) format is one of the most common formats on the PC. DV movies intended for transfer to DVD are typically stored in AVI files. But knowing that a file is in the AVI format doesn't tell the whole story. AVI is nothing but a file "container," holding video that has been compressed with a codec. And what's a codec? Good question. It stands for compressor/decompressor, and it's the actual data translator that is responsible for displaying a video. AVI files can be encoded by any of several different codecs, and so if a video is not playing properly on your PC, it's probably because you don't have the right codec installed on your computer.

- ■ **ASF**   The Active Streaming Format was designed by Microsoft back in the heyday of the Internet, and it's primarily designed for Web-based movies that stream to your PC. You will probably never need this format in real life.

- ■ **DivX**   The fairly new DivX format is a codec that plays inside an AVI file. DivX files are common on the Internet, being that DivX seems to be the format of choice for folks who swap video (television shows and movies, for example). Windows doesn't come with a DivX decoder, and so you have to get one yourself if you plan to watch content made with this format. Just visit www.divx.com.

- ■ **MPEG**   Now we're talking. The MPEG format (which is named for the standards body that designed it, the Moving Picture Experts Group) is one of the oldest compressed video formats in the business. The MPEG format is commonly used on the Internet and in PC-based videos, but its resolution is pretty low. MPEG has been superseded in many applications by MPEG-2, which offers dramatically better quality. DVDs and digital camcorders both use MPEG-2 compression, as do satellite television and personal video recorders like TiVo. MPEG-2 is one of the most common formats around.

Is It Time for HDTV?

Now that a sizable number of people have high definition television (HDTV) sets in their living rooms, and cable and satellite companies are offering HDTV programming during primetime hours, you might be wondering if it isn't time to start recording in HDTV. After all, you can buy a consumer-priced HDTV camcorder from JVC for well under $2,000—which is about what Dave spent on his first lousy S-VHS camcorder a decade ago!

Here's our take: It's still waaaay too early to think about getting an HDTV camcorder. Sure, shooting video in HDTV is cool, but what do you do with your raw footage when you're done? None of the currently available consumer video editing packages for the PC or Mac allow you to transfer and edit high-def video. And even if there were a program that would let you create a cohesive film from your raw video, how would you show it off? You'd have to store the video on a camcorder tape, because DVDs and other common playback systems can't handle HDTV yet either. So, the smart money says to wait another two or three years before plunking down money on an HDTV camcorder.

- ■ **QuickTime** Apple's video format of choice, QuickTime, uses the MOV file extension and is utterly ubiquitous on Macs. It's pretty common on PCs as well, given that a lot of Web-based content is provided in QuickTime format.

- ■ **RealVideo** RealVideo is a proprietary format owned by RealNetworks and used in such video software as RealOne. RealVideo is a good streaming video format, but one that is not nearly as popular as it was three or four years ago.

- ■ **SVCD and VCD** The Super VideoCD and VideoCD formats come to us straight from Asia, where people routinely bootleg movies and pack them onto CDs. In both of these formats, the quality is utterly abysmal: something between what you get from a bad VCR and watching a movie reflected off the back of a really shiny quarter. While some people may appreciate watching *Die Hard* that way, we suggest that you pass. The advantage of these formats is that you can make CDs that play like DVDs in some DVD players. But, as we said, the quality is bad. And not all DVD players support these formats.

■ **WMV**   The Windows Media Video format is a highly compressed video format designed by Microsoft to play movies in the Windows Media Player. WMV is actually a pretty good file format for any video intended for the Web, your PC, or download to a Pocket PC.

Where to Find It

Web site	Address	What's there
Apple Computer	www.apple.com	iMovie, Final Cut Express
DivX	www.divx.com	DivX codec
Pinnacle Systems	www.pinnaclesys.com	Pinnacle Studio 8
Sony Corporation	www.sonystyle.com	Sony DCR-IP5 and other camcorders

Chapter 2

Preparing Your PC or Macintosh for Digital Video

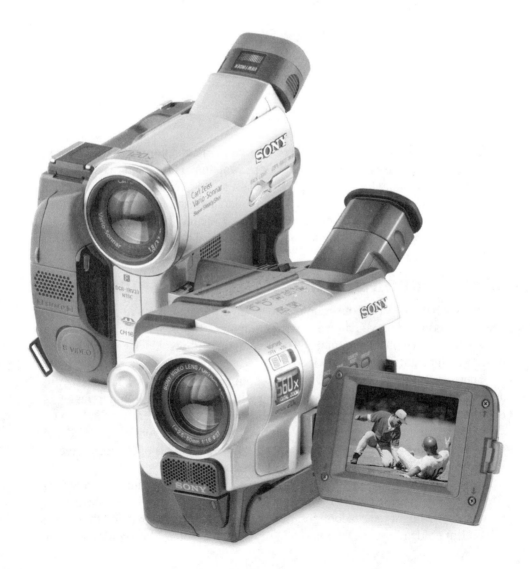

How to...

- Make sure your computer is powerful enough for DV

- Meet the minimum requirements for DV software

- Decide if you should upgrade the processor and memory

- Determine how much hard disk space you'll need

- Make sure you're equipped with FireWire ports

- Add inputs for analog video sources

- Choose a DVD burner

- Decide between PC and Macintosh systems

DV production revolves around three core components: your digital camcorder, your editing software, and your desktop computer. This chapter is all about the computer: the kind that you need, how fast it should be, how you can upgrade your machine to better accommodate digital video, and so on. We also tackle the always sticky question of PC versus Macintosh, while looking at various off-the-shelf and mail-order systems that are ideally suited to DV.

The Key Components of a DV-Ready Computer

We know what they say about people who assume things, but we're going to go ahead and assume that you already own a computer. (If not, skip ahead to "What to Look For in a New DV Computer.") The pivotal question is: Does your computer have "the right stuff" for digital video?

There are two definitions of DV-ready computer equipment: what we tell you, and what the makers of the editing software will tell you. We're going to make recommendations, based on experience, for the kind of equipment we think you should have for enjoyable desktop DV production. However, you can also fall back on the minimum system requirements specified by the makers of Pinnacle Studio 8 for Windows and iMovie 3 and Final Cut Express for Macintosh.

Here's a perfect example: Pinnacle Studio 8 requires a minimum of a 500 MHz AMD or Intel processor and 128MB of RAM. If your computer is four or five years old, you might have a configuration that's pretty close to that and think, "Cool, I'm golden!" Let us be blunt: Not only are you not golden, you're not even among the precious metals. Studio 8 will run on a system like that, but the phrase "molasses in winter" comes to mind.

Similarly, the software requires just 300MB of hard disk space for installation, but that's a speck of a drop in the bucket compared to what you'll need for actual video editing.

With so many different computer makes and configurations out there, we can't make a blanket statement like "If your system was purchased prior to 2001, you're probably going to need some upgrades—or an entirely new system." However, with that caveat in mind, if your system was purchased prior to 2001, you're probably going to need some upgrades—or an entirely new system.

> NOTE *There's a law of diminishing returns when it comes to upgrades. If your system is more than a couple of years old, it probably makes more sense to replace it entirely than to buy piecemeal component upgrades. That's because even something seemingly as simple as a new processor will have a cascading effect, requiring a new motherboard, RAM modules, and other upgrades to go along with it.*

Let's take a look at some of the key components of a DV-ready system and why they're important. In the subsections that follow, we're also going to give you the minimum system requirements for Pinnacle Studio 8, iMovie 3, and Final Cut Express, as well as tell you what your upgrade options are and whether they're worth pursuing.

> NOTE *Even though iMovie 3 comes with the latest Mac systems, we'll cover its requirements because users of older Macs can buy iMovie as part of the iLife bundle (www.apple.com/ilife/).*

Processor and Memory

You've probably heard the expression: "You can never be too rich or too thin." Where DV is concerned, your computer can never have too much processing power or too much memory. (By "memory" we mean RAM, not storage space. We'll get to hard drives in a minute.) The bare process of transferring video from your camcorder to your computer requires a fairly fast system, and more memory will come into play when you're adding special effects and rendering the final movie.

We should point out that where desktop computers are concerned, "speed" is a somewhat arbitrary and relative term. Ideally, whatever you're doing on a computer, be it editing DV or viewing web pages, you want it to happen as quickly as possible. The speed of the processor is not the sole determinant of how quickly a computer runs, but it is a key one.

So is RAM. DV editing is a hard drive–intensive task, and the more RAM your computer has, the less time it will have to spend accessing the hard drive—a process that slows things down considerably.

All that being said, speed may not be that important to you—at least, not so important that you're willing to spend big bucks on upgrades or a new computer. If you're just not sure whether your computer has the horsepower to do DV effectively, there's no harm in taking a wait-and-see approach. In other words, don't run out to the computer store and drop $2,000 just because we tell you to. See how your computer fares with the software. If it's too slow for your liking, *then* start thinking about new gear.

Pinnacle Studio 8

- **Minimum Requirements**   A 500 MHz Pentium or Athlon processor and 128MB of RAM.

- **Our Minimum Recommendations**   An Athlon XP or Pentium 4 processor and 512MB of RAM.

- **Upgrade Options**   It's fairly easy (and relatively inexpensive) to add more RAM to a PC, but a processor upgrade usually requires a new motherboard—and possibly new RAM modules as well. Unless you're what we like to call a gearhead (or "Dave"), you're probably better off buying a new system than trying to perform a processor upgrade.

Final Cut Express

- **Minimum Requirements**   A 300 MHz PowerPC G3 processor and 256MB of RAM.

- **Our Minimum Recommendations**   An 800 MHz G3 or a 667 MHz G4 (or faster) processor and 512MB of RAM.

- **Upgrade Options**   Again, adding RAM is a cakewalk. For some Mac models, adding a processor upgrade is pretty easy, too—particularly the mini-tower-style Power Macintosh series.

iMovie 3

- **Minimum Requirements**   Any PowerPC processor and 256MB of RAM.

- **Our Minimum Recommendations**   A PowerPC G3/500 or faster and 512MB of RAM.

■ **Upgrade Options**   Same as for Final Cut Express: If your Mac came with iMovie 3, you don't need to do any upgrading, and any Mac that has a built-in FireWire port will run iMovie 3. That said, more RAM and a processor upgrade will speed up iMovie considerably.

What Mac Model Is Best for DV?

For a number of years now, Apple has worked to make digital video editing a consumer pursuit, and Macs have been built with FireWire ports and have included iMovie. So, as you might imagine, nearly any Mac model on the market today is a great choice for editing video, particularly home and small-business videos that you've created using your DV camcorder. There is, however, a pecking order among Mac models.

■ **Power Mac**   The Power Macintosh G4 and G5 are far and away the best Mac models in terms of pure speed and functionality. (Even a Power Macintosh G3 can be a good choice.) These models support the most RAM, can accept additional internal hard drive, and offer the fastest processors and subsystems for dealing with the hard work of video editing and special-effects rendering. They are particularly well-suited for the high-end editing in Final Cut Express and Final Cut Pro.

■ **PowerBook**   Next comes the PowerBook G4 notebook, which, again, tends to offer a high-speed processor, a larger hard drive, and support for a lot of RAM. Many professional video editors swear by their PowerBook G4s, which enable them to edit video "in the field" using the same tool—Final Cut—that they would use in an editing studio. Older PowerBook G3s are not as capable for editing (only the very last models included FireWire ports), but they can be upgraded and so used.

■ **Consumer Macs**   Finally, iMacs, eMacs, and iBooks—Apple's consumer line-up—all offer various advantages for video editing, particularly with iMovie. (Final Cut will run on any of these machines, too.) The iMac G4 models and eMacs are as fast as PowerBook G4s and tend to offer large hard drives and internal DVD writers. They also have the same drawback of limited or no internal space for upgrades. The iBooks and older iMac G3 models bring up the rear speed-wise (as of this writing they're still based on PowerPC G3 processors—albeit fast ones), and they may have smaller hard drives and limited RAM. Still, the latest iBooks are very solid for iMovie editing, with some models offering a "SuperDrive" DVD burner just as their more powerful siblings do.

Hard Drive

Have you ever found yourself perusing the computer-store ads in the Sunday paper and thinking, "What in the world would I ever need a 160GB hard drive for?" DV is your answer. Every single application and piece of data on the average computer user's hard drive probably doesn't fill more than 20GB (unless that user likes PC gaming), but the average DV user can burn through that quantity in one sitting. That's because video recorded onto MiniDV tape consumes about 215MB of disk space per *minute*, or about 13GB per hour. That means if you fill one 60-minute MiniDV tape—just a single one, mind you—you'll need 13GB of available hard disk space when you copy the video to your computer for editing.

NOTE   *Just so you're clear on the math, a gigabyte is one thousand megabytes.*

And it doesn't end there. Let's assume you're planning to make a DVD. Not only do you need 13GB for an hour of raw video, but you'll need another 5GB in order to render the finished movie in preparation for DVD. And don't think that if you have 20GB available, you're okay. You're not. If you run the hard disk down to nearly empty while making your movie, the process will probably fail because the computer needs extra hard disk space for all sorts of things, including "scratch" space to write temporary files while the movie is being made.

Bottom line: Try to have about twice as much hard disk space available as you think you'll need to complete a project. And that, we suspect, puts you up into the 80GB range for most projects. Now you can probably see why you might want a 160GB drive.

Pinnacle Studio 8

■ **Minimum Requirement**   For the program itself, 300MB; a drive capable of at least 4MB per second throughput (meaning that the hard drive can read 4MB of data to memory every second—check with the manufacturer to see if your drive meets that spec), and all the space you can spare for video.

■ **Our Minimum Recommendation**   A bare minimum of 60GB, but you'd be better off with 120GB or more. In fact, two 120GB drives would be quite nice.

■ **Upgrade Options**   Hallelujah! Most computers have room to add a second hard drive (an ideal option, because you can use it exclusively to store video), and the drives themselves are surprisingly affordable. After a quick visit to CompUSA.com, we found a 160GB drive selling for just $100 (after a mail-in rebate). As for performance, all new drives are capable of transferring data much faster than 4MB per second.

Final Cut Express and iMovie

- ■ **Minimum Requirement**   For the Final Cut Express installation, 40MB; iMovie 3 takes up about 70GB of disk space.

- ■ **Our Minimum Recommendation**   An internal hard drive that's smaller than about 30GB is nearly impossible to work with for DV (particularly if it's also used with other applications and documents). Although we're aware that some DV-compatible Macs have shipped with much less, if you're in that boat, getting more space—at least 40GB – 60GB—is a good start.

- ■ **Upgrade Options**   If you're using a mini-tower-style Power Macintosh model, you can add internal hard drives. In most cases, any off-the-shelf ATA drive will do, so grab one of those 160GB drives that PC users like Rick drool over. If you have a portable or all-in-one Mac (an iMac, eMac, etc.), then swapping the internal drive is tougher. Instead, look for an external FireWire hard drive of the highest capacity you can afford. (Ideally, the drive should use the "Oxford 911" chipset—check the box or the description for the drive.)

Adding an Extra Hard Drive

Remember how we mentioned that it's often easier to replace your PC than to upgrade components one at a time? One big exception to that rule is file storage space, which is pretty easy to upgrade. Hard drives get cheaper and bigger every year. Last year, 80GB was pretty good, but 160GB drives are now common on store shelves. And the prices continue to fall, making them a really smart buy.

When we talk about a hard drive upgrade, we're not talking about removing your existing hard drive and replacing it with a new one. Sure, you could do that, but it's a big pain in the neck, because you have to install an operating system and transfer all of your personal data. It's far, far easier just to add a second hard drive to your computer and to continue to use your existing drive—just not for video.

To see if your PC is a good candidate for a second hard drive, shut it down and open up the case. Many computers have "tool-free" cases that you can open easily; for other PCs, you'll need a small screwdriver to deal with the screws that fasten it. In either case, once the PC is open, check to see if there's space to mount the hard drive. You can mount it in one of the drive bays or perhaps at the bottom or side of the case, where there are some mounts for exactly that purpose. If there's room available, it's easy to install a hard drive yourself.

TIP   *If you don't want to mess around inside your PC, you can add an external hard drive instead. These days, USB 2.0 and FireWire hard drives are both inexpensive and fast enough for video work. And they install in just minutes by doing nothing more than plugging in a cable. We highly recommend these sorts of external drives, especially if you're skittish about working inside the computer case.*

How to ... **Install a Second Hard Disk Drive**

Once you know that you have a place to put the drive, follow these basic steps:

1. Before proceeding, ensure that the PC is switched off and that you are fully grounded. You can purchase a static grounding mat or a strap that attaches to your wrist at any local computer shop. Alternatively, as long as the computer is still plugged into the wall outlet, you can ground yourself by touching the metal cage surrounding the computer's power supply. If you leave the computer plugged in for grounding purposes, be absolutely sure the computer is switched off before you open it up and start working.

2. Remove the new hard drive from its packaging and review the enclosed instructions.

3. Configure the hard drive, depending on how you are installing it and the sort of PC you own. If your computer is new, it may use Serial ATA (SATA), which is a faster, smarter, more modern way to connect hard drives. You can connect only one hard drive to each SATA cable, which is long and thin. These drives are a snap to attach. If you have an older PC with a traditional wide ATA ribbon cable, you usually need to set a jumper on the hard drive to CS (cable select, usually the third jumper position—but be sure to check the key printed on the drive or the user guide).

4. Use the screws that came with the kit to mount the drive in the PC. Connect the power cable and ATA cable to the hard drive.

5. Without closing the case, switch the computer on. When the PC starts to boot, go to the BIOS screen (often by pressing DELETE or F1 early in the boot sequence). Check to see that the computer recognizes the new hard drive. If it doesn't, make sure that you set the jumper properly, that the drive is connected to the correct IDE channel, and that the power cord for the drive is fully seated.

6. If all is well, shut down the PC, and seal the case.

7. Finally, use the software that came with your hard drive to format the disk and prepare it for operation in Windows.

Installing RAID to Protect Your Videos

There's one problem with using a hard drive to work with video: eventually, all hard drives fail. No matter how new, fancy, or expensive your hard drive is, the day will come when it stops spinning. And when that happens, all of your video will be irrecoverably lost.

Now mind you, that's often not a big deal for video. The video will reside on your computer only for a short time. After you're done editing it, you'll probably move the finished movie to videotape or DVD. But what if your hard drive fails in the middle of a big, time-consuming, important project? You could lose a lot of data and have to restart the editing of your movie from scratch after installing a replacement drive. That's why I am an advocate of using a RAID controller in your digital video editing computer.

What exactly is RAID? RAID stands for Redundant Array of Inexpensive Disks. It is a combination of two or more hard drives, controlled in such a way that they act as one virtual drive. Long used by large businesses, RAID systems have traditionally been too expensive and complicated for "normal folk." That has changed, though, and RAID now offers a way to painlessly and securely back up 100 percent of your data (including digital video) in real time, with absolutely no effort on your part. No more delayed backups, tape rotation schemes, archives, or forgotten data files. In some ways, RAID is the perfect backup solution.

RAID comes in many "flavors," usually called *RAID implementations* or *RAID levels*. Large businesses have about a dozen RAID levels to choose from, each designed for some specific purpose. RAID 6, for instance, delivers "independent data disks with two independent distributed parity schemes." If you actually need that, you'll want to find a good book on RAID—we can't help you. We don't even know what that sentence means.

But more typical users can choose from three handy RAID levels. RAID 0 is called a "striped array." It writes alternating blocks of data across two separate hard drives. The result? In Windows, for instance, two 120GB hard drives appear as a single 240GB hard drive. And because the data is being distributed across multiple channels, data access is much faster than if you had a single, large hard disk drive. The downside, of course, is that if either drive fails, 100 percent of your data is irretrievably lost unless you maintain a separate backup solution. RAID 0 is the most vulnerable way imaginable to store your data. And that's not our goal.

Instead, you want RAID 1. This "mirror array" treats two identical hard drives as a single drive and writes the same data twice, once to each physical drive. There's no performance advantage such as you get with RAID 0, but there's not much of a penalty, either. That comes in stark contrast to the process of mirroring data to a second drive using backup software, which eats system resources and slows down your PC in a very noticeable way. With RAID 1 arrays, if one drive ever fails, your PC continues to function as if nothing happened, and all of your images are preserved. Of course, you're warned during the boot sequence if the RAID array isn't running perfectly, and you'll know it's time to replace the bad drive.

The final option, RAID 0+1, is the most expensive solution. Using an array of four drives, RAID stripes data to one pair of drives while duplicating everything on the second pair. The result: Higher overall performance while a real-time backup is also maintained. The downside, of course, is that you must purchase four identical hard drives.

To install a RAID system on your PC, you'll usually need a RAID controller card (although many new computers come with RAID built into the motherboard) and two (or perhaps even four) *absolutely identical* hard disk drives. The drives should be the same brand and model number. Installing a RAID setup isn't difficult, but if you aren't handy inside a PC, you might want to take your computer in to a shop for the surgery.

NOTE   *If your RAID 1 hard drive is ever infected by a nasty virus or becomes corrupted, both drives will be equally affected. And so it isn't a bad idea to continue to perform periodic backups of your hard disk. What RAID ensures is that you'll never be stung by the physical failure of a hard drive—and that's very reassuring to say the least.*

Monitor

Nearly any monitor will do for DV, but we want to make a case for a big screen. A big-screen monitor not only makes everything...well, bigger...it also makes it practical to run your computer at a higher resolution. That means more information fits on the screen, which makes for a more comfortable—and practical—video editing environment.

Pinnacle Studio 8 and Final Cut Express don't have specific monitor requirements, but iMovie is pickier. It won't launch on a display that's set to a resolution lower than 1024×768 pixels. Most iMovie-compatible computers are compatible with that resolution, which is ideal for a display that's between 15 and 17 inches in size.

If you're buying a display or adding one to your computer, 19-inch monitors represent the sweet spot in terms of price and performance, and we think that your eyes will thank you for it. DV editing software tends to require a complicated interface with many small windows and controls; the more screen "real estate" you have, the better.

NOTE   *Steer clear of LCD monitors. We highly recommend a good old-fashioned CRT-based monitor instead of one of the new breed of flat-panel LCDs. The latter have about one-third the color range of CRT monitors, meaning that you will not truly know how a video will look on television (or even on most computer monitors) if you use an LCD display.*

One other suggestion: Instead of looking for a ludicrously large monitor (anything over 19 inches), consider dual monitors instead. Windows XP makes it easy to add two displays to your computer, and most modern video cards have dual monitor support as well. With two monitors, you can put the video application on one screen while you arrange supporting windows (such as video, sound, and still-image applications) on the other. And some video editing programs even directly support dual monitors, letting you distribute various interface components on two screens for easier access.

Inputs

Someday, digital camcorders will be able to wirelessly beam video straight into your computer—no cables required. (Interestingly, a few models already come with Bluetooth wireless technology built in, but that's mostly for transferring still photos, not full-motion video.) Until then, we need to rely on a hard-wired interface between camcorder and computer. For the most part, that means FireWire.

NOTE
FireWire is Apple's trademark for the technology it developed that eventually became a computing standard called IEEE 1394, or just 1394. Sony, in a highly successful effort to confuse people, decided to name its FireWire ports i.Link. However, rest assured that i.Link is no different from everyday FireWire or IEEE 1394.

FireWire was originally developed by Apple as a high-speed interface for Macintosh computers to connect with various external devices—like, oh...digital camcorders. In fact, all digital camcorders by definition have a FireWire interface. It wasn't long before Windows-based computers adopted the FireWire spec, and you'll now find one or more FireWire ports on most mid-range and high-end PCs. All new Macs, for their part, come with at least one FireWire port—and usually two.

Put simply, if you plan to transfer video from your digital camcorder to your PC, your PC needs a FireWire port. Most late-model systems have at least one, if not among the other expansion ports, then among the connectors on the sound card. If your machine doesn't have a FireWire port, you can easily install a FireWire expansion card like the one shown in Figure 2-1.

See Chapter 4 for more information about working with FireWire.

NOTE
There are actually two types of FireWire port—FireWire 400 ports, like the one shown in Figure 2-1, and FireWire 800 ports, which use a differently-shaped 9-pin plug. Ultimately, the two are compatible (FireWire 800 is faster, but otherwise "backward compatible"). The biggest pain is that you may find you have to juggle cables a bit. Most DV-to-FireWire cables are FireWire 400; you need an adapter to connect a FireWire 400 cable to a FireWire 800 port.

Analog Inputs

If you have an analog camcorder or want to transfer video to your computer from another analog source (such as a VCR), a FireWire port won't do you much good. Most analog devices have *composite* or *S-video* outputs (or both), meaning you'll need composite or S-video inputs on your computer.

FIGURE 2-1   FireWire ports look like the ones on this FireWire expansion card. This card is designed for computers that don't have a FireWire port.

If you plan to copy a lot of analog video to your system, you may want to consider an internal video-capture card. PC users might want to consider something like ATI's All-in-Wonder, which combines a robust 3-D accelerator (great for games and, of course, video editing) with analog inputs for video capture.

For Macintosh users, most PCI-based solutions are higher-end options, such as the Aurora IgniterX. The Canopus ADVC1394 in an interesting hybrid—both an analog AV card and a FireWire adapter for PCI-based Power Macs.

Of course, these upgrades are fairly major. The path of least resistance lies in an external video-capture system, one that plugs into a USB port on your computer and provides all the ports you need for analog input. One such option for PC users is the Dazzle Digital Video Creator 80, which just so happens to come with Pinnacle Studio QuickStart—a slimmed-down version of our beloved Studio 8. (That's because Pinnacle recently acquired Dazzle.)

Macintosh users have a lot of options for external devices, because analog-to-FireWire converters are fairly common. Dazzle makes the Dazzle Hollywood DV-Bridge for Mac and Formac makes the Studio DV, for instance.

> **TIP**
>
> *Some DV camcorders, particularly on the higher end of the price spectrum, offer analog-in as well as analog-out ports. What does that mean? It means that you can not only play your recorded video to your television or VCR, but that you can reverse the equation and feed images from your television or VCR to your camcorder so they can be viewed or recorded to DV tape. That arrangement gives you an instant analog-to-DV converter, because when you record from your VCR (or similar device) to your camcorder, you're creating a DV recording that you'll be able to use with your video editing software.*

DVD Burner

A DVD burner is one of the easiest pieces of the puzzle. Few new computers come with one, although they're increasingly available as a time-of-purchase option. A DVD burner is a must-have accessory if you want to turn your finished movie into something that you can watch using a DVD player—and we suspect that that's the goal for many DV moviemakers.

In the relatively short period of time since DVD burners for computers were unveiled, prices have dropped and performance has increased. At press time, you could buy a new drive for as little as $150.

Ah, but should you spend a little more on extra features or speed? Let's take a look at some key considerations regarding DVD burners, particularly with respect to PC owners (Mac advice can be found in the next subsection):

Internal or External   First decision: Do you want a drive that goes inside your PC or one that resides outside? Internal models cost less, but you need an open drive bay, an available IDE channel on the motherboard, and a willingness to venture inside your PC. If one or more of those requirements fills you with dread, consider an external DVD burner. They require nothing more than a FireWire or

USB 2.0 port, and they can move easily from one computer to another. But they cost about $100 more, on average, than internal drives do.

Formats Supported   We're pacifists. We don't like war. We especially don't like standards wars, like the one that continues to muck up DVD burning. Blank DVDs come in five different flavors, each with a different storage capacity and player compatibility: DVD-R, DVD-RW, DVD+R, DVD+RW, and DVD-RAM. DVD-RAM is now used primarily for data storage, and so we can take at least that format out of the equation. Your best bet is to buy one of the new breed of multi-format DVD burners, which can record to any of the four main types of DVD media. By the way, nearly all DVD burners can also write to CD-RW discs, so that they can churn out music CDs for you as well.

■ **Read and Write Speeds**   Like CD burners and CD-ROM drives before them, DVD burners started out slow but are finally getting faster. When shopping for a drive, you're probably going to see a ton of seemingly meaningless numbers, such as "4× DVD-R," "2× DVD-RW," "24× CD-RW," and so on. Here's the scoop: Higher numbers mean faster performance. Faster performance means that it takes less time to burn a disc.

TIP   *A good place to look for reviews of the latest DVD burners is Cnet (reviews.cnet.com).*

DVD Formats Explained

We'll be honest: There are enough recordable DVD formats out there to give anyone a headache. DVD-R. DVD+R. Good grief. What do all the designations mean? Which ones work well for playback in DVD players? Let's cut through the mush and explain:

- **DVD-ROM** DVD-ROM is the ordinary DVD that you play on your computer or home theater. They're prerecorded with commercial content such as movies, reference software, and games.

- **DVD-RAM** Forget about this format for video work. DVD-RAM has one really big advantage: It can be recorded and erased repeatedly, like a floppy disk or hard disk. But serious compatibility issues arise between manufacturers. And because DVD-RAM discs are typically housed in cartridges, they can't be played in stand-alone DVD players, even if they happened to be format-compatible (which they aren't).

- **DVD-R** DVD-R is a recordable format similar to the old CD-R discs that most people are familiar with. In other words, DVD-R discs record data only once, after which the data becomes permanent on the disc, and the disc is done—you can't rerecord on it. That may sound like a disadvantage, but DVD-R discs are reasonably inexpensive, and the data that you copy to them is preserved more or less forever. The data can not be erased or overwritten. DVD-R is one of the oldest recordable DVD formats, and it is very compatible with standalone DVD players.

- **DVD-RW** The DVD-RW format is a *rerecordable* format similar to CD-RW. Bottom line, the data on a DVD-RW disc can be erased and recorded over many times, in the same manner as a floppy disk or hard disk. The discs themselves are a bit more expensive, though, and you probably don't want to make home movies in this format, because it's possible to accidentally erase them. However, if you want to create "test" discs before committing your film to DVD-R, you can, because most DVD players can read this format.

- **DVD+R**   DVD+R arrived at the party a bit later than DVD-R, but it's now fairly common. Like CD-R and DVD-R, DVD+R records data only once, after which the data becomes permanent. Early incompatibilities plagued this format, but these days, most DVD players can read DVD+R just fine.

- **DVD+RW**   Finally, there's DVD+RW, another rerecordable format. The data on a DVD+RW disc can be erased and recorded over many times. Like DVD-RW, these discs are a bit more expensive and probably not ideal for long-term storage of data such as home movies.

Macintosh DVD Considerations

Apple includes what it calls a "SuperDrive" on many of its models. A SuperDrive is a DVD-RW drive that can be used to create DVD movie discs. (In the past, Apple has shipped Power Macintosh G4 models with DVD-RAM drives, but those drives were not compatible with the software that enables you to create DVD movie discs.)

The SuperDrive is the only drive that's *really* supported by iDVD, which is Apple's DVD movie disc–creation software, although you'll find upgrade vendors who offer aftermarket "SuperDrive" and "SuperDrive-compatible" external drives. In many cases, those drives are *not* compatible with Apple's iDVD, so make sure to

Which Is Better for DV: PC or Macintosh?

The PC-versus-Macintosh debate has a long and ugly history. For many people, computers are like children: a source of pride, something to be defended tooth-and-nail. Friendships have been tarnished over such comparisons. (We speak from regrettable experience.)

So why raise the specter here? If you're new to DV and want to pursue it seriously, you'll also want to look seriously at which platform to use for editing: PC or Macintosh.

For starters, neither platform is necessarily "better" than the other, though many of the old arguments still apply: PC systems tend to cost less; Macs tend to be easier to use. A lot more software is available for PCs; some software available for Macs is of a higher quality. And yada yada yada. Those are things to take into account, sure…but strictly from a DV standpoint, the playing field is fairly even.

Todd's take on this (he's the resident Mac user) is that the PC-versus-Mac debate in DV can be boiled down to a "bang for the buck" versus "wow for the buck" argument.

With a PC, the original outlay for a powerful system is usually much less than with a Mac. An extremely powerful processor with a speedy graphics card and a nice display can often be had from one of the many PC manufacturers for less than the equivalent machine from Apple. It's cheap to add and upgrade components, too. That's "bang for the buck."

Because Apple controls both the hardware and software of the "Macintosh experience," it's able to offer a bit more "wow for the buck" in that its applications—iMovie, Final Cut, iDVD—are incredibly well designed, particularly in how they work together. Apple puts an extraordinary amount of engineering into its applications, and it knows how to make them work with the Mac OS and native technologies such as QuickTime. So, even with a relatively inexpensive SuperDrive-equipped eMac, for instance, you can do your editing in iMovie 3 and seamlessly export the movie to iDVD, which can then be used to graphically build your DVD movie interface and burn the disc.

Your decision, then, probably boils down to which operating system (Windows or Mac OS) you're more comfortable with and which software you like more for digital editing. Pinnacle Studio 8 is a Windows-only product; iMovie and Final Cut are strictly Mac. You need to weigh the features and limitations of the programs and decide for yourself which one best suits your needs. And then there's the final test: If you're not a computer guru yourself, you should buy the computer platform used by the computer guru that you can most rely on—the one who will take your call at 2:00 A.M.

read the fine print. You may need to use a third-party application to create a DVD movie disc. Also, in most cases, an external DVD-RW drive cannot be used to *play* DVD movies on your Mac—that requires an internal DVD drive. If you have the option, purchasing a Mac model that includes an internal SuperDrive is ideal.

Where to Find It

Web site	Address	What's there
Crucial Technology	www.crucial.com	Memory upgrades
Pinnacle Systems	www.pinnaclesys.com	Dazzle Digital Video Creator 80
		Dazzle DV-Hollywood Bridge
Apple Computer	www.apple.com	iMovie, iLife, Final Cut
Formac Electronic	www.formac.com	Studio DV converter
Canopus Corporation	www.canopus.com	Mac and PC digital video cards and converters
Aurora Video Systems	www.auroravideosys.com	IgniterX analog/digital video card

Chapter 3

Using Your Camcorder

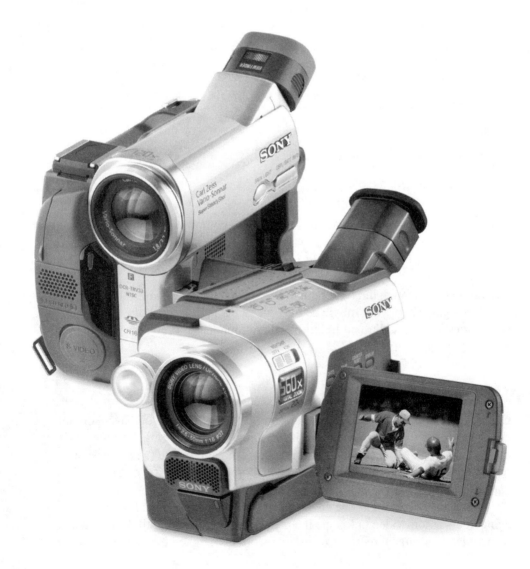

How to...

- Charge your camcorder battery
- Operate in various video modes
- Manage your library of tapes
- Create a storyboard
- Make an animatic version of your production
- Hold your camcorder for steady, usable video
- Use a dolly and a Steadicam for better video
- Get the best audio on location
- Color-correct a video
- Optimize exposure in a video
- Use night video modes

So, you think that you're ready to start making your movie. You've got a camera, some video editing software, and perhaps even a DVD burner so that you can copy the finished product to a disc that will play in the DVD player in your living room.

But it all starts with the camera, and that's what we'll look at in this chapter: how to actually shoot your movie using your camcorder and perhaps use some accessories such as additional lighting and microphones—if you want to get fancy. Ready? Let's get started.

Camcorders Explained

Obviously, in a book about digital video, we're assuming that you have a digital camcorder. But if you're new to all this, you might be wondering: Just what is a digital camcorder? And how is it different from the alternative (whatever that would be—an analog camcorder, I guess)? Do you need a digital camcorder? Or can you make do with something else?

Let's start by looking at the different sorts of camcorders. Traditional analog camcorders record video onto tape in an analog format—hence the name "analog camcorder." The signal these camcorders record is designed for playback on television and other NTSC video systems. NTSC is simply the broadcast standard used in the United States; in Europe, the equivalent is PAL.

Analog camcorders fall into a few major categories, distinguished by the tape format they use. Most analog camcorders use VHS tapes, which are essentially the same as the tapes you use to record *Friends* on Thursday nights. (To be really precise, most analog camcorders actually use mini-VHS tapes, which are the same as VHS, only in a smaller cassette so that the cameras themselves can be built more compactly.) Another major format is 8mm. There aren't many 8mm VCRs; 8mm is really designed just for camcorders, and you need to convert your 8mm tapes to VHS to play them in a regular VCR.

VHS and 8mm are both capable of recording video with a resolution of about 240 lines per frame. Broadcast television, in contrast, transmits about 500 lines of video per frame, which means that analog camcorders work with half the resolution that your television is capable of playing.

In addition to VHS and 8mm camcorders, there are S-VHS and Hi8 models, which can record about 400 lines of video per frame, more closely approximating broadcast video quality. Hi8 was pretty popular in its day, but S-VHS was never really a household name in camcorders.

You may have any one of those four kinds of camcorders tucked away in your closet. But if you've owned even an S-VHS or Hi8 camcorder, you may have noticed that image quality is difficult to control. If you wanted to combine video from one or two different tapes, rearrange scenes, and perhaps add some special effects, you'd have to record from one tape deck to another, essentially making a copy of the original video in the process. The completed video would become a "duplicating master," and any copies that you made for friends, family, or co-workers would be copies of that tape. In other words, an edited tape would be a copy of a copy, or even a copy of a copy of a copy. And each copy would be significantly lower in quality than its predecessor. As a result, analog video was never really a good solution for doing fancy editing.

All that background on analog camcorders goes to explain why digital camcorders are so much better. Digital camcorders record video in digital form onto a high-quality magnetic tape—like storing a digital picture or a Word document on disk. When you want to edit the video, you transfer the footage from the camcorder to a PC using an IEEE 1394 cable, also called FireWire (see Chapter 4 for details). The transfer over the cable preserves the data exactly as it was shot: there's no dreaded "generational loss" such as videographers experienced with older analog camcorders. Digital video data can be edited without losing a single pixel of image quality, and the finished video can then be sent back to a tape in the camera. Or you can copy the finished video to a VHS tape, CD, or DVD, or simply keep it on your hard drive.

Digital Camcorder Standards

Not surprisingly, there are many kinds of digital camcorders on the market. The industry's two formats are sort of like VHS and 8mm—totally incompatible with each other (the tapes are different sizes). However, camcorders of both format types can connect to a PC through the same type of FireWire cable we talked about earlier.

The most common kind of digital camcorder is called a DV (short for Digital Video) camcorder. To be accurate, these are actually mini-DV, because consumer camcorders use smaller, "mini" versions of the DV tape created for professional broadcasters. All of the manufacturers currently offering digital camcorders sell a mini-DV version. Competing with mini-DV is the proprietary Digital8 format from Sony. Digital8 is similar to mini-DV (it offers the same 500 lines of resolution, for instance), but with one big difference: Digital8 camcorders can play older 8mm and Hi8 tapes as well. Thus, if you have a library of Hi8 videotapes (for example), you might consider a Digital8 camcorder. If you don't have that legacy collection of old video, then Digital8 really has nothing unique to offer you. You could purchase a DV or Digital 8 camcorder and get similar results.

Getting Around Your Camcorder

Thankfully, your camcorder is a very simple gadget. For the most part, you can turn it on, press "Record," and shoot your video with exposure and focus set to "Automatic." There's not much to fiddle with; you can get great results right out of the box.

Let's step through the process of shooting your first video clip.

Charging and Using the Battery

The battery that accompanies your camcorder is, in all likelihood, a lithium ion rechargeable. Such batteries generally take three to five hours to fully charge and provide between two and four hours of operating time before they need to be recharged. You should make an effort to fully charge the batteries before first use. If you only half-charge the battery before its first use, you may not be able to exploit the full potential of the battery in the future.

Your camcorder probably also works with two or more styles of battery (see Figure 3-1):

- **Normal Capacity**   This kind of battery typically comes with your camcorder. It offers a modest amount of power. You'll need to charge it more frequently, but it's smaller and lighter.

- **High Capacity**   This kind of battery is usually optional and more expensive. It's larger and heavier, but it may deliver two or even three times the run time of a standard battery. Here at the How To Do Everything mansion (a palatial estate on Cayman Brac, occupied by roommates Dave, Todd, Rick, and Halle Berry), we generally stick with high-capacity batteries. Sure, they're another expensive item to buy along with the camcorder, but they minimize the risk of running out of juice in the middle of the day.

What do you need to know about charging and using your batteries? Here's a quick laundry list of tips to remember:

- Lithium ion batteries don't suffer from "memory" effects like older NiCad and NiMH batteries sometimes did. That means it's okay to charge them however you like, whenever you like. There's no need to totally discharge them first.

- Don't leave batteries in the charger too long. After the batteries have charged, take them out of the charger and store them. With some chargers, leaving lithium batteries in place for many hours after they're fully charged can cause them to overheat, shortening their life.

FIGURE 3-1   The Sony high-capacity battery is quite a bit larger than a standard battery, but it offers hours of extra run time.

■ No battery lasts forever. Every time you charge a battery, you slightly shorten its maximum run time. Eventually, your battery will no longer hold a charge. The lesson? Don't top off your camcorder batteries every time you run them down by a few minutes or you'll end their careers before their time.

■ If you'll be doing a lot of shooting throughout the day, you can often get better performance from a battery by leaving your camcorder switched on. If you keep switching the camcorder on and off, you'll needlessly waste power as the camera repeatedly steps through its warm-up and shutdown sequences throughout the day.

■ Camcorder batteries don't perform as well in the cold. If you're shooting outside in winter, a common trick is to take two batteries with you. Leave one in your pocket, where it will stay warm, and swap it for the battery in the camera when that one dies. Put the "dead" battery in your pocket to warm up. It'll probably run for a while longer after it thaws.

Loading Tape

Digital camcorders are still analog devices in the sense that they use good old-fashioned magnetic tape for information storage. When you open the tape door on your camcorder, the tape mechanism should open automatically. That action requires some power, so make sure that a battery is installed in the camcorder or that the camcorder is connected to an AC adapter. You can see an open miniDV tape mechanism in Figure 3-2.

TIP *If the camcorder tape mechanism doesn't open and close the way it is supposed to, don't try to "help it" by hand. It's broken, and needs to be serviced. If you manhandle it, you'll only compound the problem and make the damage worse.*

When you load a tape cartridge into the mechanism, be careful to slide it in properly—don't force it. If the cartridge is upside down or backwards, it won't easily slide any further than about halfway in. The cartridge should enter the mechanism with the tape itself entering first and the rollers facing down into the tape transport mechanism. Gently push the cartridge into the chassis. Look for the "Push" label, and be sure to apply pressure only there. Once the cartridge is loaded, the mechanism will retract into the camcorder on its own with no further effort. The process may be slow; just be patient.

FIGURE 3-2   Don't manhandle the tape mechanism. The mechanism is meant to be pushed in only one location, which is usually clearly marked.

Using the Camcorder Mode Controls

It's the moment of truth: You're ready to make some video. Shooting video can be as easy as turning on the camera and punching the "Record" button, but you'll do your best work if you become really familiar with the camcorder's controls, button layout, and features.

To start shooting, generally all you need do is to power the camcorder on and press the Record button, which is usually red. Most camcorders cluster the power and Record controls together, making it easy to switch the camcorder on and to start recording with a flick of the thumb (see Figure 3-3). But remember that it can take several seconds to power up a camcorder and prepare it for recording. If you anticipate needing to shoot quickly, it's a good idea to keep the camera powered on. Depending on the camcorder, you may have as many as four modes associated with the power switch. Here's what you should look for:

■ **Off** Off is pretty much what it sounds like: Don't expect to do much with the camcorder in the Off mode—except, perhaps, hold this book open to the page you're trying to read. The Off mode shuts the camera down completely. You should always put the camcorder into this mode after you have finished a shoot, or when you are preparing the camcorder for storage or travel.

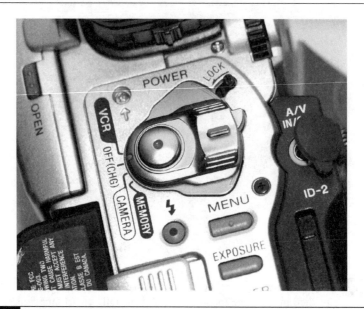

FIGURE 3-3   Most digital camcorders put all of the mode settings in one place, near the power switch.

- **On, Video, or Camera**   The On, Video, or Camera mode (identified a bit differently depending upon the camcorder that you're using) lets you record video to tape. You'll generally want to set your camera to this mode so that you can start making your masterpiece. Then, press the Record button to start the tape rolling; press Record again to stop. Most cameras use an indicator light in the viewfinder to tell you when you're actually recording. A red light usually signals Record.

- **VCR or Playback**   Using the VCR or Playback mode, you can review tape you've already shot. In this mode, the camcorder works like a portable VCR: you can rewind, fast-forward, and play the tape. VCR or Playback is also the mode that you'll want to use when you connect the camcorder to your PC for transfer of video to the hard disk.

- **Still or Memory**   In Still or Memory mode, you can use your camcorder to store still pictures as if the camcorder were a digital camera. Most camcorders have two still modes: one for storing stills on tape, interspersed with your video clips, and one for storing stills to a memory card (usually one from Secure Digital or Memory Stick). Memory cards are easy to pop out of the camera and insert into a memory card reader on your PC. If you use the Memory mode, be sure to switch back to the regular Video mode afterwards so that you can capture more movies.

> **TIP** *This might sound silly, but becoming extremely familiar with the recording indicator is important. More than once, Dave has missed taping something underwater because he mistook the Ready light for the Record light, and captured nothing to tape.*

Managing Tapes

Tape management can become a major issue for folks who make a lot of movies—especially if, like Rick, you tend to be sloppy and senile. These tips will help you to stay on top of your tape collection:

■ Always make sure that your tapes are completely rewound before you start shooting and after you're done. All tapes—blank, full, or somewhere in between—should be rewound at the end of each project unless you intend to continue shooting on a particular tape. That way you won't accidentally overwrite video you've already shot or lose track of what's on each tape.

■ Use easily readable labels to identify every tape in your collection. Color-coded labels can be good for identifying separate projects. Using the "1 of 3," "2 of 3" format can help keep track of all the tapes associated with one project. All tapes start out looking alike. If you're not careful, you won't know which are blank and which have important video on them. And you certainly shouldn't use cues such as "if it's rewound, it's blank," because it's all too easy to accidentally rewind a tape and end up recording over it. That's why you should get into the habit of rewinding *everything*.

■ You might want to consider establishing a *run sheet*. Instead of writing the tape contents on the small stickers attached to each tape, just write a number. Then, on the run sheet, list the tape numbers in numerical order, and, beside each number, write down exactly what should be found on the corresponding tape.

■ After you transfer your video to your computer and edit and burn your completed movie, be sure to replace the tape labels so that the tapes can be used again without confusion. If you leave old labels in place, you might accidentally confuse Tape 2 from last month's vacation with Tape 2 from your current school pageant video.

Working with a Storyboard

Many movies need little advance preparation. If you're shooting a simple vacation video, you'll probably just record a lot of tape whenever the mood strikes you, with some vague plan to edit it down to something interesting after you get home. With a little luck and skill, that might work fine. But if you want to create something a bit more coherent—perhaps tell a story with your movie—then a storyboard might be for you.

A storyboard is simply a graphic depiction of your movie, usually told in the form of panels in comic-book style, like this:

Timmy walks to the house

He opens the front door

and climbs up the stairs

where Uma attacks him

3

Each panel represents a scene in the movie. You can put as much or as little effort into the graphics as you like. If you're a talented artist, you might want to make detailed sketches that depict the contents of the scene. If you're like Dave—you can't even draw poker—then a simple, stick-figure rendering is fine. A good storyboard has brief notes under each panel that explain what happens in each scene.

The idea here is not to create a work of art, but to create a visual guide that prepares you to shoot the video. It also shows you how the current scene relates to other scenes so that you can properly position your sets, actors, and cameras, and know when to start and finish taping. Think of your storyboard as a set of instructions, like the ones supplied with assemble-it-yourself furniture.

Once your storyboard is complete, you have a few options:

- ■ You can use the storyboard as a rough guide to the movie you're making. Use it to set up and tape all the scenes in your movie. This approach can come in handy even for an informal family event like a birthday party. If you storyboard it ahead of time, you'll know the shots you want to get when the big day comes.

- ■ You can shoot the event first, then review your footage, and build the storyboard afterward to give yourself some idea of how to approach the editing and production process. This approach is backward to the way that big Hollywood types do it, but then again, they have a multimillion dollar budget…so there!

- ■ You can also proceed to another step often used in Hollywood—make an *animatic*. An animatic is a full-length version of your movie, shot on video using a camcorder, but entirely from storyboards. If the first scene is 30 seconds long, for instance, you shoot the Scene One storyboard panel for 30 seconds, adding the appropriate voice-over dialog as you tape. You then switch to the next storyboard panel, and read the dialog for that scene. When you're done, you'll have a video that you can import into your video

Did you know?

Animatics Are Handy for Special Effects

Just as Hollywood editors do, you can use animatic technique to create special effects in your movies. The storyboard frames act as placeholders in your live-action movie, letting you see what you need to do to bridge the gaps between scenes and how long the special effects need to be.

Want to see animatics in action? Many commercial DVDs include special features that show parts of the project in development, sometimes with animatics inserted in the place of finished effects. Recently, Dave rented the special edition of the John Carpenter classic *Big Trouble in Little China,* and it included extended production clips with animatics still in the place of completed special effects. A very cool rent!

editor and watch on the small screen. As you capture live-action scenes, you can import them into the movie project, replacing the corresponding animatic scenes as you go. Using this approach, you can watch your movie take shape, and see, at every step, how the missing scenes fit in, because they're represented by storyboard frames.

Handling Your Camcorder

Once you start shooting, you should strive to master some basic skills.

First and foremost, learn your camera's controls inside out. Your fingers should instinctively know how to find the zoom, for instance, because if you take your eyes off the viewfinder for a moment to locate it, the video will jiggle. Your eye should be on the scene you're taping, not on the location of the camcorder controls. And make no mistake: that kind of familiarity takes practice. Get comfortable with your camera by shooting a lot of test tape before you tackle something that others will see.

Your camcorder has two viewfinders: an optical one and a digital one. Which should you use?

In general, it's easier to use the digital viewfinder to frame your scene, because you can stand back from the camera and use your peripheral vision to anticipate where to point the camera next. If you use the optical viewfinder, you can be surprised by changes in the scene that take place outside the viewfinder's scope.

Choosing a Shooting Position

Hold the camera securely. That generally means with both hands—but if you use only one hand, be sure to use the camera strap to secure the camcorder tightly against that hand. When you move the camcorder, do so slowly…smoothly…fluidly. Avoid fast or jerky motions. Not only do you risk causing "streaking" in the recorded video, but you make watching that video hard on the audience's eyes—to the point of motion sickness in some viewers. You don't want a nauseous audience, do you?

Here are some common handling techniques to become comfortable with:

■ **Eye Level**   Hold the camcorder to your eye to get a natural, handheld, eye-level view of the world. For a steadier shot, you might want to brace yourself against a wall or door jamb. Too much handheld video makes everything you do look like *The Blair Witch Project*. Stick with wide-angle shots, because handheld zoomed close-ups are far too jittery.

■ **Waist Level**   Hold the camera near your waist for a more casual, MTV-like feel. If you tilt the digital viewfinder, you can still see what you're shooting. Camera motions that are more exaggerated and obviously "handheld" are acceptable when shooting from this perspective, but be careful not to overdo it.

■ **Pan**   When you're trying to follow action, such as a moving car or a running dog, pan with the motion. Hold the camcorder close to your body and tuck your elbows in for stability. Then track the moving subject, carefully keeping it in the viewfinder as you twist at the waist. (Keep your feet firmly planted on the ground.)

■ **Tripod Mount**   The problem with handheld shots is that they look...well, handheld. Video shots that use a tripod-mounted camcorder are significantly steadier and more professional-looking. And don't be fooled: No matter how steady your hands, a handheld shot *always* looks handheld. Even if you wobble just a little, keeping the subject more or less centered, the scene boundary will jiggle, and that's a dead giveaway. Thankfully, your camcorder

3

has screw threads on the bottom for a tripod. Keep in mind that tripods for video are a bit different than those for still photography. Your old camera tripod may not be the perfect tool for the job. Nonetheless, you can keep the pan head of your old tripod a bit loose and use it much like a video tripod—steady enough for stationary shots, but able to track motion in a pan as well. You can safely zoom with a tripod, because your platform is dramatically more stable than if you were holding the camera.

■ **Steadicam Mount**   If you want truly Hollywood-like video, a Steadicam is the solution—but only for the really dedicated, committed videographer. The Steadicam is a clever gadget that revolutionized moviemaking about twenty years ago when it was first invented by a filmmaker named Garrett Brown. Until then, shooting stable, steady film from a moving camera was really hard. Shots would always shake and jitter enough that they didn't look professional. The Steadicam is a special arrangement of weights and balances. It allows you to move with your camcorder, yet shoot rock-solid video. Several Steadicam-like devices are available, but generally they're all priced well beyond what a hobbyist can afford. All except for the Steadicam JR Lite, that is:

This version of the Steadicam sells for under $500. It's small and light enough to provide rock-solid handheld video with almost any common digital camcorder. Very large and heavy camcorders may require a larger Steadicam, though.

■ **Dolly Mount**   No, we're not suggesting that you mount your camcorder on a little girl's doll. In the film world, a dolly is a cart that rolls along a predetermined path, allowing the camera—and hence the audience—to move through the scene and experience a real sense of motion. A dolly shot can add a really professional look to your video, so give it a try. A real dolly is probably priced outside your budget, but you can improvise. Mount the camcorder on a wagon, baby carriage, wheelchair, or some other small wheeled contraption, as in Figure 3-4. Keep the same perspective throughout the shot. Don't zoom while using a dolly, because that's visually confusing in most situations. And one word of caution: Be sure to move with the dolly. Don't give it a shove and hope for the best. Dave knows someone who tried that particular cinematic technique and ended up with nothing more than a spare camcorder battery, if you know what we mean. And keep in mind that a dolly—especially a makeshift one—works best when you have a clear, smooth path to travel along. Otherwise, the camera will shake, rattle, and roll. In that case, you're probably better off with a Steadicam.

TIP *You might want to invest in a monopod. That's a one-legged tripod, available at most photography stores. It's handy for panning, as well as for quick-and-dirty image stabilization without a complete tripod. Yet a monopod is really small and compact, which makes it great for traveling. Indeed, it's especially good as a support during long handheld sessions, when your arm can get really tired and start shaking the camera.*

FIGURE 3-4   From personal experience, we can say that this Radio Flyer dolly works best when one person sits inside and operates the camcorder while another person pushes and steers.

Zooming for Success

Using a zoom lens, you can change the magnification of the scene you're taping. Your camcorder's *zoom range* is what lets you switch smoothly from a wide-angle to a telephoto shot, or anything in between. But what you may not realize is that your zoom control actually changes several elements of your video at once—the most important of which are called *focal length* and *depth of field*.

What are those things? How are they related?

Well, imagine taping a scene with your camcorder. When the zoom control is all the way "out" (set to wide-angle mode), you can see more in the frame at one time than when the lens is "zoomed in." Your camcorder has a wider field of view than any normal human eye, which is why the shot is called "wide-angle." We also say that the lens has a *short focal length*.

Whaaaa?

"Focal length" is the measure of the distance from the lens to the point behind the lens where the image is in proper focus. Shorter focal lengths create low-magnification, wide-angle images. The greater the focal length, the greater the magnification. A lens with a long focal length is called a "telephoto."

So how are these controls useful to us? First, there's the obvious application: You can use a zoom to get a closer look at something without physically moving closer. That's the way most people instinctively use a zoom lens. However, there's more to it than that.

Consider this: A zoom also has the ability to "compress" a scene. When you zoom way in on a subject that's quite distant, the foreground and the background "squash together," giving the scene less depth. As you zoom out and see the same subject with a wider-angle lens, you also add a sense of depth back into the image.

Zoom lenses offer one other important effect: they vary the *depth of field* in the scene. "Depth of field" is the measure of how much of a scene is in sharp focus. If you are taping a subject close to the camera (for instance), check out the background: it'll be blurred or out of focus. That's because the camera can't focus sharply on everything at once. (Neither can your eyes, but you rarely notice that fact because your brain tries to keep that lack of focus a secret most of the time.)

In general, you get the greatest depth of field when the camcorder is set to a short focal length. Check it out—the more extreme the zoom, the shallower the depth of field. You can take a few lessons from this knowledge and apply them in your own movies:

■ To keep both the foreground and background of a distant scene in sharp focus, get closer to your subject and set the lens to a short focal length. Don't take the video from far away with the assistance of zoom.

■ To keep the viewer's attention on a single element in a scene, reduce the focal length by zooming in. Alternatively, you can manually change the aperture setting, if your camcorder allows that adjustment.

■ Shooting very wide or very telephoto is unnatural. It draws attention to itself. If you want the video to look as if seen through the eyes of a human, set the focal length to a more "normal" level somewhere in the middle.

It's also worth pointing out that the zoom control is rather like a novelty toy at Christmas: something that initially fascinates, but that quickly grows tiresome. What we mean is that excessive zooming is distracting and amateurish. Try to zoom slowly; abrupt zooms are extremely distracting. And zoom infrequently. If you zoom constantly in a video, you'll give your audience a headache. And keep in mind that the zoom controls on some camcorders are so twitchy that it's all but impossible to achieve a smooth zoom. Practice ahead of time, and see of there's a way to slow the zoom rate.

Finally, a few words about digital zoom: Don't use it.

The digital zoom on a camcorder is a fancy electronic gizmo that magnifies the image captured by the image sensor to provide a higher apparent level of magnification than the ordinary optical zoom can provide. Your standard optical zoom may be 5×, 8×, or even 10×, but camcorders typically offer another 100×, 200×, or even 500× magnification by digital zoom.

Sounds great, right?

The problem is that digital zoom dramatically lowers the quality of the video. Beyond 50× or 75×, the quality is so bad that it's downright embarrassing. We highly recommend that you root through your camcorder's menu system until you find a way to completely disable the digital zoom. That way, you won't accidentally barge into the digital zoom range by pressing the camera's Zoom button for too long.

Working with Sound

Your camcorder came with a built-in microphone, and so you're all set to start recording, right? Right.

Well, kind of. You can obtain perfectly acceptable results with the built-in mic in your camera, but you should understand its capabilities and limitations. If you

Bluescreening

When Dave was about 12 years old, he sat in a darkened theater and saw *Star Wars* for the first time. It was an utterly magical experience. Remember when Obi-Wan tried to disable the Death Star's power system from a platform that seemed poised thousands of feet in the air? Dave still does. He can vividly remember the queasy feeling in the pit of his stomach as he watched that scene.

Of course, Alec Guinness, the actor playing Obi-Wan, was standing no higher than the top of a kitchen stepstool. Only through the magic of *bluescreening*— also known as *digital compositing*—did the scene seem to be death-defying. When Dave learned about the magic of compositing, he was hooked—not just on science fiction, but also on the art of making science fiction as well. What you may not realize, though, is that you can do your own compositing with a simple camcorder and any of several different video editing packages.

What is bluescreening? In simple terms, it's the act of filming live actors in front of a solid-colored backdrop (often blue, hence the name). Afterward, on the computer, you tell the video editing software to digitally remove the background color throughout the entire scene. Then, behind that scene, you can *matte* (layer) a second video source, which "shows through" the transparent areas that were created by removing the background color. Voila! You've combined two video tracks in such a way that you have inserted someone into video taken a thousand miles away.

What do you need for bluescreening? A screen, for starters. And it doesn't have to be blue. Any solid color will work, and green is actually easier to work with. You also need good, even lighting. After your video is complete, you'll need a video editing program that can remove color from a video track. Pinnacle Studio 8—the program with which we spend most of our time in this book—cannot do color removal, but other programs such as Adobe Premiere and Ulead MediaStudio can. (And Mac users can accomplish some bluescreening in Final Cut Express or Final Cut Pro.)

Bluescreening is covered in more detail in Chapter 5, along with another software package called Visual Communicator Pro, from Serious Magic Inc. Visual Communicator is designed expressly for bluescreening. It even comes with a huge green screen that you can tape in front of. (For more information, visit www.seriousmagic.com.)

need to go beyond what the camcorder mic can offer, we'll show you how to upgrade to a higher-performance microphone.

Unless your camcorder is an older model, it probably has a stereo microphone built in. (Many older models record only in mono.) The built-in microphone will get the job done most of the time. Because it's built in, you needn't worry about hauling around or setting up an external mic, and it will capture high-quality audio up to a range of about 25 to 30 feet. On the other hand, when you use a built-in mic, you have to consider these issues:

- **Range**   A built-in mic can't capture a distant scene that you're shooting with a telephoto lens.

- **Audio Quality**   Your camcorder mic is limited as compared with true DVD audio. That means that certain situations—recording a musical event, for instance—might call for a better microphone.

- **Stray Audio**   Your camcorder mic can capture unwanted noise in the vicinity of the scene that you're taping—for example, wind or the sound of the camcorder itself taping.

- **Sound Level**   You have no effective way to control the sound level as audio sources change their distance or orientation with regard to the camera.

In some situations, then, you might want to connect an external microphone to your camcorder to better capture audio. Can your camcorder accept an external microphone? Probably. Check for an input like this one:

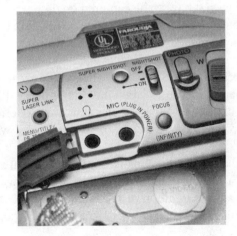

Keep in mind that, in most cases, you'll need a microphone that supplies its own power, through either an AC adapter or batteries. If the mic can't supply its own power, you probably can't use it with your camcorder. And check your camcorder menus; you may have to expressly enable the external mic input, or manually disable the built-in mic when using an external microphone.

The most common external microphones come in three varieties:

- **Cardioid**   A *cardioid microphone* is a directional mic that is most sensitive to the area directly in front of the microphone housing. It's useful for situations in which you want to capture the sound from a specific scene that's fairly close to the camera, and yet prevent background noise from interfering with the shot.

- **Shotgun**   A *shotgun microphone* is the long, boom-shaped mic that you've no doubt seen used on movie sets. It is the audio equivalent of the telephoto lens: It picks up distant sounds and is especially useful when combined with the telephoto lens setting on your camcorder.

- **Lavalier**   The clip-on personal microphones often used for interviews on television are called *lavalier microphones.* They isolate the sound to just the person speaking, making them very handy for noisy environments or when you want just a single individual to be recorded.

B Unit Recording

All of your audio does not have to be captured on digital video tape through your camcorder. You can use other recording devices. Some examples are digital audio recorders (models intended for dictation are available in office supply stores), digital music recorders/players, and even old-fashioned analog tape decks. These gadgets come in handy when you want to record audio for sound effects, for narration or off-screen interviews that will be overlaid as an additional track on top of the video sound, or for atmospheric effects such as background noise, room noise, and equipment sounds that will be included in the video.

Dave has used the Archos Jukebox Recorder with great success (visit www.archos.com). You can attach a microphone to this device and record very high quality digital audio for later transfer to computer. Not only is a digital audio recorder like the Jukebox Recorder lightweight and unobtrusive, but it

3

frees up the camcorder for other tasks—meaning that you can have one person recording audio in one location and another person recording video elsewhere. One caveat: It's virtually impossible to perfectly synchronize second-source audio with your video unless you have highly sophisticated gear. So, don't try recording audio that you'll want to sync to onscreen lips or use in another low-tolerance-for-error synchronization situation.

Creating Foley Effects

Believe it or not, when the Beatles recorded their classic movie theme *Yellow Submarine* in 1966, the Fab Four didn't have access to a wealth of sound effects and sound effect–making equipment in their Abbey Road studio. And, I'm willing to bet, neither do you. So, if you're making a home movie and want to include sound effects—whether it's a slipping sound when someone trips on a banana peel, or the laser gun sound when your toddler comes charging into the scene with a spaceship in hand—you can do exactly what the Beatles did: wander the halls in search of homemade effects.

The art of making special sound effects from everyday items is called Foley Effects, named for Jack Foley, a studio technician who pioneered the art.

Finding Foley Materials

If you want to add your own sound effects to your movies, you'll need the tools of the trade. Thankfully, almost any object can be used for sound effects. Here are some ideas to get you started:

- Wearing shoes, walk on different sorts of surfaces (such as hardwood floors and carpet) to emphasize the sound of footsteps on tape. You'll want to do the walking while you're watching the video, though, so that you can match the rhythm of the person walking on the screen.

- Coconut shells (cut in half) are great for mimicking the sound of clopping horses. Remember *Monty Python and the Holy Grail*? It really works!

- Crinkle cellophane to reproduce the sound of fire.

- Swat a desktop with a rolled up telephone book to create powerful impact sounds for scenes of two people fist-fighting.

- Flushing in a bathroom certainly worked just fine for the Beatles when they needed water sound effects.

- Fill a balloon with small beads, and then inflate the balloon. If you flick the balloon sharply, you can easily make a sound like a gun firing. Shake the balloon quickly back and forth to get the sound of an automatic machine gun.

- If you have an electronic keyboard, don't forget that special sound effects are probably built into it: laser blasts, thunder, car engines, rain, and more.

As you'll see in Chapters 7 and 8, sound effects like these can be added to the audio track in your video editor just as music can. You can also track down premade effects on the Internet. You'll find more about that in those chapters.

Making the Recording

Ready to add some sound-effects magic to your home video? If you're recording standard sound effects, such as crinkling paper, footsteps, or rattling spoons, you'll need to bring the recording device to the sound effect. You can record sound using your camcorder (for best results, attach a reasonably directional external microphone to the camera), or you can record directly to a computer or digital music recorder.

You'll need to experiment a little, but in general you'll want to keep the mic about three to five feet away from the noisemaker. For most sounds, any distortion is bad—so keep the sound level on your recording device moderate. But for certain sounds—gunshots, for example—feel free to overdrive the mic. Increase its level to maximum to get a fuzzy, slightly distorted tone.

If you're recording sound effects from an electronic keyboard, you'll want to plug the keyboard output (an audio output jack usually resides on the back of the instrument) into the audio input of the sound card on your computer.

You can do some cool things with your sound effects. Want to capture the essence of someone walking out of a room? Don't move your feet…move the microphone instead. As you walk in place, have someone else slowly move the microphone away from you—from a close three feet to a distant ten feet. And you don't have to stick with plain vanilla sound. Almost any computer-based sound editing program will let you speed up or slow down sound or add interesting effects such as "flanging" (a digital whooshing effect) that can lend a sci-fi aura to your effects.

Working with Light

When you make a movie, you're painting moving pictures with light. Light determines how good the video looks, and so it helps to have some understanding of how to make the best use of light in your movies.

Correcting the Color Balance

First, you need to understand that light is not all the same. The color of artificial light is dramatically different from that of natural outdoor light, for instance. In fact, every kind of light has unique properties. And that means that different kinds of light—morning, afternoon, evening, tungsten, fluorescent, and gymnasium—all have different colors.

Your camcorder has a way to adjust for these different light sources. It's called *white balance,* and it helps to keep the colors in your video natural regardless of the kind of light you use.

Photographers and scientists have gone to the trouble of cataloging the different color temperatures exhibited by various light sources. Higher temperatures appear warm (slightly reddish). Cooler light sources tend to add a blue tone. It's not at all unlike the way a flame has different colors at its outside and center. Why? Because the different parts of the flame are burning at different temperatures.

As a point of comparison, the chart that follows shows the color temperatures, measured in the Kelvin scale, of several common light sources.

Source	Color temperature (degrees Kelvin)
Candlelight	2000
Sunset	3000
Tungsten light	3200
Fluorescent light	5000
Daylight	5500

If your camcorder is balanced for one kind of light source (daylight, for instance), and you photograph a scene that is illuminated by a very different temperature of light (such as candlelight), the resulting image won't reflect the true colors in the scene. What should be white will turn out looking somewhat reddish. Ordinarily, we don't notice those color shifts because the human brain is very good at interpreting what the eyes see. The brain adjusts for color temperature so that white almost always looks white, no matter what color light we're seeing it in. Of course, cameras aren't quite that smart. And that's the reason for a white-balance adjustment.

The white balance setting on your camcorder allows you to specify the exact color temperature of the scene. In many cases, the camera can automatically adjust to conditions, but the results are often a little inaccurate. You're better off doing it yourself—especially when shooting indoors.

> **TIP** *If you get into the habit of manually adjusting the white balance, remember to reset the white balance to auto at the end of each shoot. Otherwise, when you shoot outdoors, you might forget that your camera is balanced for fluorescent light. The results could be quite funky.*

Some camcorders let you choose from a small collection of white-balance presets, such as Indoors and Outdoors. How you change your white-balance setting varies depending on the camcorder that you own, but, typically, the process is fairly simple. For the specifics on your camcorder, check the accompanying user guide. The process goes something like this:

1. Switch your camcorder on, and set it to normal record mode.

2. Press the menu button on the camcorder to see a set of menus in the LCD display.

3. Find the option for white balance.

4. Scroll through the white balance options until you find the lighting condition that best matches your scene.

5. Press the menu button again to switch off the menus. You can now shoot your video.

Sometimes the available white-balance presets just won't get the job done. If you are in a tricky lighting situation, such as a room that has both incandescent light and candlelight, you may need to set the white balance manually based on the actual lighting conditions in the room.

TIP

One of the most difficult lighting situations on planet Earth is a school gymnasium. Because of the way gyms are lit, no white-balance preset ever seems to work properly. For best results—and to avoid the inevitable yellow cast in your video—try to arrive early and manually set the white balance with the help of a white card.

How to ...   Set the White Balance Yourself

Setting the white balance manually may sound complicated, but it's really not that hard. Before you start, you'll need just one additional item: a white surface that the camera can use to set the white balance. Typically, you can get by with a small square of white poster board or typing paper. Here is how to go about it:

1. Ask your subject or an assistant to hold the white card or paper. Make sure that the card is located where you're actually going to be taping. You want to be measuring the actual light in your anticipated scene. Zoom in so that the white surface fills the viewfinder.

2. Activate the menu system on the camcorder LCD display.

3. Find the white balance controls in the menu system.

4. Scroll until you find the option to set white balance manually. Select the manual option while continuing to point the camera at the white card (which should take up most, if not all, of the frame).

5. Exit the menu system.

Your camcorder will use the new white balance value for all future video, so be sure to reset the white balance to automatic when you're done shooting. Otherwise, if you try shooting a day or two later in very different lighting conditions, your results may be quite bizarre because the white balance will be completely askew. If that's the case, just reset the white balance to fix the problem.

TIP *You might want to intentionally set the white balance incorrectly on occasion. You can mess with white balance to simulate an alien landscape or to show the world through the eyes of someone who is ill, for instance.*

Controlling Camcorder Exposure

Controlling exposure using a camcorder really isn't all that different from controlling exposure using a still camera. Just as still cameras do, camcorders open a *shutter* for a brief time, allowing light to enter. In the camcorder, that light interacts with a light-sensitive computer chip called a charge-coupled device (CCD), and an image is recorded. In still photography, just a single image is recorded, but a camcorder records an image *(frame)* 30 times each second from the moment you start recording.

And there's another half to the exposure equation: When the shutter opens, the amount of light that reaches the CCD is determined by the size of the *aperture* (the opening that admits the light). The shutter speed and the aperture size, working together, determine the video exposure.

Most consumer camcorders are designed to handle the complexities of exposure automatically. Few give you much manual control over the shutter speed and aperture setting in any meaningful way. Indeed, most camcorders offer you only these semiautomatic methods of adjusting exposure:

■ **Programmed Autoexposure**   Many everyday video situations—for example, actors on a stage, night shots, or a day at the beach—can confuse the exposure system in a camcorder because the scene is filled with high-contrast brights and darks in the same frame. That's why many camcorder models offer a handful of programmed autoexposure modes with descriptive names such as Spotlight, Sports, and Beach. Just dial up the appropriate exposure at the camcorder menu, and you'll get pretty good results.

■ **Backlight**   Strong light behind a subject can massively underexpose your scene. Examples include situations such as shooting outdoors against a bright sky or indoors with the subject near a window. If your camcorder has a Backlight mode, those situations are exactly the times to turn it on. The background will probably "blow out" (overexpose), but that's likely okay. Your priority in this instance is that the subject be properly exposed. If your camcorder doesn't have a Backlight control, then look for a manual way to overexpose the scene a bit. Specifically, you want to overexpose the scene somewhat with manual exposure compensation.

■ **Manual Exposure or Exposure Lock**   Sometimes, you'll want to pan the camera between two or more subjects in a single scene, and the exposure will change constantly as you shift the point of view. In such a situation, your best bet is to lock the exposure at some "compromise" value between the extremes. Not all camcorders will let you do this, though.

TIP
If you need to pan continuously between two subjects, consider shooting them with two different cameras. That approach avoids the need to constantly change position and focus.

Shooting at Night and in Low Light

Not all of your video must be shot in daylight. Most modern digital camcorders are equipped with a slew of features for low-light and even no-light operation. In general, you have three tools to work with:

■ **Low Lux Mode**   Although the terminology varies from one manufacturer to another, a low lux setting usually increases the sensitivity of the CCD (the camcorder image sensor), making the overall video brighter. This solution increases the amount of digital "noise" in the video, however, and so it's a last resort for shooting video in low light.

■ **Slow Shutter Speed**   By adjusting the shutter speed of your camcorder to a ridiculously slow value, such as 1/8 or 1/4 second, you can, in near

Do You Need Extra Lighting?

Hollywood sets are filled with lights. Yet most low-budget hobbyist videos use few or none. Why? Because lighting is very complicated and rather expensive. The cheapest way to add extra lighting to a video set is to put a video light on your camcorder; however, the results are often harsh and artificial. A somewhat more involved solution is to invest in one or more *sun guns,* which are handheld or tripod-mounted lights that help to fill in the lighting in your scene. One of the most common ways to use additional lights is to point a second light at your subject to soften the effect of the primary *(key)* light. You can also add a third source to blast light on the subject from behind. That type of light—called a *back light,* not surprisingly—can give a subject a certain depth and definition, separating it from the background.

Our advice? Avoid production lighting, at least until you're ready to move up to a more professional level, which requires a giant leap forward in time, money, and research.

darkness, capture video that looks as if it were shot at noon. Sort of. The downside to this approach is that anything that moves will be rather blurry, so save this technique for stationary or nearly stationary subjects.

■ **Infrared** Infrared mode uses an infrared transmitter to blast your scene with infrared radiation. The camera then records the infrared imagery. The result is monochrome video (usually blue or green) that resembles military action shot through night-vision goggles. If you wish, you can convert such video to true black and white using the video editing software on your computer.

Where to Find It

Web site	Address	What's there
Adobe Systems	www.adobe.com	Adobe Premiere
Archos	www.archos.com	Archos Jukebox Recorder
Serious Magic	www.seriousmagic.com	Visual Communicator Pro
Ulead Systems	www.ulead.com	Ulead MediaStudio

Part II

Edit Footage and Apply Effects

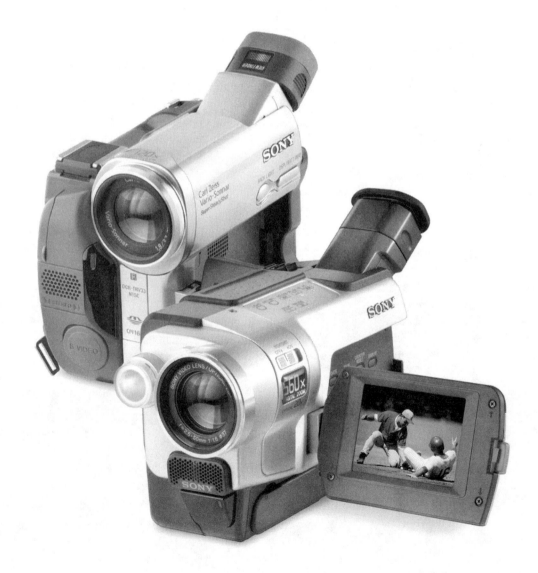

Chapter 4

Getting Video into Your Computer

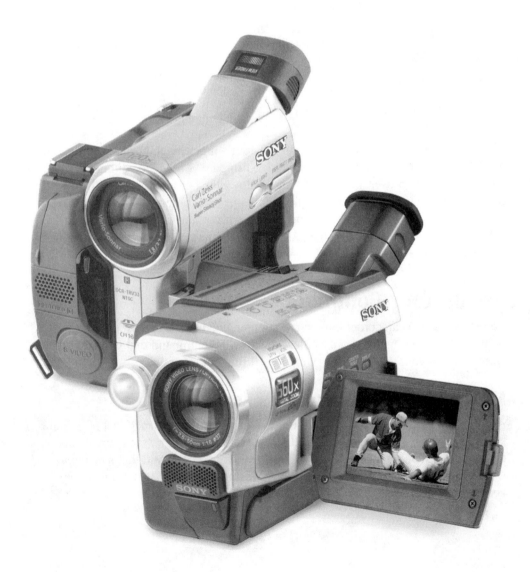

How to...

- Prepare your computer for capturing video
- Connect your DV camcorder
- Modify the capture settings in Studio 8
- Decide on video quality
- Decide where to store captured video
- Begin the capture process
- Capture video from an analog camcorder
- Import analog video into your video editor

Once your film is "in the can," so to speak, it's time to put it "in the computer." That means connecting your camcorder, firing up your video editing program, and punching the proverbial Record button. However, before you begin the transfer process—this "capture" of footage shot with your camcorder—you should make sure that your computer is properly prepped. That not only means checking to see if there's enough space to store the video, but also fine-tuning your hard drive for optimal performance.

Preparing Your Computer

Before you plug a camcorder into your computer, you need to do two things: one is optional, the other mandatory. Needless to say, we recommend that you do both. Don't come crying to us when... Well, you'll find out in a minute.

Making Space for Captured Video

As you learned in Chapter 2, DV consumes a lot of hard disk space. That 60-minute tape in your camcorder may look small, but if you want to dump the entire contents to your computer, you need about 13GB of available space. And that's *per tape*. Depending on how much video you plan to download to your system, you may need a larger hard drive—or a second one (see Chapter 2 for more information).

TIP

If you decide you want a second hard drive, the path of least resistance is usually an external drive. Maxtor's OneTouch is available in a variety of capacities for both PCs and Macs, and it's speedy enough to permit copying of video straight from your camcorder. Surprisingly, external drives don't cost much more than their internal counterparts. At press time, the 160GB Maxtor 5000DV was selling for $250—only about $50 more than a comparable internal drive.

Step one is to determine how big your current hard drive is and how much space is available on it. (Advanced users, feel free to skip ahead while we walk novice users through this process.)

Here's the process for PC users:

1. Double-click My Computer, and then, in the window that opens, locate the icon for your hard drive.

2. Right-click the hard-drive icon, and choose Properties (with either mouse button) from the resulting pop-up menu. The next window that opens shows used, free, and total space on the hard drive.

Local Disk (C:) Properties ? X

| General | Tools | Hardware | Sharing | Quota |

Type: Local Disk
File system: NTFS

■ Used space: 68,075,814,912 bytes 63.4 GB
■ Free space: 11,947,900,928 bytes 11.1 GB

Capacity: 80,023,715,840 bytes 74.5 GB

Drive C   Disk Cleanup

☐ Compress drive to save disk space
☑ Allow Indexing Service to index this disk for fast file searching

OK   Cancel   Apply

OR

> If you have Windows XP, a single click of the hard-drive icon should reveal its size and the available space in the Details panel on the left side of the window.

Mac users can check the available hard disk space this way:

1. On the desktop, or in a Finder window, select the hard drive you want information about.

2. Choose File | Get Info from the menu or press COMMAND+I.

3. Look for the "Available" entry in the General section of the window.

If you have enough space to accommodate the amount of video you plan to capture, you can skip ahead to "Connecting Your Camcorder." But let's say that just 20GB are free, and you have two tapes' worth of video to copy. That means you need to free up at least 10GB or so. (Why do you need 30GB free if two 60-minute tapes require only 26GB of space? Simple: You don't want to leave yourself with zero space when you're done transferring the video. The operating system on your computer needs some free space in which to function, and so does your video editing software.)

Reclaiming Hard-Disk Space

If space is tight on your hard disk, it may be time to consider upgrading to a larger drive or, better yet, adding a second drive just for video (see Chapter 2). That said, there are steps you can take to clear some additional space on your currently crowded disk.

- Uninstall programs you no longer need.

- Uninstall games you no longer play.

- Check your Downloads folder (particularly if you're an America Online user) for old and unwanted downloads. Delete them.

- Search for AVI, MPEG, QuickTime files (that is, video clips), MP3, and other large files and delete the ones that you don't need to keep.

As you now know, audio, and especially video, can consume a lion's share of disk space.

■ Search for digital photos and offload them to CDs. If you have a digital camera, chances are that you have lots of pictures eating up space on your disk. By moving them to CD, you'll not only have a reliable backup, you'll free up extra room.

■ Empty the Recycle Bin or Trash. There could be gigabytes' worth of already-deleted files in there. But until you actually empty the contents, those files still take up space.

All of those steps combined might not be enough to free the space you need, but if all you need to reclaim is just a gigabyte or two, try those options before you spring for a new hard drive.

Optimizing Your Hard Drive for Captured Video

Your second task before capturing video should be to optimize your hard drive. We say "should" because optimization is optional: you don't need to do it, but we highly recommend it. (Heck, you should do it once in a while anyway, whether you're capturing DV or not.)

Optimization is a two-step process: check the disk for errors, and then defragment it so that all the files are in contiguous chunks rather than in scattered... well, fragments. The latter step is particularly important, because a highly fragmented disk can slow computer performance and possibly even lead to video-capture errors (specifically, gaps in the video because the hard drive has to work overtime to find contiguous space). That's already more technical detail than you need. Just trust us when we say to defragment your disk, okay?

These tasks can take a considerable amount of time, so plan ahead by doing them a day or two before you plan to capture your video. Defragmenting in particular is usually a very slow process; it can take several hours to complete.

TIP   *Start defragmenting before you go to bed. It'll usually all be done in the morning. But if you start in the middle of the day, your computer will be a paperweight for hours. On the plus side, more time to watch TV!*

Optimizing Your PC

First, you need to check the hard disk for errors. Such errors usually occur when the computer crashes or you reboot without shutting down, but they can also happen in other instances—very often without your knowledge. You can't defragment a disk that has errors, and so error-checking has to be the first step.

NOTE *The illustrations that follow show Windows XP, but previous versions of Windows are virtually identical when it comes to error-checking.*

Here's the procedure:

1. Shut down all application programs that are currently running on your system. Once that's done, right-click each icon in the Windows System Tray (at the right-hand corner of the Windows Taskbar), and shut down everything that can be shut down. That means virus checkers, pop-up stoppers, firewall programs—everything. (You should disable or shut down your Internet connection as well, so that your computer stays protected from outside snooping.)

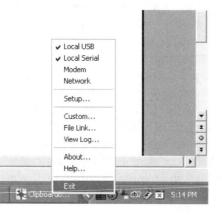

2. Double-click My Computer, and then, in the window that opens, locate the icon for your hard drive.

3. Right-click the hard-drive icon, and choose Properties from the resulting pop-up menu.

4. Click Tools. The Tools tab looks like this:

5. In the area labeled Error-Checking, click Check Now. A window containing two options opens. Click the box that reads Automatically Fix File System Errors, and then click Start.

NOTE   *You may see a message advising that some program is using the hard drive and that the error-checking session needs to be scheduled for the next reboot. If you pick "Yes" and restart your PC, the session will start automatically.*

Depending on the speed of your processor and the size of your hard drive, the error-checking process could take two minutes or it could take twenty. When it's done, your best bet is to move right on to defragmenting, because all the other programs are already shut down—something that's required for defragmentation as well as for error-checking.

To defragment the hard disk, do this:

1. Click Start, and choose All Programs | Accessories | System Tools | Disk Defragmenter.

2. Click the disk that you want to defragment (usually it's C:) to select it, and then click Defragment.

3. The disk defragmenter starts by analyzing the hard disk, a process that should take no more than a few minutes. Assuming the analysis reveals that the disk does indeed need defragmenting, the process begins automatically.

Now you wait. And wait. As noted earlier, defragmentation can take many hours to complete. Make sure that you don't do anything else with your computer during the process.

After you've checked the hard disk for errors and defragmented it, restart the computer, and skip ahead to "Connecting Your Camcorder."

Optimizing Your Macintosh

Mac OS X doesn't have a built-in disk defragmenting tool, and so if you're headed down that path, the best plan is to use a third-party optimizer such as Norton Disk Doctor from Symantec (www.norton.com) or Micromat Drive 10 (www.micromat.com).

If you don't use a disk defragmenter, you can still get slightly better results by using the Apple Disk Utility to fix your disk and your permissions periodically. Here's how:

1. Launch Disk Utility by double-clicking it in the Utilities folder inside your main Applications folder.

2. Now, choose a disk or disk volume in the list to the left, and select First Aid.

3. On the bottom right-hand side of the window, you'll see the Repair Disk option. Click that option to check for errors, and repair them on the selected disk.

4. Also near the bottom of the window is the Repair Disk Permissions command. That command can help to speed up certain operations on both the disk you're using for movies and your main disk, if they're different.

TIP

One way to get around needing any sort of defragmenting utility is to use a particular drive or drive partition as a scratch disk exclusively for video editing. When you're ready to edit a new video on that drive, you can reinitialize it (erase it, in Mac OS X parlance) and begin work anew. A reinitialized disk is, in effect, defragmented because it has no fragments of files stored on it. You can also use the Disk Utility to create partitions on disks, but partitioning a disk destroys all the data that's already on it, and so that's something you probably want to do either with a new disk (such as an external model) or at the point where you're willing to reinstall the Mac OS and all of your applications and documents from backups.

Connecting Your Camcorder

If you already know how to successfully connect your camcorder to your computer, you're in luck—you probably don't need to read this section at all. Go ahead and plug that baby in, fire up your video editing software, and meet us at the upcoming sections on capturing video. For those of you still taking Camcorder 101, stick around.

In the upcoming sections, we're talking solely about digital camcorders. If you have an analog camcorder, the process for capturing video is quite different. See "Capturing Video from an Analog Camcorder" for the details.

TIP *Before you go any further, now would be a good time to connect AC power to your camcorder. It's going to be running for upwards of 60 minutes (specifically, the running time of the video you're going to transfer), and you don't want the battery to poop out in the middle.*

Connecting to a PC

As you learned in Chapter 2, most DV camcorders have FireWire (also known as IEEE 1394 and, in Sony parlance, i.LINK) interfaces. That means your PC needs to be equipped with a FireWire port to which your camcorder can connect. Consult your system manual if you don't know where to find the port or what it looks like. With any luck, there'll be one right up front, probably alongside a pair of USB ports. Refer to Chapter 2 if you need help adding FireWire to your machine.

Your camcorder should have come with a FireWire cable for connecting it to your PC. If yours didn't (and some models, such as the Sony Handycam DCR-TRV33, come with a USB cable instead—which is unsuitable for our purposes), you should be able to find a generic FireWire cable at your local computer superstore.

> **TIP** *If your computer's only FireWire port is at the rear of the machine and your camcorder cable is short, you might want to pick up a longer cable, just so the camcorder doesn't have to sit in an awkward location (such as on the floor) during the capture process. A 6-foot cable should cost you no more than about $8, and FireWire cables are standard—you don't have to use the one that came with your camera.*

Connecting to a Windows XP System

If you're using Windows XP (and we really hope you are, because it has built-in drivers for FireWire devices like camcorders), plug the cable into the camcorder and into the PC, then switch on the camcorder and choose playback mode (usually labeled "Play" or "VCR"). In a few seconds, you should hear a sound indicating that Windows has detected the camcorder, and you should see a few "installing new hardware" messages. (You know, when Windows works, it really is a thing of beauty.) Wait a minute or two until you get the all clear ("Your new hardware is installed and ready to use"), and then run Studio 8. Now, skip ahead to "Capturing Video in Studio 8."

Connecting to Other Versions of Windows

If you're using a version of Windows earlier than XP, you might need to install some drivers. (See the manual for your camcorder.) More than likely, however, you'll just connect the camcorder to the PC as stated above, and then switch it on and put it in playback mode. Don't be surprised if nothing happens—prior to XP, Windows didn't always acknowledge the presence of FireWire devices. Even so, you shouldn't have any trouble—or need any additional drivers—if you're using a recent version of Windows (for example, Windows 98SE or Windows Me).

Start Studio 8, and then click Capture (see Figure 4-1). Now you should be ready to roll, as it were. Skip ahead to "Capturing Video in Studio 8."

Connecting to a Macintosh

As of this writing, only the Power Macintosh G5 has a FireWire port up front on its case, but most modern Macs have one either on the side or at the rear. Some of the latest models offer both FireWire 400 (the original) and FireWire 800 ports. You'll likely want to plug into the FireWire 400 port if you're using the cable that came with the camcorder.

Album   Player

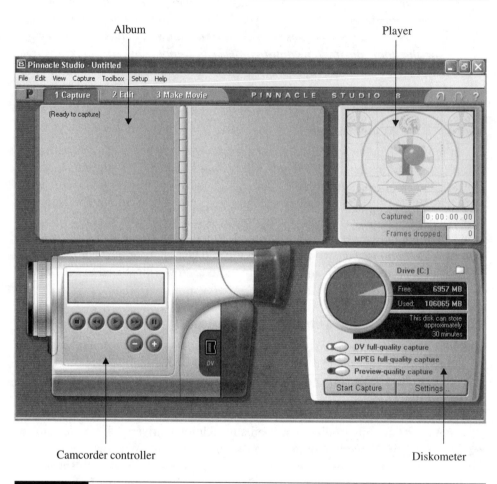

Camcorder controller   Diskometer

FIGURE 4-1 The Capture screen in Studio 8 consists of the Album, the Player, the Camcorder controller, and the Diskometer.

As long as you're using Mac OS 9 or later, connecting your camcorder should be simple: plug the cable into the camcorder and into the Mac as directed by the camcorder manual. You won't see any immediate reaction from the Mac (nothing shows up on the desktop, for instance), but you should now be able to launch iMovie or Final Cut and see that the camcorder is recognized.

With connection accomplished, see Chapter 6 for more on the video import and capture process in iMovie and Final Cut.

Capturing Video in Studio 8

You'll be glad to know that capturing video in Studio 8 is quite easy. Here's the process in a nutshell:

1. Choose the hard drive on which the captured video should be stored.

2. Assign a name to the video you're capturing: "Bob's wedding," for example.

3. Click Start, and go get a cup of coffee.

Okay, that's it! Thanks for stopping by. See you at the next chapter; have a nice day.

Just kidding.

We need to go into just a bit more detail, otherwise we'd have to rename this book *How to Do One or Two Things with Your Digital Camcorder.* Let's take a look at the Studio 8 Capture screen and some of the procedures and settings therein.

Navigating the Capture Screen

The Capture screen in Studio 8 is used expressly to import video from a camcorder (or other sources, but this isn't an "other sources" kind of section). The screen is divided into roughly four quadrants, as you can see in Figure 4-1.

These areas function as follows:

■ **Album**   The Album shows thumbnails of individual scenes from your captured video; if scene detection is turned off, it shows a single thumbnail of the entire capture.

■ **Player**   The Player window shows the video that's arriving from the camcorder.

■ **Camcorder Controller**   You can actually control your camcorder from within Studio 8. All the basic controls are here: Play, Stop, Fast-Forward, Rewind, and Pause. You can also advance frames one at a time by clicking the plus and minus buttons (but that's rarely necessary; you can do that kind of precision editing after the capture ends).

■ **Diskometer**   The Diskometer is the most important area of the Capture screen. It's where you choose the storage location of captured video and adjust the capture settings.

Inside the Diskometer

Dave, who's always been a closet Bee Gees fan, thinks Diskometer is pronounced "Disco-meter." As it happens, the Diskometer has nothing to do with disco and everything to do with your hard drive (a.k.a. hard *disk*—get it?). The Diskometer is where you select the hard drive that you want to use for storing video. It's also where you choose some important capture settings. Let's take a look at what the Diskometer shows:

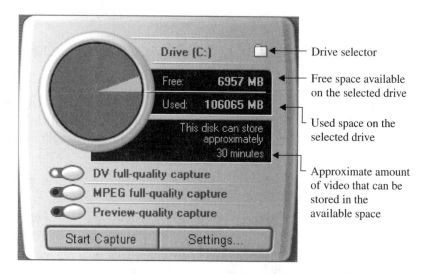

If you have just one hard drive in your system (usually drive C:), the Diskometer shows it by default. If you want to capture video to a different hard drive, click the yellow folder next to the drive letter, choose the drive you want from the Save In menu, and then click OK. (You can also specify a folder if you want, or you can create a new folder.) Notice that the Diskometer now shows the newly selected drive, complete with new free-space and approximate-storage information.

Below all that you'll see three choices for video capture:

- ■ **DV Full-Quality Capture**   "DV full-quality" is the default setting and the one that we highly recommend you use. It captures the best possible video quality from your camcorder.

- ■ **MPEG Full-Quality Capture**   Without getting overly techie about it, the "MPEG full-quality" option captures video in a compressed format, the idea being to save hard disk space and to let you edit video a bit more quickly. (The files are smaller, and therefore less demanding of your PC.) But you sacrifice some image quality in that equation, and therefore we recommend sticking with the DV option—especially if you plan to burn to DVD. MPEG is fine, though, for lower-quality videos, such as videotape, Video CD, and web-sized movies. Consult the Studio 8 documentation if you want more information on this feature.

■ **Preview-Quality Capture**   The "Preview-quality" option is a holdover from the days when hard drives were smaller and cost a lot more. It captures video in a low-quality format that consumes much less space than DV quality does. At the same time, it stores time-code information from the tape. You can then edit and assemble your movie as you normally would. When the time comes to render the finished product, Studio pulls only the necessary scenes (this time in DV high-quality format) from the camcorder, thereby using the minimum possible hard disk space. If you need to use this feature, consult the Studio 8 documentation for further instructions.

Adjusting Capture Settings

Most users won't need to do the slightest bit of fiddling with the Studio capture settings. However, you might want to peek at one or two of the options before starting your capture.

After making sure that DV Full-Quality Capture is selected in the Diskometer (you can tell by the little light next to the option), click Settings. A window opens that looks like that shown in Figure 4-2.

Notice that it has four tabs and that Capture Format is the currently selected tab. That's not the one you want. You may need to adjust the settings in this tab at a later date, but most users will never need to touch them. No, the tab you want is Capture Source. Select it, and you see the information shown in Figure 4-3.

Pay no attention to the top half of the window; it's the bottom half you're interested in right now. Let's quickly discuss scene detection and data rate, and then you'll be ready to go forth and capture.

Scene Detection During Video Capture   Scene detection is arguably one of the most valuable features of Studio 8. As your footage streams into the computer, the software automatically detects major breaks in the action (usually a stop in the recording) and creates a scene. The result is that you wind up with a number of shorter clips rather than one all-encompassing one.

For example, suppose your camcorder tape contains lots of footage of your kids. There's a birthday party here, a trip to the zoo there, and lots of other events and occasions. Scene detection automatically divides those different recording

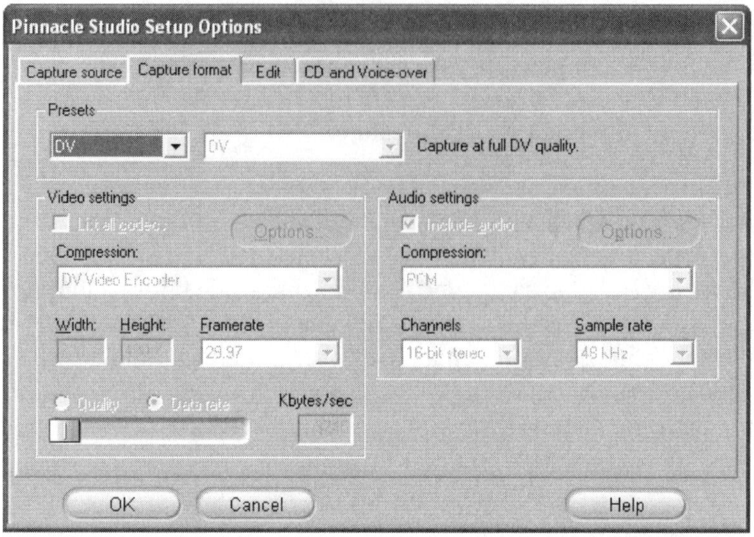

FIGURE 4-2 It's rare that you'll need to make any changes in the Capture Format tab, but that's what first appears when you click Settings.

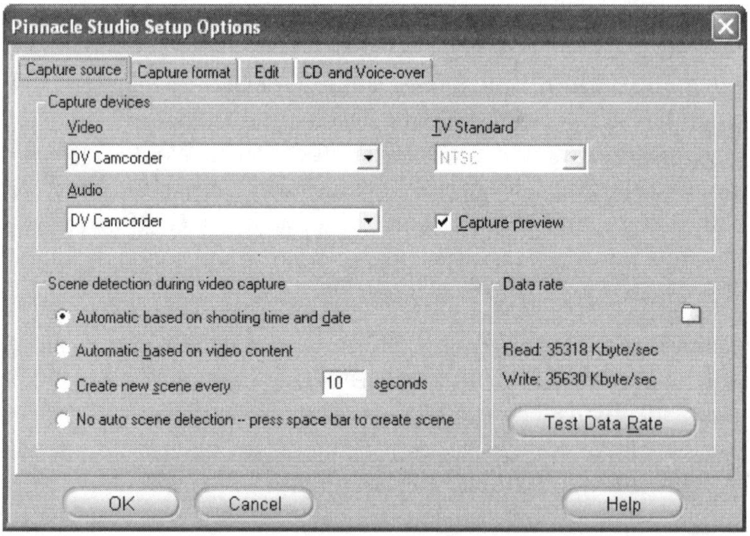

FIGURE 4-3 The Capture Source tab enables you to modify settings like automatic scene detection and data rate.

sessions into individual clips, thus making the editing process much, much easier. If you had 30 or 60 minutes' worth of video in a single giant clip, you'd have to work a lot harder to find the scenes you want, to split the clip into pieces, and so on.

Studio provides four fairly self-explanatory options for scene detection. The first, Automatic Based on Shooting Time and Date, uses the camcorder's time and date codes to divide scenes. If you have some very long recording sessions on your tape, you might want to choose Automatic Based on Video Content, which analyzes the images and looks for dramatic changes in the scene.

Finally, there may be times when you don't want scene detection at all, or you want to break scenes up manually. For that, select the fourth option, No Auto Scene Detection – press Space Bar to Create Scene.

Data Rate   Data rate refers to the speed at which the computer hard drive can read and write data. As long as the two numbers listed are higher than 4,000 Kbytes per second (Kbps), you're in good shape. If they're lower, then your computer (or its hard drive) is too slow to capture smooth, uninterrupted video. Might be time for an upgrade.

Starting the Capture Process

Once you've chosen your desired hard drive, capture quality, and capture settings, the time has finally come to... capture! Use the onscreen camcorder controls to make sure that your tape is rewound (or advanced to the desired start position), then click Start Capture. You'll see a box just like that in Figure 4-4.

Type a name for the video you're about to capture. You can also specify a duration for the capture process. If you have, say, 30 minutes of video on a 60-minute tape, you can tell Studio to stop recording after 30 minutes. Or you can just leave the default value (which usually reflects how much recording time is available on your hard drive). Studio is smart enough not to record blank tape to your hard disk, and so you don't have to worry about the disk filling up with empty video.

Click Start Capture, and you're off to the races! Your camcorder should start playing, and you should see video in the Player window. Now, go get yourself a cupcake: You've earned it!

NOTE   *You may or may not hear audio during the capture process. If you do, it'll be coming from the camcorder, not the computer. Don't worry if you don't hear anything; most video editors don't play audio during capture to preserve the computer's horsepower for capturing video error-free. The audio track will be there when the time comes to review and edit your footage.*

FIGURE 4-4   You should enter an easily identifiable name for the video you're about
to capture.

After the Capture

When the capture process is complete, click Edit. You'll see all your scenes in the
Album, ready for assembly and editing, as shown in Figure 4-5.

Congratulations! That wasn't too painful, was it? Now you're ready for
Chapter 5.

Capturing Video from an Analog Camcorder or a VCR

Here's a common scenario: After you upgraded to a DV camcorder, your old
analog camcorder sat in a closet collecting dust (and all your old videotapes
along with it). Or maybe your old analog camcorder is still your primary everyday
camcorder. Either way, you've got footage that needs to move from that camcorder
to your computer, and there's no FireWire port on the camcorder to make it happen.

However, what the camcorder likely does have is a set of composite video and
audio jacks, the kind you see on the back of nearly every television and VCR.
Problem is, most computers *don't* have jacks like that, so you're still up the video-
transfer creek without a paddle.

You have two options at your disposal:

- Connect your camcorder or VCR to an analog video input device.

- Connect your camcorder or VCR to the analog inputs on your digital
  camcorder—if it has them.

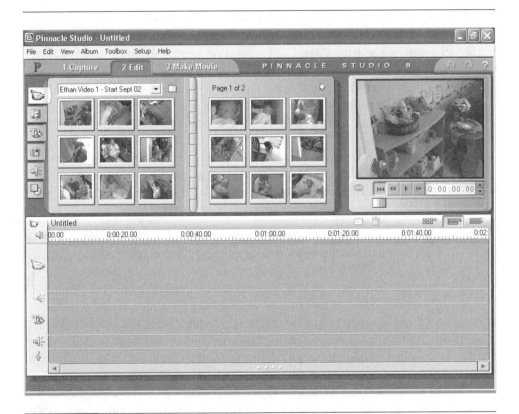

FIGURE 4-5   When the capture process is complete, you'll see scenes in the Album
ready for assembly and editing.

Capturing Through an Analog Capture Device

Let's start by talking a bit about the analog-input solutions we first described way
back in Chapter 2. With the right video card or external accessory, you can capture
analog video almost as easily as you can DV video over FireWire. Analog capture
cards are available that slip into a PCI slot on your PC. You can also get a video
card (with video inputs) which, when used with the audio input on your sound
card, lets you capture analog video. Or you can get an external capture device that
connects via your computer's USB port.

Which should you choose? Here are some pros and cons:

- **PCI-Based Capture Cards**   PCI cards for analog video capture provide excellent video quality, because they connect to the innards of your computer via a high-speed data bus. These cards usually have both composite video and S-video inputs, which means they can accommodate any kind of video connection. They usually also include audio inputs, simplifying the connection process. The downside of these cards is their installation complexity: you need to open your computer, find an empty PCI slot, add the card, and then install driver software after you put everything back together. If you're not shy about opening your computer and you have a PCI slot to spare, we think that this solution is a good one.

- **Video Card**   Older video cards usually came with just one connection— a VGA port that plugged into your computer monitor. More modern video cards have two VGA ports so that you can attach a pair of monitors, and some might even have an S-video output to display data on a television. But a special breed of multimedia video card goes above and beyond the call of duty by supplying a complete set of video input and output ports. Video cards like that are great for capturing video, and they typically have very sophisticated computer graphics features as well, which makes them a blast for games and other applications. Advantages? They're all-in-one devices that use only a single slot, they offer excellent video-capture quality, and they typically come with a bunch of other goodies as well—such as the ability to capture television shows to your PC using TiVo-like software.

- **External Capture Device**   An external device is the easiest sort of gadget to install. Usually, you just plug it into an available USB port and install some software. You're then ready to capture without ever having to open your PC. However, many of these gadgets have a serious liability: they're not really fast enough to capture a full 30 frames per second of video without losing frames or making other errors during the capture process. If you buy one of these devices, you're better off with USB 2.0, which is dramatically faster than the older USB 1.1 devices. USB 2.0 should be able to keep up with analog video, but only if your PC also has USB 2.0 ports. If your PC is a few years old and supports only USB 1.1, your spiffy new USB 2.0 capture device will run at old USB 1.1 speeds. And those lost frames will add up to glitchy, stuttering video. Our advice: Avoid these devices unless you have a new, fast PC with USB 2.0 ports.

Wondering where to look for the right gadgets? Check out your local computer store. Or rely on our advice, and look into one of these devices:

Device	Comments
ATI All-in-Wonder	The ATI Technologies All-in-Wonder family of video cards is the perfect solution for someone who wants a broad selection of video input and output ports on a sound card. These cards come with all kinds of cool stuff, such as video cables, a remote control, and buckets of helpful software. But the bottom line is that they can capture video from a VCR or analog camcorder without glitches. All-in-Wonder is our top choice for analog video capture.
AVerMedia DVD EZMaker PCI	If you have a PCI slot to spare, the EZMaker package from AVerMedia captures video flawlessly via completely analog video ports. If you don't want to mess with your existing video card, this is a second-best option.
ADS USB Instant DVD 2.0	If you simply want to connect your camcorder or VCR to an external box and be done with it, you'd be hard pressed to find a better solution than the ADS Tech USB Instant DVD 2.0. The "2.0" means that the device supports USB 2.0, which is dramatically faster than USB 1.1, and should be able to capture your video error-free. We'd still prefer a faster solution (like the internal products), but this product should get the job done.

In a nutshell, here's how to use one of those analog devices to capture your video:

1. Either the camcorder or the video-capture device should have come with a video-transfer cable. That cable has red, yellow, and white connectors on both ends. Use it to connect the camcorder to the video-capture device.

2. Following the instructions supplied with the video-capture software, record the footage on your computer using the highest available quality setting. Usually, that setting is DVD or MPEG-2. Make sure to give the resulting file a descriptive name, and save it in a folder where you can easily find it again.

3. If you're a PC user, the next step is to fire up Studio 8, open your project (or use the analog video as the basis of a new one), and click the little yellow folder that appears in the Album. You can now navigate to the folder that contains your captured video. Select the file, and click Open.

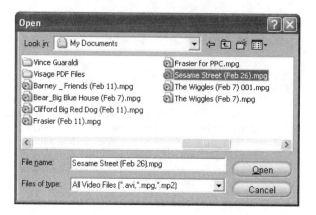

OR

If you're a Macintosh user, you'll import the footage using the Import command in your editing application. In iMovie, choose File | Import, and use the Open dialog box to navigate to the file. When you find the file, select it, and click Open.

Capturing Through Your Digital Camcorder

Analog capture devices are great if you enjoy adding stuff to your PC, but we might be able to give you a shortcut through the whole analog capture issue. Does your digital camcorder have analog video inputs? If it does, you can connect your analog camcorder or VCR to the digital camcorder, and then plug the digital camcorder into your PC via FireWire.

TIP   *It may not be immediately obvious that your camcorder has analog video inputs. Not all do, and some use the same set of A/V cables for both input and output, complicating the job of figuring things out. The easiest solution is to check your camcorder user guide.*

Using your existing digital camcorder to capture analog video is easy and (even better) inexpensive. Here's what you need to do:

1. Plug your analog video source (camcorder or VCR) into the video and audio inputs on your digital camcorder. You may need to use a special cable that came with your digital camcorder.

2. Connect the digital camcorder to your PC using your FireWire cable.

3. Turn on the PC, camcorder, and analog source. Set the digital camcorder to VCR or Playback mode.

4. Check your camcorder manual or onscreen menu for a setting that recognizes the analog video inputs. There probably is one, and you'll need to activate it before you can see analog video.

5. Insert your analog videotape into the analog source, but be sure that you don't have any videotape in the digital camcorder.

6. Launch Pinnacle Studio 8 on your computer and start recording digital video. Wait a few seconds until you know that the capture is really under way.

7. Press Play on the analog camcorder or VCR. You should see the analog video appear in the viewfinder of the digital camcorder and in the capture window on your PC.

8. When playback finishes, stop the capture. Your video is now on the computer and can be edited like any other digital video.

NOTE   *If you leave a videotape in the digital camcorder, the analog source won't transfer to your PC. Instead, when you click Capture on the PC, the digital camcorder will start its own videotape rolling, and that's what you'll capture. Always remove the tape from the digital camcorder when capturing video through the analog inputs.*

Where to Find It

Web site	Address	What's there
ATI Technologies	www.ati.com	ATI All-in-Wonder video cards
ADS Tech	www.adstech.com	ADS USB Instant DVD 2.0
AVerMedia	www.aver.com	AVerMedia DVD EZMaker PCI
Symantec	www.norton.com	DiskDoctor
Micromat	www.micromat.com	Micromat Drive

Chapter 5

Editing Your Masterpiece on a PC

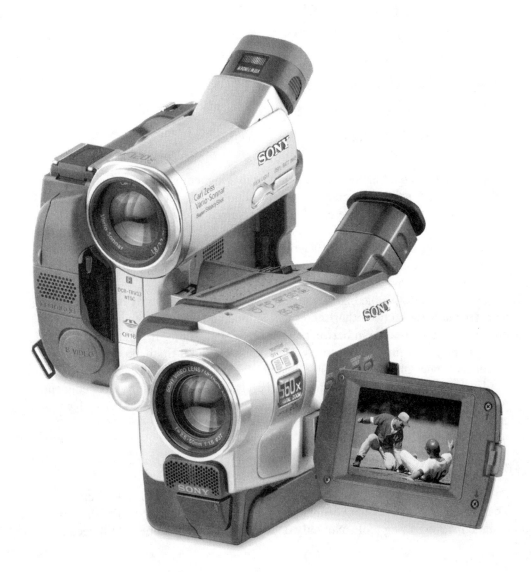

How to...

- Manage video files on your PC

- Use the Edit mode in Studio 8

- Use the Timeline to navigate around a project

- Add scenes to your production

- Trim and reposition your clips

- Split scenes in two

- Add video transitions between scenes

- Modify your video with visual effects

- Composite video for clever bluescreen effects

What's the most fun and exciting part of making a movie? Some people might tell you it's the videography: actually shooting the scenes with a camcorder. And although those folks are entitled to their opinions, we feel differently. The coolest part of the process is actually editing all those hours of raw footage into a coherent story. It doesn't matter whether you're making a movie of little Joey's birthday party, your last summer vacation, or your dog; it's your skill as an editor that makes your movies fun to watch.

In the old days, people had to splice lengths of film together by hand. To insert a new scene between two others, they'd literally cut the film into two pieces and connect the new footage in between. That made performing sophisticated edits difficult, time-consuming, and tricky. Dave knows about it firsthand: as a teenager, he edited movies that he had recorded on his dad's Super8 movie camera.

These days, of course, it's a whole new ball game. You can comfortably edit, cut, paste, splice, move, and delete your digital video movie all on a PC. That's what this chapter focuses on.

Working with Video Files

For much of this book, we use Pinnacle Studio 8 for our video editing examples. That's because Studio is an excellent program that contains nearly all of the most common video editing tools. Not only does it have all the features you'll need for your own movies, it's also an easy and inexpensive way to get into video. For those occasions when Studio 8 doesn't quite get the job done, we'll switch to other popular video programs.

For now, let's look at Studio, which is pretty representative of most video editing programs. Figure 5-1 shows the main Edit screen. At the upper right, you can see a video window called the Monitor. A Project Album is at the upper left, and the video editing Timeline is on the bottom. The essence of video editing in Studio 8 is to take clips from the Project Album and arrange them in the Timeline in the order that you'd like them to play.

To get started, you'll want to make sure that your video clips are loaded into the Album.

5

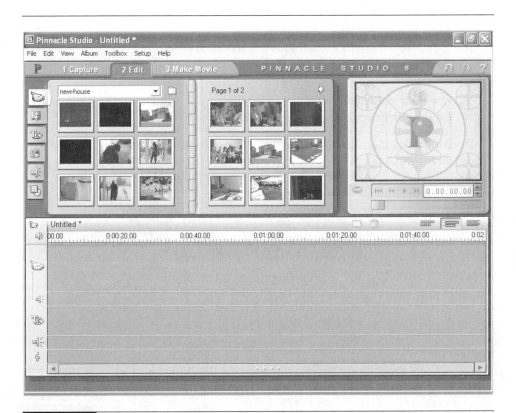

FIGURE 5-1   In Pinnacle Studio 8, making a movie is a matter of dragging clips from the Album or video library to the movie Timeline, and editing it via the Monitor.

But what exactly is the Album? It's really just a holding bin for all of the media you might want to use in your video. It shows thumbnails of your video clips, transitions, still images, sounds, and more. The first tab, Videos, shows a single video clip at a time. If you've captured a video in one large file with scene detection switched on, you'll see lots of thumbnails. Each one is a scene from the video. The thumbnails are sort of like bookmarks: no matter how many thumbnails you see in the Album, it's all just one video file.

If you have more than one video file in the current folder, you can access the others by clicking the folder's drop-down list. There, you'll see a list of all the other video files in the current folder.

To change folders, click the Folder icon to the right of the drop-down list.

If you have already used Studio 8 to capture video from your camcorder (see Chapter 4), your scenes should be ready and waiting for you. Use the Folder icon to find them, and they'll appear in the album.

If a video file on your PC hasn't had its scenes autodetected, you can convert that video into multiple, easy-to-use scenes now. Just follow these steps:

1. Use the Folder icon to find the video file on your hard disk. The thumbnail for the video should appear in the Album.

2. Right-click the video thumbnail, and choose Detect Scenes by Video Content.

Copy	Ctrl+C
Paste	Ctrl+V
Combine Scenes	
Split Scene	
Subdivide Scenes	
Detect Scenes by Video Content	
Detect Scenes by Shooting Time and Date	
Set Thumbnail	
Find Scene in Project	
✔ Icon View	
Details View	

After a few minutes (depending upon the length of the video), the various scenes should appear in the Album.

NOTE   *Editing on a Mac? Check out Chapter 6 to dig into iMovie and Final Cut.*

Saving Your Work

In video editing programs, the "project" concept covers just the act of keeping all of your video files, edits, titles, and other doodads in one place. A project is not a finished movie, and selecting File | Save does not render your video into a finished, watchable product (see Figure 5-2). Rather, a project is just a lot of little digital pointers to various video clips that, when *rendered,* will play back as a finished movie.

When you start a new video, be sure to use the File menu to create a new project, and *save your work often.*

Some video programs require that you identify the details of your project right up front—such as if you're planning to input DV files or save your work as a DVD.

FIGURE 5-2   Saving your project doesn't render the various clips, effects, and titles as a completed movie. That happens when you "make the movie" or "render" the production (depending on the terminology that your video editor uses).

Other programs don't bug you with those details when you're first getting started. Either way, be sure to name your project so that it's readily identifiable. Save your work every 15 minutes or so. If you don't save regularly, and if your PC happens to crash after three hours of intense video editing, you won't lose the video files themselves (they're already saved on your computer); but you will lose all of the meticulous editing and arranging of the video clips, and that can be frustrating.

Understanding the Timeline

In Studio 8, all of the action really happens down in the Timeline, and so it's important to understand the various control parts. First of all, note the various rows *(tracks)* in the Timeline. The top track is the *video track*. It depicts all of the clips in your video production. Under the video track are tracks for titles and additional audio.

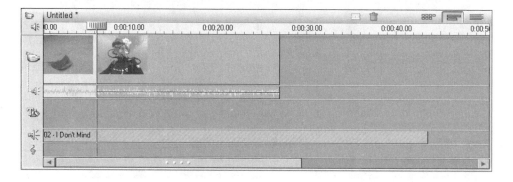

NOTE   *We're calling those video and audio tracks at the bottom of the screen the "Timeline" throughout most of this book. That's because most video editors use a timeline motif for working with video clips, and it's really the most logical and straightforward way to do it. Keep in mind, though, that Studio 8 also has a storyboard mode that you can use instead.*

The Timeline has a time strip running across the top. You can zoom in or out of the Timeline to see more (or less) of your production.

Some video editors provide a screen control that you can use to zoom the Timeline. In Studio 8, just position the pointer in the time strip. Click and drag the pointer as shown in Figure 5-3.

Dragging to the left shrinks the timescale so that you can fit more video into the window. Dragging to the right expands the timescale, letting you zoom in on as

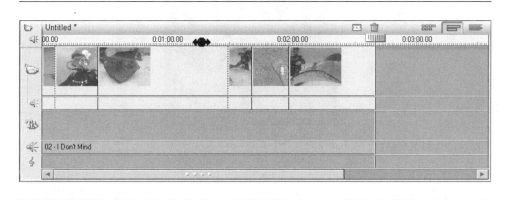

FIGURE 5-3   You can drop new clips between existing scenes in the video track.

little as a few minutes or seconds of video. If you zoom in so far that there's more video than will fit on the screen, notice the scroll bar at the very bottom that you can use to move around in your production:

Once you have placed a few video clips in the Timeline, you may want to watch the video or move to a specific point in the production. You have a choice of several methods:

■ In the Monitor, press Play to start the video. You can also use Fast-Forward and Rewind, or you can enter the exact time of the scene in hours, minutes, seconds, and frames. (There are 30 frames of video each second.)

■ Drag the Monitor *scrubber* to quickly browse through the video. ("Scrubber" is the name for the drag button under the Monitor that you can use to cruise through the video.)

■ Drag the Timeline scrubber. It works in the same way as the Monitor scrubber does. Indeed, when you drag one, the other moves automatically at the same time. However, the Timeline scrubber tends to offer much more precision in navigating to a specific point within a video clip.

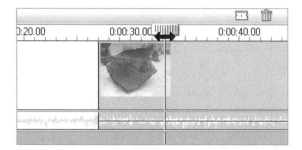

Finally, it's worth pointing out that not all video editors use a Timeline metaphor to help you edit your video. For instance, some programs use a storyboard concept instead. In a storyboard layout, you don't see a Timeline with hours and minutes at all. Instead, when you drag video clips to the production zone, you see simply a collection of video thumbnails laid out in sequence (see Figure 5-4).

Studio 8 offers a storyboard option: click Storyboard View on the right-hand side of the Timeline. The button to return to Timeline View is right next to it, and a third icon lets you see your clips in a text view known as an Edit Decision List (EDL).

Want our advice? The Timeline is the most flexible and user-friendly way to edit your video, and so we suggest sticking with that.

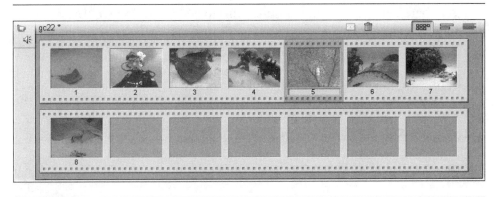

FIGURE 5-4   Pinnacle Studio 8 lets you use either a Timeline or a storyboard metaphor when editing video. Use whichever method you find the most comfortable.

Adding Scenes to the Timeline

After the preceding buildup, you probably think that adding clips to the Timeline is an onerous, multistep process that takes hours to master. Here's the exact, step-by-step process:

1. In the Album, find a thumbnail that you want to put into your movie.

2. Drag it from the Album to the top track in the Timeline, and drop it there.

That's it. Not too hard, right?

It's important to remember that the video clips in your Timeline are not new files stored somewhere on your hard disk. And that means you can't delete the original video clips while you're still working on the production. The clips that you see in the Timeline just represent—point to, if you will—portions of the original video file. If you move, rename, or delete the original file, your video editor won't be able to find your clips to complete the movie.

NOTE   *At this early stage of the game, don't worry too much about the order in which you drop elements into the Timeline. It's very easy to shuffle things around later on. For now, you just want to concentrate on moving stuff in.*

From here, you can continue to find clips to add to your video. Drag the new clips to the Timeline. As you drag-and-drop clips into the Timeline, you have two choices:

■ To append a new clip to the end of the movie, drop the clip to the right of an existing scene.

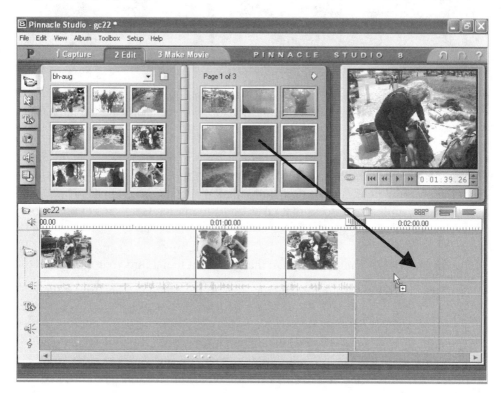

■ To insert a clip into the movie between existing scenes, drop it between two previously inserted clips (see Figure 5-5).

Want to delete a clip from the project? Just click the clip in the Timeline, and press DELETE. Of course, that action doesn't delete the clip from the hard disk; it just removes the clip from the movie project.

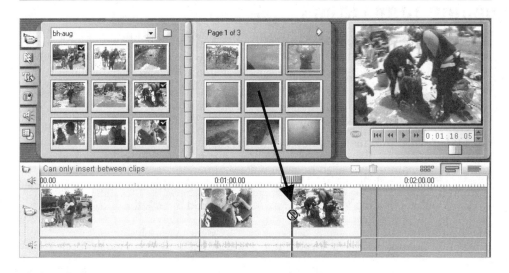

FIGURE 5-5   In a rolling edit, you shorten a clip and the very next scene automatically gets longer to preserve the total length of the movie.

Previewing Video Clips

Okay, insertion is pretty easy; but how do you know if you're inserting the right video clip into your movie?

That's easy: You preview it. To preview a clip, just double-click a scene while it's still in the Album. The clip immediately starts to play in the Monitor.

You can use the controls under the Monitor to fast-forward, rewind, and zoom directly to a particular moment in the scene. If you know when a particular event occurs in the scene, type the time into the time box, and press ENTER. (In the time box, the digits represent hours, minutes, seconds, and frames, in that order. There are 30 frames in each second of video.)

Trimming Your Video Clips

Unless you're, say, Andy Warhol or Kevin Costner, you probably shoot a lot more tape than you actually plan to include in your finished movie, and you need some way to trim the fat out of your production. So it stands to reason that your video editor should supply some method for editing out parts of scenes that you don't want or need.

In Pinnacle Studio 8, the process is very straightforward—and quite similar to most other video programs. Here's how to trim your video:

1. Drag a video clip to the Timeline.

2. Double-click the video clip. A window should open—the Clip Properties window.

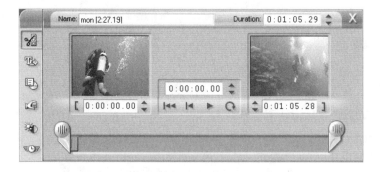

3. Use the scroll bar or Play control to advance through the scene. When you find the point in the clip that should be its true beginning in the video (the *set-in point*), mark it by clicking the open bracket under the left video thumbnail. Alternatively, you can drag the big slider to the right to mark the set-in point:

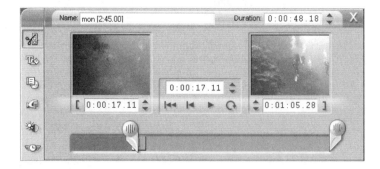

4. Likewise, find the point at which you want the clip to end in the video, and click the close bracket or use the other big slider to designate the *set-out point.*

The marked set-in point tells your video editor where a given clip is to actually begin playing when it appears in the final production. By using set-in and set-out points, you can trim your clips without ever really discarding or deleting video. The unused parts of the scene are still there; the editor simply doesn't use them in this particular project.

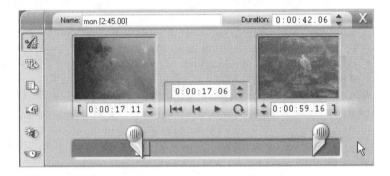

Whichever method you use to establish set-in and set-out points, notice that, in the Timeline, the length of your video changes as you make modifications in the Clip Properties window. When you're happy with the results, close the Clip Properties window by clicking the Close box.

Studio 8 provides one monitor for viewing your finished production and a pair of monitors for editing clip properties. In some programs, such as Premiere from Adobe, two monitors are open onscreen all the time: one shows the project, and another includes trim controls for editing individual clips in the Timeline (see Figure 5-6).

We again need to emphasize something very important about trimming clips: the actual video file is not affected by this editing step. No video is actually discarded, and no video is lost. In fact, you can double-click a clip in the Timeline at any time and change the set-in and set-out points—none of the changes are permanent.

TIP   *You can trim clips in the Timeline without ever opening the Clip Properties window. Just grab the edge of a clip and drag it to the left or right; you can see the changes to the clip in the Monitor.*

FIGURE 5-6   Adobe Premiere uses dual monitors for viewing the production video and
editing clips. Notice that the set-in and set-out points for starting and
ending clips look similar no matter which program you use.

Using Ripples and Rolls

If you use a video editing program such as Adobe Premiere, you will no doubt see
a few common terms that Pinnacle Studio 8 doesn't use. Here are some that you
might run across:

- **Ripple Edit**   Suppose you want to edit the duration of a clip—shorten its
  set-out point, in other words—without affecting the duration of the clip that
  follows it in the Timeline. (As you shorten a clip, for instance, the entire
  following clip slides to the left to fill the gap.) You can use the Ripple tool to
  drag the ends of the video clip, changing its characteristics without affecting
  the other clips in the video. (This is the way that Studio 8 works all the time,
  by the way.)

- **Rolling Edit**   What if you want to change the length of a clip in the middle of a movie, but it's very important that you not change the total length of the production? You need to cut a few seconds from the end of scene 3, for instance, but you need scene 4 to lengthen in response, keeping the total video length the same. That's when it's time to use the Rolling Edit tool to drag your clips around. There's no way to perform a rolling edit automatically in Studio 8, but in Figure 5-7 you can see a rolling edit in action in Premiere.

- **Slide Edit**   Here's another puzzler for you. Suppose you have at least three clips in a row in your movie, and you want to slide the middle clip to a point earlier or later in the movie without affecting the video production's overall length (that is, the earlier clip would have to get shorter and the later clip would have to lengthen automatically in response to whatever you do with the middle clip). The Slide tool lets you move a clip to the left or right, and the clips on either side will get shorter or longer accordingly, keeping the video's total length a constant. (There's no way to slide a clip in Studio 8. You have to adjust all the set-in and set-out points manually to achieve the same objective.) See Figure 5-8.

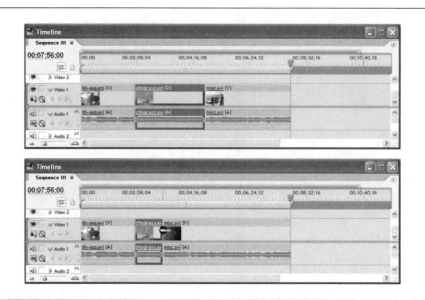

FIGURE 5-7 When you perform a slide edit, you "slide" a clip in the movie without changing the total length of the film.

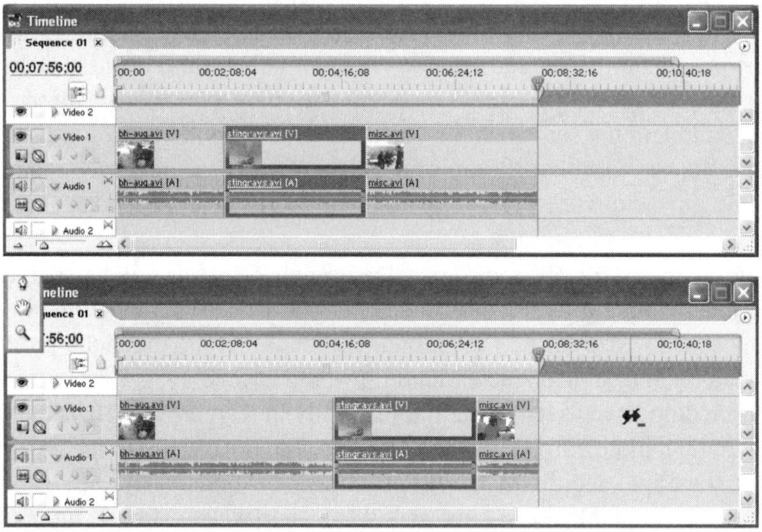

FIGURE 5-8 You can vary the intensity of an effect through the length of a clip using the Start, Hold, and Finish tabs.

Of course, all of the trim tools only work to the extent that you have extra video in the clips beyond the set-in and set-out points. Remember the way you used set-in and set-out points to shorten clips earlier in the chapter? What comes into play here is the extra, unused video beyond those edit points—video that the audience usually wouldn't see. You can only slide a clip as far as you have extra frames beyond the set-in or set-out points.

Splitting and Joining Clips

Suppose you have a lengthy scene in the middle of the movie that you'd like to cut in half. (Perhaps you want to insert a different scene in the middle to break up the flow of the action.) That's easy to do. Just follow these steps:

1. Drag the Timeline scrubber to the position where you want to cut the scene.

2. Right-click the scene, and choose Split Clip from the resulting pop-up menu.

    That's it. Where once there was one scene, now there are two. The video editor actually created a duplicate clip and established the set-in and set-out points for both clips so that it appears, in the Timeline, as if the one clip was simply cut into two.

    Anything that can be cut can be rejoined. If you decide that you don't like the split, select both halves of the split clip, right-click, and choose Combine Clips from the pop-up menu.

Adding Transitions to Your Movie

Half the fun of making your own videos is the opportunity to include extra goodies such as television-style transitions that change the scene in subtle or dramatic ways. Most video editing programs come with at least a few dozen transition effects, and often you can buy more.

Many, many kinds of transition effects have been created over the years. Some of the most common are these:

■ **Fades and Dissolves**   Fade and dissolve effects replace one clip with another through a full-screen transition in which one clip fades out as the other appears. In general terms, a fade is a gradual change in brightness from one scene to another, and a dissolve is a random or patterned exchange of pixels at full intensity from one scene to the next.

- **Wipes, Pushes, and Slides**   Wipe, push, and slide effects move the old clip out of the way to "make room" on the screen for the new one.

- **Peels**   Much like a wipe, a peel effects transition in a "page turning" style.

The variety of effects ranges into the hundreds, if not thousands. Many advanced effects involve animated graphics. If you've ever watched the television show *Home Improvement*, you've seen that style of transition.

> **TIP**   *Use fancy transitions sparingly. They may look cool to you during the editing process, but they can quickly cheapen the look of most finished movies. Stop and ask yourself if you've ever see a video frame spinning off into the distance or breaking into pieces during a movie, television show (Home Improvement notwithstanding), or even commercial. We think that plain, old-fashioned fades and dissolves are the best—and most professional-looking—transitions you have at your disposal.*

Adding a Transition in Studio 8

In Pinnacle Studio 8, as in most video editors, adding a transition is pretty simple. Follow these steps:

1. In the Album, click the Transitions tab to switch to the transitions library. Like the Videos tab, the Transitions tab has a drop-down list at the top. You use the drop-down list to choose other transition folders:

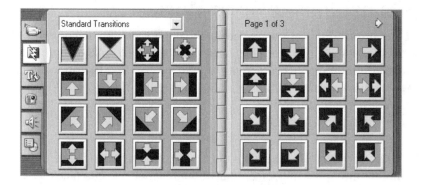

2. Pick a folder. Standard Transitions, which should be the default, is fine for now.

3. Click a transition. You should see a preview of the effect in the Monitor. Click other transitions to review your various options.

4. When you find a transition that you like, drag it from the Album into the Timeline. Drop it between two existing video clips.

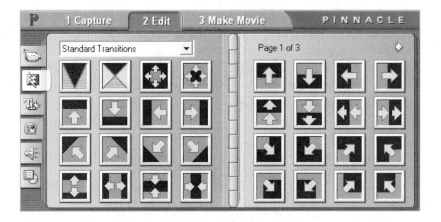

5. As soon as you drop the transition into the Timeline, the scrubber moves to the start of the transition. That means you can press the Play button under the Monitor to see what the transition will actually look like.

> **TIP** *A faster way to start playing your video from the scrubber's current position is to press* SPACEBAR. *This method should work in almost any video editing program.*

Editing Transitions

Once the transition is in place, you can use the scrubber to play it over and over again to see if you like the way it works with your actual video clips. The result may be a bit different from the preview that you watched before actually adding the transition. If you don't like the effect, you have four choices:

■ **Delete It**   Just select the transition in the Timeline, and press DELETE.

■ **Exchange It**   Drag a different transition from the Album to the Timeline, and drop it on top of the original transition. The transition automatically changes to the new one.

- **Change Its Length**   If you want the transition to be longer or shorter, grab it on the right-hand side and drag it left or right to change its length. Notice that this adjustment works like a ripple edit: the total length of the video does not change. Instead, the transition takes an equal amount of time from both the before and after clips to perform the effect.

- **Modify It**   Transition effects can usually be modified. Studio 8 simplifies the process by allowing only a single kind of edit: you can reverse the direction of the effect. Other programs sometimes offer more options. To edit a transition in Studio 8, double-click the effect in the Timeline. The Clip Properties window opens in the Album area. Click the Reverse box, and test the effect to see which version you prefer.

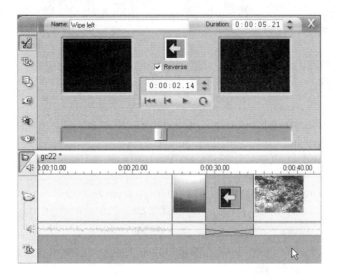

Adding More Transitions

Okay, we warned you. We said that you should stick to the simple stuff like fades and dissolves. But we can see it in your eyes: you want to explore the wide, wide world of transitions, and you're eager to add even more to your repertoire than the meager 150 or so that come with Pinnacle Studio.

   The good news is that, unlike many video editors, Pinnacle Studio 8 allows you to add more transitions. Pinnacle offers the Hollywood F/X transition add-on package, for instance, which includes almost 300 additional transition effects.

Did you know?

How to Build a Scene for a Good Transition

When you apply transitions to your video clips, you should consider extending the set-in and set-out points so that only non-essential action is lost in the transition. Some programs, such as Adobe Premiere, automatically try to use the wasted space outside the set-in and set-out points for transitions. Other editors, such as Pinnacle Studio, do not. You should experiment with your video editor to see how it works.

You can get the Hollywood F/X package from your local computer store in a regular boxed version, or you can download it from the Pinnacle web site. Either way, it costs about the same (about $50 for the Plus version or $100 for the Pro version, which has extra tools such as a sophisticated text generator).

Once you install Hollywood F/X, the extra transitions appear in the usual place—the Album at the top of the screen—and they can be used in your movies just like any other transition. As much as we try to avoid really flashy effects, even we are wowed by the really cool organic and real-world transitions.

Applying Fancy Video Effects

If you've ever seen MTV or a low-budget science fiction show filmed in Toronto, then you have no doubt been exposed to the magical world of digital video effects. Many video editors come with at least a small handful. Some of the effects are a bit over-the-top goofy, but many can be used to spice up your video production, making it look like a big-budget film.

Okay, we're exaggerating. But effects can at least make it look as if you *have* a budget. Available effects range from simple color adjustments to more sophisticated tricks such as solarization and pixilation of the video display. Some programs even let you add digital swirls, snow, and wave-like distortion, or render the video as a "negative." The fanciest effect of all is combining two video clips into a composite shot.

Video Effects in Studio 8

Unfortunately, Studio 8 is one of the most conservative video editing programs; it offers just a handful of simple effects. To find to them, double-click a clip in the Timeline. When the Clip Properties window opens, click the fifth tab to open the Visual Effects window:

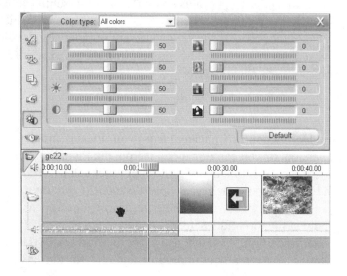

All of the effects work pretty much the way they do in an image editor such as Adobe Photoshop Elements or Paint Shop Pro. The difference is that any change you make to the settings affects not just a single image, but every frame of video in the currently selected clip.

Here are the eight video tricks that Studio 8 offers:

■ **Hue**   The Hue control changes the color bias of the clip.

■ **Saturation**   The Saturation control changes the color saturation. You can intensify the colors by sliding the controller to the right, or drain the scene of color by sliding to the left. Moving the controller all the way to the left turns your scene black and white.

■ **Brightness**   The Brightness control is just what it sounds like: a method of adding or removing brightness from the scene.

■ **Contrast**   The Contrast control is often used in concert with the Brightness control. As a rule of thumb, change the contrast at one-half to one-third the rate you change the brightness.

- **Blur**   Want to give the impression that your video is being viewed through the eyes of someone who has lost their glasses? Using the Blur control, you can dial anything from a soft-focus buzz to a headache-inducing sheen.

- **Emboss**   Using the Emboss control, you can render your entire movie as if it were embossed on sheet metal.

- **Mosaic**   The Mosaic control pixelizes your video. This classic "digital" look tells the viewer that the scene is being seen through the eyes of a computer or killer robot.

- **Posterize**   The Posterize control reduces the total number of colors in the video. This reductive filter was often used in music videos—until even Whitesnake got tired of using it.

To apply effects to the currently selected clip, choose one or more effects in the window, and watch the results in the monitor. When you're happy with the result, click the Close box on the Clip Properties window. That's all there is to it.

Controlling Video Effects in Other Video Editors

If you use another video editor, video effects are probably activated in a similar fashion. And many other programs do something that Pinnacle Studio 8 cannot do: they can change the effect over time. When you apply an effect—a blur, for instance—to a scene in Studio, the effect remains exactly the same in intensity throughout the entire scene. In many other programs, the ongoing intensity is adjustable.

For instance, one of our all-time favorite video editors is VideoWave Movie Creator from Roxio. (It used to be sold by a company called MGI.) VideoWave has three different modules loaded with video effects:

- **Darkroom**   In Darkroom mode, you can recolor images with a few great presets.

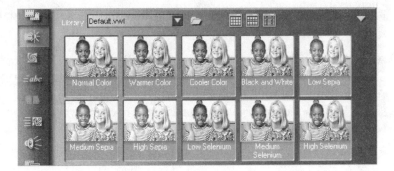

■ **Special Effects** In the Special Effects mode, you'll find a collection of interesting special effects that are, perhaps, most useful for sci-fi-themed videos.

■ **Video Mixer** Using the Video Mixer, you can combine two different video clips in interesting ways. Just drag a second video clip into the Video Mixer monitor, and vary the settings until you achieve an effect you like.

Let's set the behavior of an effect in VideoWave:

1. Double-click a clip in the Timeline to select it, and then click Special Effects in the VideoWave toolbar. You should see the clip in the Monitor and the library of effects onscreen.

2. Pick an effect—Oil Painting, let's say—and drag it to the Special Effects monitor.

3. At the bottom of the screen, you should see tabs for Start, Hold, and Finish. Click Start to make sure it's selected, and then set the Effect Level to **0**. Assume that you want the effect to start about a quarter of the way into the scene. Slide the scrubber over about 25 percent of the way. Then, under the Monitor, click Set Effect Start Position.

5

4. Now, click Hold. This is the meat of the effect, so set the Effect Level to about **60**. Where should the peak occur? Move the scrubber a bit to the right (to the middle of the scene), and click Set Beginning of Effect Hold. Drag the scrubber further to the right, and click to set the end of the hold period.

5. Finally, click Finish, and set the effect back to **0**. Drag the scrubber a short distance to the right of the hold range, and click Set Effect End Position (see Figure 5-9).

6. Click Apply, and play back the effect in the Monitor to see if it came out the way you wanted. If not, you can correct it.

Notice the color-coded bar with the timeline in the Special Effects monitor. It shows the timing of the effect: The red portion is the "hold" period (when the effect is at its height). The white portions mark the time from the start to the hold and from the hold to the finish. As you can see, this is a very powerful way to control effects in your videos. And VideoWave is far from being the only program

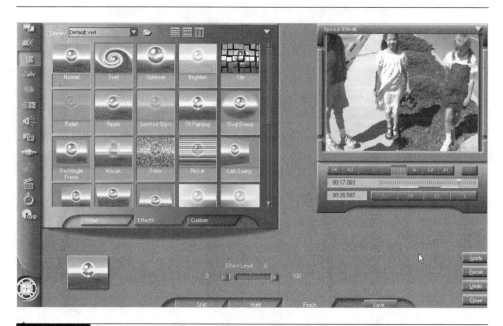

FIGURE 5-9   You can control the special effect level and duration in Roxio VideoWave.

that allows you to add timed effects. Premiere, for instance, uses *keyframes*: you can set a series of keyframes in your video to trigger changes in the effects.

Trying Your Hand at Slow (or Fast) Motion Video

Movie makers have few more effective tools to tug at the heart strings than slow motion. When that big moment comes—the bride walking down the aisle, the little leaguer hitting the ball, the car slamming into the fire hydrant (okay, maybe that last one is emotional for different reasons)—seeing it happen in slow motion is dramatic. And the moment resonates a lot better than when it happens in real time.

Thankfully, most video editors include some method of adjusting the playback speed of video clips. That means you can slow down (or speed up) video clips throughout your production.

TIP   *You probably already realize that speeding up a video is a common technique for comic effect (think Charlie Chaplin), but faster-than-normal video can have practical, non-comic applications as well. You can make a speeding car or plane seem to be moving faster than it really is, for instance.*

In Pinnacle Studio, you can finagle the speed of a video this way:

1. Double-click a clip in the timeline. The Clip Properties window should open in the Album area.

2. Click the very last tab, which looks like a clock with wings (hey, don't look at us—we didn't design the thing).

3. Now, by moving the Speed slider at the left, you can vary the playback speed of the clip. You can change the playback from about 10 percent of the ordinary speed up to as fast as five times normal.

4. The Strobe slider, to the right of the Speed slider, offers another cool effect. Instead of smoothly animating the clip, it turns the images into a strobe-like montage of stills. Strobing can be highly effective for dramatic effect if used sparingly.

5. When you're happy with the effect, click the Close box to accept the changes.

That's all there is to it. But both slow- and fast-motion effects are best used only occasionally. Here are a few last tips to keep in mind:

- Video is usually captured at 30 frames per second. Real Hollywood slo-mo is typically captured at 100 frames per second or more. As a result, slow motion in home movies can't approach the level of professionalism found in commercial films. Your original camcorder video simply hasn't captured enough frames, and so slo-mo often appears jerky. If your video editor gives you a "smooth frames" option (like the one in Studio 8), use it to smooth out the stutters. But remember that the number of frames per second in the original capture is why your slo-mo won't look as good as the ones on the big screen.

- Want to make a movie slower or faster than the program allows? Apply the speed effect and then render the movie (see Chapter 11 for details). Next, load the rendered slo-mo clip back into Studio 8 and apply even more slow motion to it. You can repeat that process as often as you like to get really slow or fast video, but remember that the overall quality of the effect will definitely start to suffer.

- Want to add some slow motion to a specific moment in the middle of a long clip? Just split the clip on both sides of the slow-motion section, and then apply slow motion just to the middle clip of the three.

■ Remember that most video editors will mute the audio for any scene that isn't playing at normal speed.

Compositing Video

Thank goodness for technology. It's getting easier and easier to add certain kinds of video effects. A decade ago, bluescreening—the art of matting two video clips together so that your subject appears to be somewhere he or she isn't—was a studio trick that cost lots of money and was hard to accomplish without very sophisticated gear. Lately, Dave has pulled off some very convincing bluescreen effects in his basement with a camcorder, a big green backdrop, and a program like Visual Communicator Pro or Adobe After Effects.

There are many ways to composite two video clips, and you can use compositing to achieve all sorts of goals:

■ **Special Effects**   You can line the windows of a car with blue or green material, shoot actors in the stationary vehicle, and later composite a moving road in the widows.

■ **A "Virtual Set"**   You can shoot someone against a green or blue backdrop, and then later replace the backdrop with video from a completely different location—like the scene in Figure 5-10.

■ **Over-the-Shoulder Video**   You can play news anchor by compositing video into a green or blue board over your subject's shoulder.

FIGURE 5-10   Bluescreening is an easy way to add a professional-looking effect to your video. You need to obtain a large backdrop, though, and to make sure it's well lit.

Once you have the bluescreen video, though, what do you do with it? How do you composite it?

As we mentioned back in Chapter 3, you can use a program such as Visual Communicator Pro to composite two video sources. The downside of using Visual Communicator is that you have to record the bluescreen video directly to the PC from a camcorder connected via a FireWire cable—which is not always convenient. We prefer to shoot both sources at our leisure and combine them in a video editing program. There's no way to do that in Studio 8, but you can do it in many other applications. In Roxio VideoWave, for instance, here's all you have to do:

1. With the background video already in the Timeline and selected, click Video Mixer in the toolbar.

2. Drag the bluescreen video from the library into the Video Mixer monitor. This second layer of video is the one on which you're going to work digital magic to create the composite.

3. At the bottom of the screen, set the video size to **100%** for all three positions—Start, Hold, and Finish (see Figure 5-11). Also, make sure that the Position is the center of the screen.

4. Click Remove Color, then click Color to open the Color dialog box.

5. Click Pick a Color, and then click on the blue (or green) background in the monitor. If the backdrop has large variations in color because of light and shadow, try to pick a mid-tone. Click OK to close the dialog box.

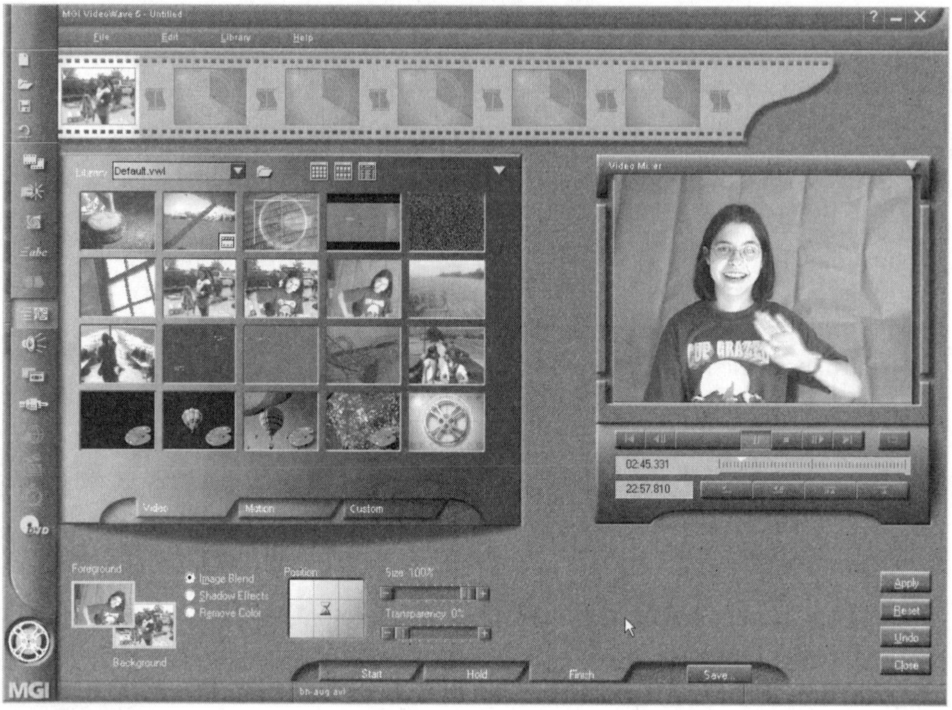

FIGURE 5-11 Bluescreening is easy to do in video editors like Roxio VideoWave.

6. Slowly increase the Tolerance until all of the bluescreen is replaced by the underlying video, but not so much that the subject starts to disappear as well.

As you can now appreciate, it's important to make sure that your subject and the foreground use colors very different from that of the bluescreen. In Figure 5-12, you can see how the established tolerance level lets some of the background video show through, but not yet quite enough to completely erase the bluescreened portion of the image.

> **TIP** *Here's an easy special effect you can do with bluescreen—dress your subject in clothing that's the same color as the screen. When you apply the color replacement effect, you can render some body parts invisible.*

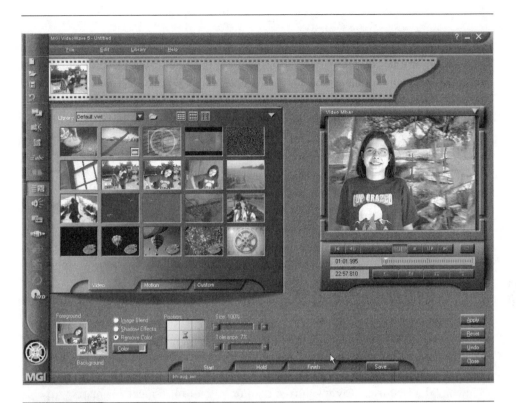

FIGURE 5-12   By appropriately setting the Tolerance, you can erase just the screen, allowing the background video to show through. Here, the tolerance isn't yet quite high enough; you can still see the screen.

Probably the king of bluescreening is the Keylight plug-in that comes with Adobe After Effects. Setting up a bluescreen effect with After Effects takes just moments, and a wealth of easy-to-use tools makes it easy to eliminate the background without blowing out the subject at the same time. Our favorite trick: you can reposition the foreground or background video—handy if you have a "talking head" scene and want to move the person to the side to give the viewer a better look at the background video.

Don't forget that if you have more than one video editing program and you like different features in each program, the video files are interchangeable. You can render a composite in VideoWave or After Effects, for instance, and, provided that you save the finished product as a DV-quality AVI file, you can import the composite into another video editing program where you can add different effects or titling, or burn a DVD.

Leave the Editing to Your PC

Believe it or not, you can entrust the job of editing your movie to the computer itself. That's an attractive proposition for some folks—after all, editing clips into a coherent movie is often the hardest, most time-consuming part of making a home movie. If your computer volunteers to edit clips for you, why not let it?

Yeah, we know: it sounds too good to be true. And in many ways, it is. Your computer isn't smart enough to correctly assemble clips to actually tell a story based on your script, storyboard, or animatics. But if all you need to do is assemble clips into a home movie and set it to music, a company called muvee Technologies has an interesting program you might want to try.

Simply put, muvee autoProducer converts your raw, unpolished footage and still images into a compelling music video. Just import your video, select the soundtrack, and then choose details such as the movie's style, tempo, and clip order. From there, autoProducer analyzes your video and matches the clips to the music so that changes occur at the appropriate times. You can choose from among two dozen styles, some of which have very specific themes—for example, silent movies or black-and-white television. You can save the finished product in a variety of ways, including to DVD.

The autoProducer software won't assemble an epic drama for you, but it's well worth trying for simple home movies that are set to music. You can download a free trial at www.muvee.com or buy autoProducer for just $49.

Where to Find It

Web site	Address	What's there
Adobe Systems	www.adobe.com	Adobe After Effects
muvee Technologies	www.muvee.com	muvee autoProducer
Pinnacle Systems	www.pinnaclesys.com	Pinnacle Studio 8
Roxio	www.roxio.com	VideoWave 5

Chapter 6   Editing on a Mac

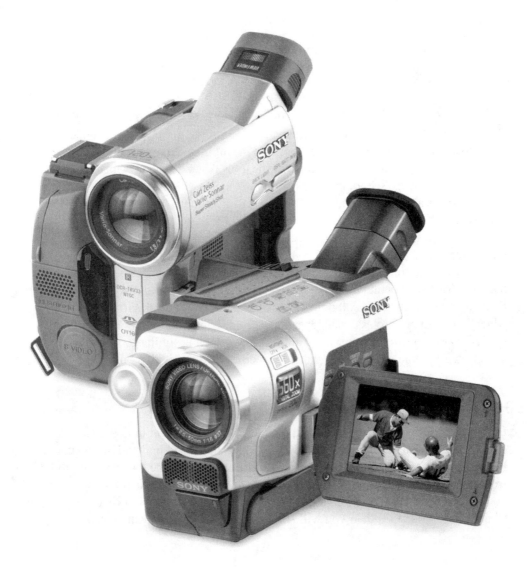

How To...

- Choose your tool: iMovie or Final Cut (Express or Pro)
- Set up your camcorder and import video
- Master basic editing in Clip Viewer mode
- Edit in the timeline
- Add overlaps and overlays
- Add transitions between scenes
- Add special effects

For Macintosh owners, the desire to edit digital video is one that's easily fulfilled. Apple includes iMovie, its own free video editing program, with any modern Macintosh equipped with FireWire (IEEE 1394) high-speed input ports. iMovie makes video editing easy, offering most of the tools that a consumer would need for editing home movies, school projects, or small-business videos. For professional editing, Apple also offers Final Cut Pro and its "prosumer" (and considerably less expensive) sibling, Final Cut Express. Both packages offer amazing editing tools, which make possible a very sophisticated final project—one aimed at commercial video, television, or even a film festival.

All of these applications use straightforward and familiar metaphors to import the video you've shot and then to edit and arrange video clips into scenes for your final project. You can then add transitions, special effects, and titles to give your edited video a more professional appearance. This chapter looks at how the editing process works in iMovie and Final Cut Express (which is similar to Final Cut Pro) and discusses some of the issues that are specific to editing video on a Mac.

Choosing Your Tools

Before we discuss specific software applications, it's important to note that video editing requires a relatively powerful Macintosh, as discussed in detail in Chapter 2. Perhaps most important is your choice of operating system: the latest editing tools from Apple Computer are designed for the Mac OS X. In fact, the latest versions no longer work with earlier versions of the Mac OS. If you're using Mac OS 9 (the "classic" Mac OS) then you will still be able to edit video using iMovie (version 2 or earlier) or Final Cut (version 3 or earlier). All later versions require Mac OS X 10.2 or above.

Along those same lines, video editing is a demanding process, and so you'll need a computer with plenty of power and enough storage space to deal with the huge files created when you edit video. See Chapter 2 for a detailed discussion of system requirements.

The Entry Point: iMovie

If you've got a DV–compatible Mac equipped with FireWire (IEEE 1394) ports, then you've probably already got some software you can use for video editing: iMovie. Apple makes iMovie available for free on most Macs, and it can be downloaded for free from Apple. (It's also available as part of the iLife package, which bundles the latest versions of iMovie, iTunes, iDVD, and iPhoto, and, at the time of writing, was available for $49.)

iMovie is great for projects in the beginner-to-intermediate range. It gives you the ability to import and edit footage, and to add transitions, titles, special effects, and music. You can even accomplish some fairly sophisticated sound edits using iMovie. For most hobbyists and many small-business editors, iMovie works great.

Moving to the Next Level: Final Cut

The high-end editing application from Apple, Final Cut, comes in two versions, Pro and Express. Either version of Final Cut is a wonderful tool for taking your video editing skills to the next level. For many, Final Cut Express (currently $299 from Apple Computer) offers all of the capabilities you need for DV editing, including an advanced timeline-based approach that enables you to layer video and audio tracks, to make sophisticated edits easily, and to add a slew of special effects and effects transitions. (You'll see what all that means later in this chapter. For now, suffice to say that Final Cut Express is more capable than iMovie in this respect.)

Final Cut Pro goes even further. It provides you with the ability to edit a variety of video formats and to edit video that was shot in 16:9 aspect ratio (for HDTV or for transfer to film). It also provides a number of filters and tools designed specifically for professional applications and needs.

NOTE   *In this chapter, we refer to "Final Cut" in a general sense when we we're discussing something that both versions can do. For features that are exclusive to one version or the other, we'll name the specific version (Final Cut Express or Final Cut Pro).*

Weighing the Pros and Cons

So, which package should you choose?

Because iMovie is free for most Mac users, it's a great place to start and learn video editing. It offers tools that easily allow it to be used in business video projects and video that you edit for the Web. It can also be used effectively in school projects, video creation for non-profit organizations, and even for documentary videomaking. There's absolutely nothing wrong with the quality of video that is produced and edited using iMovie.

Final Cut Express is handy for *non-destructive editing,* which is something you'll find extremely handy if you begin to add video editing to your professional tool belt. To fit your clips together, iMovie requires you to crop them (select portions) and delete the rest. In Final Cut, you simply make portions of the clip visible or invisible (that's the non-destructive part) while editing them together. It's an easier way to work with multiple video clips, because it gives you the ability to create extremely smooth "cuts" and transitions.

Likewise, Final Cut uses a layered approach to video editing in the timeline. That approach gives you much more flexibility than you have in iMovie. Although iMovie is capable of many of the edits and transitions found in Final Cut, most of them are easier to accomplish in Final Cut once you're familiar with the interface.

As for Final Cut Pro, the decision to move up to this level of capability really depends on your budget and your technology needs. Final Cut Pro ($999) is more advanced than Final Cut Express and works in conjunction with other high-end video editing tools from Apple (for example, Logic, DVD Studio Pro, and Shake, all available at www.apple.com). Moreover, as mentioned, you can use it for professional-level editing in a variety of video formats. If you're shooting wedding and corporate videos with DV camcorders only, then you can get away with Final Cut Express. If you're doing anything more sophisticated at a professional level—particularly if you need to work with multiple formats, third-party video editing hardware, and so on—then Final Cut Pro is worth the investment.

If your Mac is equipped with an internal DVD-R drive (often called a "SuperDrive" by Apple), any of the video editing applications can work with iDVD to create DVD movies. And, of course, any of them can be used to export your edited video to your DV camcorder or to QuickTime (Apple's proprietary compressed video format) as digital movies that can be saved on a hard disk or shared over the Internet.

For most of us, a decision to start with iMovie is a good one. If you outgrow iMovie, you can move on to Final Cut and let your budget dictate which version, Pro or Express, seems to make the most sense.

Setting Up and Importing

To move your captured footage onto your Mac for editing, you'll need to connect it to the video source (in most cases your DV camcorder). This is usually as simple as connecting a FireWire (IEEE 1394) cable between the camcorder and the FireWire port on your Mac. Most camcorders come with the necessary cable. If yours didn't, replacements can be bought in most electronic or computer stores. However, you'll want to make sure that it's specifically designed for camcorder-to-computer connection, because the camcorder end is smaller and shaped differently.

Once the cable is connected to the camcorder, connect the other end to an available FireWire port, which should be at the back or the side of the Mac, depending on the model. If you already have devices plugged into the FireWire ports on your Mac, you may be able to plug your camcorder into one of those devices, because FireWire connections can be "daisy-chained" together. A daisy-chain connection isn't always optimal (if you have the option, we recommend connecting your camcorder directly to the Mac), but such chains of devices will often work fine.

Once the FireWire connection is established, the Mac should recognize the camcorder automatically. Switch the camcorder on and set it to VCR, VTR, or Playback mode; then, launch the editing software. The exact process depends on the editing software you're using. See "Importing Camcorder Footage in iMovie" and "Importing Camcorder Footage in Final Cut Express."

NOTE *You may find it handy to use the other video connectors on the camcorder to connect it to a television set or television monitor. The necessary cable will either be an RCA-style composite (red and white for audio, and yellow for video), or an S-video cable, or a combination of the two. If the camcorder is connected to an external monitor while you edit, the monitor will show the clips being previewed through your camcorder, which can be handy for seeing what your final project will look like.*

Importing Camcorder Footage in iMovie

In iMovie, if the camera has been recognized, Camera mode starts up. Using Camera mode, you can manage your camera, view what's on it, and import the footage to your hard disk for editing. (If you aren't already in Camera mode, you can click the small camera icon to get into it; later, you can click the scissors icon to switch to Edit mode.) You're in Camera mode when the mode selector is set this way:

When the camera has been recognized, iMovie looks like Figure 6-1, which also shows you the basic iMovie interface. Note the VCR-like controls. In Camera mode, you use those controls to play the footage on the tape in your camcorder. When you find the footage you want, you can import it.

TIP *What if iMovie doesn't recognize your camcorder? First, try turning the camcorder on and off. Also, make sure it's in VCR or Playback mode. Second, check the FireWire cable connection: Is the cable firmly seated at both the camera and the Mac ends? Try relaunching iMovie, or, if that doesn't work, restart your Mac. For more troubleshooting hints, visit www.info.apple.com/usen/imovie/ on the Web and search for advice regarding your camcorder brand. Also see www.apple.com/imovie/ compatibility/camcorder.html for information about camcorders that have known compatibility issues.*

iMovie imports footage in one of two ways: either as a continuous stream (a single clip) for as long as you allow the import to continue (or until either the camcorder tape or the hard disk space runs out), or as multiple, separate clips that appear on the Clip Shelf. The type of import depends on a preference setting. Choose iMovie | Preferences, and make sure that Automatically Start New Clip at

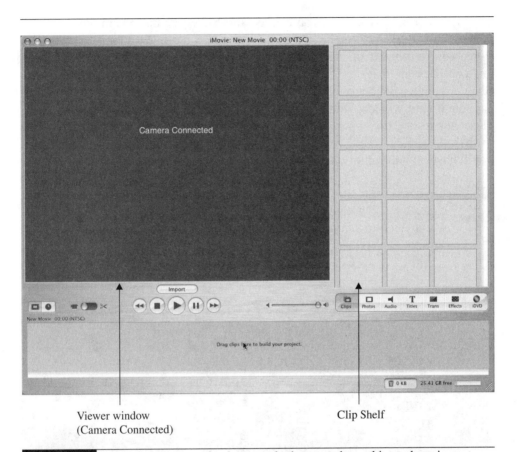

Viewer window
(Camera Connected)

Clip Shelf

FIGURE 6-1   iMovie has recognized an attached camcorder and is ready to import video footage.

Scene Break is selected if you want multiple clips to be created as iMovie detects changes in scenes. (The detection process notices when you've selected the Pause or Stop button during your filming. It isn't always 100 percent accurate, but it does a good job.)

NOTE   *Using the Automatically Start New Clip at Scene Break feature is a good idea in iMovie because it makes editing easier (editing in iMovie involves manipulating the clips from the Clip Shelf). If you don't import your video as clips, then you'll need to go through the extra step of viewing the single long clip and cutting it into smaller ones. That isn't tough, but it can be time-consuming.*

With your preference set, you can use the VCR-like buttons in the iMovie window to find the location in your footage where you'd like to start importing. When you've found it, click Import. The camcorder should start playing the video, and you'll see an image appear in the Viewer window as a new clips appear on the Shelf. Footage will continue to be imported until you click Import again, in which case the import will stop, but the camcorder will continue playing. You can also click Stop to stop the import and the playback simultaneously. That's all it takes.

Now, if you switched scene selection on or imported multiple clips manually, you'll have a Shelf full of clips that you can use for editing (see Figure 6-2).

> TIP   *As your video footage is playing, you can press* SPACEBAR *to toggle between importing and not importing clips. This shortcut method can be handy if you're interested in importing only portions of your footage into iMovie.*

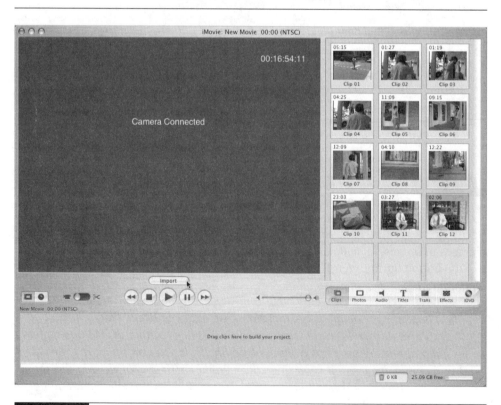

FIGURE 6-2   After you have imported some clips, iMovie should look like this.

Importing Camcorder Footage in Final Cut Express

Final Cut Express offers a slightly more advanced (some might call it more complicated) approach to importing video. An iMovie user may take a little while to get used to the approach used in Final Cut, but that approach can be a powerful way to import video.

With your camera connected to the Mac, launch Final Cut Express. In the first dialog box that appears, choose from the Setup menu the type of video you're importing. If you live in North America, your choice will most likely be the default DV-NTSC. (If your camcorder has special audio features or if you're using European or Asian PAL-standard equipment, then choose the associated video type.) You also need to choose your primary scratch disk (see note), which is where Final Cut will store important and edited files. After you choose the disk, click OK.

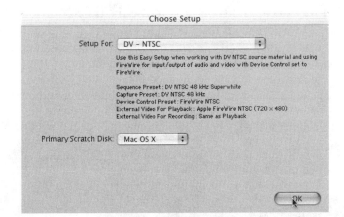

6

NOTE   *Final Cut works best when you set up a separate disk or disk partition for saving scratch files. (It also works best if that disk has tens or even hundreds of gigabytes of free storage space.) If you don't have such a disk or partition available, you can choose the main drive as your scratch disk. Video editing is very demanding on a disk partition, and so many professionals use a second hard disk or a special partition on their main disk for editing. That way, the disk can be reinitialized between major projects without causing trauma to system files and other important documents and applications.*

Once you've made those decisions, Final Cut Express appears in its default layout. You'll learn more about the editing tools in a moment, but for now let's move right to capturing video.

Choose File | Capture from the menu. The Capture interface (see Figure 6-3) opens after being initialized. If your camcorder has been detected, you'll see the words "VTR OK" at the bottom of the viewer portion of the Capture window.

You now have two ways that you can capture video: manually, using time codes; or automatically.

To capture footage manually, simply click Play and watch the video until you reach a moment that you want to import. At that point, click Now (the button on the right-hand side of the window). You then watch the video as it is being imported. When you reach the end of the material that you want in the clip, press ESC. (You should try to anticipate the start and stop points so that you can activate the controls a little in advance of the start point and a little after the stop point, just to make sure you get the footage you want.) The clip is then added to your project Browser window.

The second way to capture footage is to use the time-code tools to capture individual clips. This approach is more precise, although it takes a little extra time. To use this approach, you specify *in* and *out points* to create a *marker*. The marker is then used to import the clip.

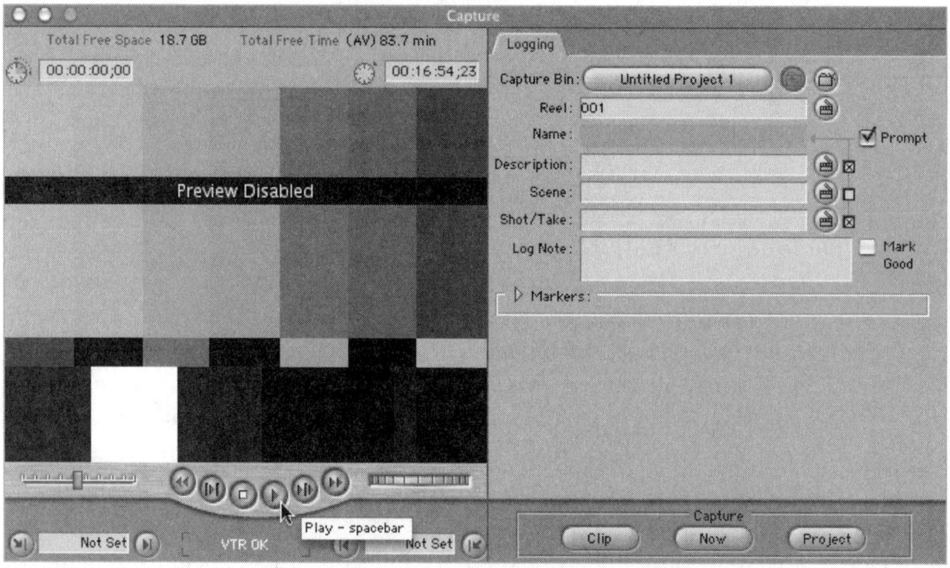

FIGURE 6-3   The basic Capture interface shows the "VTR OK" message when your camcorder has been detected.

Here's how it works:

1. On the Logging tab (the right-hand side of the window), click Markers.
   The controls to create a marker open.

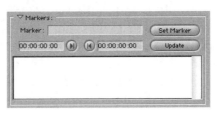

2. In the first window, enter the in point for your clip in time-code format
   (hours:minutes:seconds:frames). If you don't know the exact time code,
   you can watch the video, and click the button next to the in point at the
   moment that you want the clip to start. (The out point will change as well.)

TIP *You can watch the video in advance and jot the time code down on a piece
of paper so that you can enter the exact value later. In fact, that's the way
the pros do it: they watch all of the footage while noting all the in and out
points for the clips to be imported. This is called logging footage. Final
Cut Pro has more sophisticated options, including one for importing a
computer text file of logged footage, called an edit decision list (EDL).*

3. Next, enter the out point for the clip, or, as you're playing the clip, click the
   associated button at the moment you want the clip to end.

4. Now, if playback is still going on, stop it, and then click Clip on the Logging side of the window. The Log Clip dialog box opens.

5. Enter a name for the clip and an optional note. (The note is a good idea when you have a number of similar-looking clips and you want to be able to differentiate them quickly.) Click the Mark Good check box (we assume you're not capturing a clip that you're not interesting in using in your project), and click OK.

Final Cut now takes control of your camcorder, backs up to the selected in point, captures the clip all the way to the out point, and places the clip in the Browser window on the tab for that project.

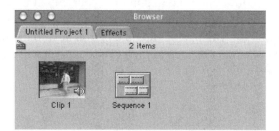

Keep going. Repeat the procedure for each clip that you plan to bring into the project.

NOTE   *The interface for setting markers might look a bit more sophisticated in Final Cut Express, but you can't enter markers for more than one clip at a time. Apple took that feature out of the Express version to make Express less expensive and Pro more attractive to professionals. In Final Cut Pro, you can create an entire EDL that contains all of the markers necessary to important all relevant clips for a project at once. That's efficient, but the Express approach should work fine for most consumer and small-business projects.*

iMovie: Basic Editing in Clip Viewer Mode

In iMovie, you can edit your videos using either of two approaches: the Clip Viewer or the Timeline. Both options are available when you switch to Edit mode. Use the same slider that you used to enter Camera mode. Click to slide it over to the scissors icon, which represents Edit mode.

As you'll see a little later in "Edit in the Timeline," using the Timeline for editing instead of the Clip Viewer is the more professional approach and the one that Final Cut defaults to. However, in iMovie, editing using the Clip Viewer is a handy way to quickly create a "rough cut" of your video project. In fact, many people can get away with editing entire projects in the Clip Viewer—to no ill effect.

The Clip Viewer is fun to use, because once you arrange the clips (represented by little 35-mm slide icons), you can immediately play back the video. If you see a clip that doesn't seem to belong, you can simply drag it back to the Shelf. And if you want to move a clip from one part of the video to another, you can do that, too.

In iMovie, the Clip Viewer is best used to arrange clips that have already undergone some editing while still on the Shelf or that have at least been carefully split into smaller clips that can be arranged to tell your story or communicate your idea. If you imported your video as one continuous stream, then you have to do at least some basic editing to create your clips. And indeed, editing clips before placing them on the Clip Viewer is often a good idea.

To view, split or edit a clip that has been imported in iMovie, you simply select it in the Shelf. Click once to select it. Once the clip is selected, the associated video should appear in the Viewer window. Using the VCR-like controls, you can play the clip and move back and forward within it.

NOTE   *If you're in Camera mode when you select the clip, you'll switch to Edit mode automatically.*

In Edit mode, additional controls are available in the Viewer window. Just below the Viewer window is the *scrubber bar,* a blue bar that stretches all the way across the viewer. On that bar is the *playhead.* The playhead shows you the current frame within the clip. You can drag the playhead back and forth to see different frames in the Viewer window and to choose different starting points for playback (see Figure 6-4).

You can do a lot more than simply play back or choose a frame within a selected clip. You can also *split* the clip and *crop* it.

Splitting a Clip

Splitting a clip is just what it sounds like—selecting a moment in the clip and choosing a split from the menu, which divides the clip in two, just as if you had taken a strip of film and cut it with scissors. Split commands are handy for splitting long clips into manageable sections that are easier to arrange in the Clip Viewer.

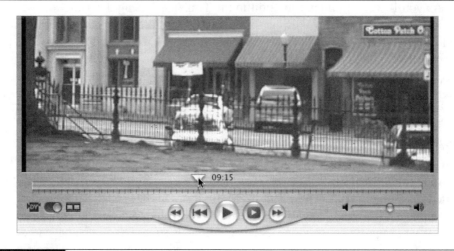

FIGURE 6-4   You can drag the playhead back and forth on the scrubber bar to see each frame of video or to select a frame.

(You might want to use Split because you imported a video as one long clip or because you want to turn one clip into a series of shorter clips that can be interleaved with other clips in your video.)

Here's how to split a clip:

1. Select the clip on the Shelf.

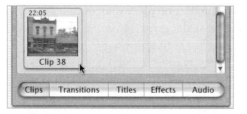

2. Drag the playhead to the video frame where you'd like the split to occur. (If necessary, you can use the left and right cursor keys on the keyboard to position the playhead more exactly, advancing or rewinding the clip one frame at a time.)

NOTE   *The frame that you're viewing when you select Split will become the first frame of the second clip (as opposed to the last frame of the first clip). That is, the split happens on the left-hand side of the visible frame. (Just so you know.)*

3. Choose the Edit | Split Video Clip at Playhead command, or press CMD+T.

4. Two clips should now appear on the Shelf.

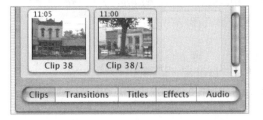

If you like, click the name of either clip and edit it to something more meaningful.

Cropping a Clip

When you crop a clip, you're actually trimming it down so that it will fit better into your overall video presentation. Cropping (like splitting) is something you can do either on the Shelf, or after you've arranged your clips in the Clip Viewer. Generally, however, it's easier to crop beforehand so that you can have a better sense of how the clips will fit together in the Clip Viewer.

When you crop a clip, you're choosing to keep the *middle* portion of the selected clip. Once you've defined that portion, you choose Crop from the menu, and the rest of the clip—the portions you haven't selected—are deleted (cropped) from the clip.

Here's how it works:

1. Select a clip on the Shelf or in the Clip Viewer.

2. The associated video appears in the Viewer window. Under the scrubber bar, locate the left and right cropping triangles. Drag the right triangle out along the scrubber bar.

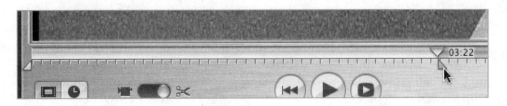

3. Using the left triangle, select the beginning of the portion of the clip that you're going to keep. Using the right triangle, select the end of the portion that you want to keep.

NOTE   *Remember, you're highlighting the portion of the clip that you want to keep, not the part that you're going to crop away.*

TIP   *You can click either cropping triangle and then use the left and right cursor keys on the keyboard for finer movement.*

4. Choose Edit | Crop. The playhead and the two cropping triangles jump back to the start of the scrubber bar, and the clip now begins at the frame you selected using the left crop triangle. It's cropped!

NOTE   *You can undo a crop immediately after making it by choosing Edit | Undo. After you've done some other editing, however, Undo may not be an appealing choice, because you would have to undo everything you've done in the meantime. If that's the case, you may be able to recover the cropped footage by selecting the clip and choosing Advanced | Restore Clip. If you haven't emptied the Trash in iMovie, you'll likely recover the edge portions of the clip so that you can try the crop again.*

Arranging Clips in the Clip Viewer

Once all your clips are split and cropped, you're ready to place them in the Clip Viewer. The Clip Viewer is used to arrange clips visually—almost like one of those projected filmstrips that you may have encountered in grade school. (Well, some of us did, at least.)

You can use the Clip Viewer not only to place the clips in your movie, but also to arrange and rearrange them. It's pretty straightforward: Just drag from the Shelf to the Clip Viewer (see Figure 6-5), and then drag the clips around on the Clip Viewer itself.

To play an individual clip, select it in the Clip Viewer and then use the Viewer window controls. The controls operate just as if you'd selected the clip on the Shelf. (To select multiple clips for playback, hold SHIFT down while you click each clip in turn.) You can even continue to split and crop clips after you've placed them in the Clip Viewer.

Building your movie is basically a question of arranging your clips in the Clip Viewer and playing them back to see how the resulting sequence looks. To play back the entire presentation, click its name just above the left-most clip in the Clip Viewer.

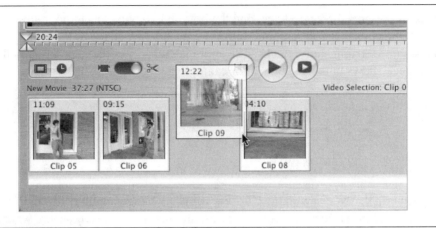

FIGURE 6-5 Adding a clip to the Clip Viewer from the Shelf is simple drag-and-drop operation.

When you click the presentation name, iMovie drops any current selections so that you can play the entire movie from the beginning. To view the results full-screen (without the iMovie interface), click the button just to the right of Play in the Viewer window:

Editing in the Timeline

The next level of editing a digital movie on a Mac involves the Timeline approach. Instead of manipulating little clip icons, you work with strips that represent the video and audio portions of your clips. In iMovie, Timeline mode is particularly handy for editing sound. In Final Cut, the Timeline approach is the fundamental editing method. It also offers considerable power and can be very handy for creating certain effects and types of edits.

The iMovie Timeline

In iMovie, click the Timeline button (it looks like a small clock) to exchange the Clip Viewer for the Timeline. The new interface shows three horizontal bars: the top bar represents the video track, and the bottom two bars, the audio tracks. By default, the clips that you imported into iMovie and then added to the Clip Viewer do not show separate audio tracks. The audio is still part of the clip, but only the video track shows in the Timeline. For example:

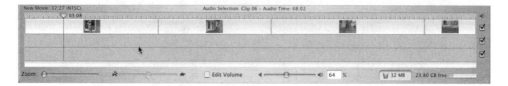

Each clip that you saw in the Clip Viewer is now a rectangular strip in the video track. Border lines that enclose a little thumbnail picture show you where each clip begins and ends.

NOTE *The Timeline has a small slider control labeled Zoom. That slider is used to change the magnification of the Timeline so that you can see fewer or more clips at once in the Timeline. Drag the slider back and forth to zoom in and out on portions of the movie.*

In the Timeline view, you will quickly realize that you can't drag clips around to change their order or to remove them. You can drag clips from the Shelf to the Timeline; you can't go the other way. If you do select and drag a clip, you'll open up some black space between the previous clip (or the beginning of the movie) and the clip that you're dragging. To remove a clip or return it to the Shelf, switching back to the Clip Viewer is the easiest way to do it.

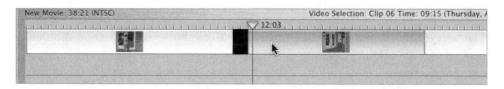

What you can do in the Timeline, however, is edit audio levels and sound. Audio editing is one of the main reasons that iMovie has a Timeline mode. (Early versions of iMovie didn't have the Timeline.) Using the Timeline mode you can change the volume of one or more clips, edit the volume in a clip (fade it up or down, for instance), and separate the audio from the clip so that you can work with the audio separately.

Changing and Editing Volume

Changing the overall volume for individual or multiple clips is simple:

1. Click the clip to select it. (For multiple clips, hold down SHIFT you while select the clips.)

2. Use the volume slider at the bottom of the Timeline interface to change the volume level for the selected clips.

Editing the volume for a clip is just a bit more complex:

1. Click the check box next to Edit Volume. A small horizontal line appears in all clips. (Note that it doesn't matter which clips are selected; the line is switched on for all of them.) That line represents the current volume level for each clip.

What that line enables you to do is change the volume of a clip over the length of that clip. It's handy for causing the volume on a clip to fade in or fade out, or to change the volume in the middle of a clip to negate the effect of a loud noise that happens at that point in the clip, for instance.

2. To change the audio level, simply click the line. Clicking creates a point on the line that can then be dragged up or down. It takes a little practice to get used to making the adjustment. For instance, to fade a clip up from no volume to 100 percent volume, you need two points: one at the beginning

of the clip that you drag down to 0 percent, and a second that you drag to 100 percent. (Alternatively, you can select the clip and pull the entire volume line down to 0 percent using the Volume slider, and then create a point that you drag up to 100 percent.)

You can use the audio line to get fairly specific about volume throughout your movie. Volume can be set to range up and down throughout the clips so that the recorded audio plays back at an optimal volume throughout the movie. (Or, at least, you can mess around and try to get close to optimal volume!)

NOTE   *To edit the volume in all clips simultaneously, first select all the clips. You can do that by selecting one clip and then choosing Edit | Select All or by pressing* COMMAND+A. *Now, use the volume slider to change the level for the entire project.*

Extracting Audio

The other audio trick that the Timeline makes possible is the ability to extract audio from a clip and to edit that audio separately. Indeed, as you'll see later in this chapter, "audio editing" within your project is another level of complexity that iMovie allows.

One of the tricks that can make a basic DV project seem considerably more professional is editing audio so that different video and audio clips play at the same time. If you watch television shows or movies carefully, you'll begin to notice that you're often hearing one thing and seeing another. It happens constantly: You hear a reporter talk while you see a fire blazing, or you hear a politician speak while you see the crowd reacting. Mastering that capability in iMovie is a great way to improve your videos.

First things first, though. To edit video and audio separately, you have to separate the audio from the video clips. In iMovie, you do that by selecting one or more clips and choosing the Advanced | Extract Audio command. A dialog box shows the progress of the command. When the extract finishes, a new audio clip appears on the Timeline beneath the video from which it was extracted.

With the audio extracted, you have a number of options. You can click Edit
Volume and see the volume line for the audio clip instead of for the main clip.
(Actually, the main clip still has its audio, but the volume is set to 0 percent now.)
You can edit the extracted audio line in the same way as you edited the audio when
it was attached to the clip.

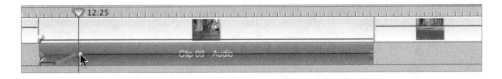

Also notice that the audio clip has crop markers (small triangles) just like the
ones you saw earlier for cropping video clips.

Those markers can be used two ways. First, you can use them to create in and
out points. Simply drag them into the audio clip a ways, and the sound won't start
playing until the in marker is encountered; likewise, the sound will stop playing
when it reaches the out marker, even though the video clip continues.

TIP *If you're have trouble selecting one of the audio crop markers, make sure
that the Edit Volume option is switched off.)*

Second, the audio clip can be cropped. With the in and out points selected,
choose Edit | Crop from the menu. That crops the audio separately from the video,
shortening only the audio clip.

Thanks to this ability to extract audio, some interesting editing feats can be accomplished in the iMovie Timeline, as you'll see in the section "Paste Overs and Intercuts."

The Final Cut Timeline

Final Cut is quite different from iMovie, and its power becomes apparent after a few hours of use. That's not to knock iMovie—it's a great program that happens to be fairly simple to use and easy to learn. However, as you attempt more complex edits, you can soon run up against its limitations. With Final Cut, you work in a sophisticated Timeline-based interface where you can not only edit audio and video tracks separately, but also layer video and audio tracks to achieve various types of edits and special effects.

The first thing you'll notice about the Final Cut interface that is different from iMovie is that Final Cut shows more than one video window (see Figure 6-6). On the left is the Viewer window, which shows the clips that you're working on. You edit individual clips in the Viewer window. The other window is the Canvas window. The Canvas window is where you see your video as it is currently coming together in the Timeline. In creating various edits and effects, you often make the choices in the Viewer window and then see the results of your handiwork in the Canvas window. All of these elements—the two windows, the Timeline, and the Browser (where captured clips are stored)—are used in concert to edit movies in Final Cut.

In and Out Points

If you read the previous section about editing in iMovie, you'll recall that we suggested cropping your clips before you place them in the Clip Viewer or Timeline. Moreover, we mentioned that cropping is *destructive*, in that it actually removes the video outside of the crop markers.

With Final Cut, the approach is a bit subtler. You still create in and out points for each clip, but Final Cut assumes that you already did the gross "cropping" when you made your edit decisions during the process of capturing the footage. Now, you should have less reason to cut away large portions of each clip. Instead of actually stripping away the video outside of in and out points marked on a video clip, Final Cut plays only the portion of the clip between the two points. The entire clip is still there if you need to change the in or out point later.

Here's how to create in and out points on a clip in Final Cut:

1. First, double-click the clip in the Browser.

Viewer window   Canvas window   Timeline   Browser

In Final Cut Express, you edit individual clips in the window on the left (the Viewer window). In the center window (the Canvas window), you see the project played back when you use the Timeline to preview the project.

2. In the Viewer window, place the playhead at the position on the scrubber bar where the clip should start—that is, where the in point should go.

3. To establish the in point, click In (located at the bottom of the Viewer window). The in point now shows on the line below the scrubber bar.

4. Next, move the playhead to the position on the scrubber bar where the clip should end. Click Out (just to the right of In).

That's it. The portion of the clip between the in and out points is what you will be working with and playing back in your project. However, you still have that other footage to work with if you need it, which is why this editing is considered *nondestructive*.

Arranging and Altering Clips

To build your project from captured clips, you start by dragging a clip from the Browser down to the Timeline. When your cursor is hovering over the Timeline, one video track (on the top) and two audio tracks (on the bottom) are highlighted. That shows you where Final Cut will place the clip when you drop it on the Timeline.

You want to aim for V1 (video track 1) and A1 and A2 (audio tracks 1 and 2, respectively) for your first clips. (The other tracks are handy for editing, as you'll learn later.) When you drop the clip on the Timeline, some colorful bars appear on the tracks, including a small video icon preview for the clip.

To build your video, add more clips to the Timeline in the same way. As you drag the new clips to the Timeline, notice that subsequent clips "snap" to the preceding clip, and arrows appear at the top and bottom of the Timeline:

While you're still in the Timeline, notice that you can double-click a clip and have it appear again in the Viewer window. There, you can set new in and out points if desired. You can also drag the edges of a clip in the Timeline to quickly change the clip length.

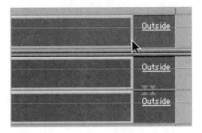

The Timeline interface also offers a razor blade tool. (You can find this tool in the Tools window, which you can toggle on and off with the Window | Tools command). The razor blade tool can split a clip in the Timeline. You'll find that the razor blade is handy to split a clip when you want to apply a transition or effect within the clip (useful for a dream sequence or music-video style special effect) or when you want to add a title to a portion of a clip.

To split a clip, select the razor blade tool, and click the point in the clip where you'd like the split to occur. You'll immediately have two clips.

TIP *After you've used the razor blade tool to split a clip or two, don't forget to use the Tool window to switch back to the pointer tool so that you don't keep splitting clips accidentally. If you do split a clip you didn't want to split, choose Edit | Undo to put the clip back together.*

Using Paste Overs and Intercuts

If you pay close attention to movies or television, you'll see something you may not have noticed consciously before: the shot changes a lot. The typical television show or film actually uses lots of different edits, moving between various camera angles, various actors or subjects, and even between a person and footage of what that person is talking about. The trick to making all of those edits work well is to maintain the quality and smooth nature of the sound. As long as the sound doesn't seem to jump around, pop, hiss, or change dramatically between camera angles, the audience will accept all sorts of back-and-forth cuts.

The main type of cut that falls along these lines is called an *intercut*. An intercut shows different clips over the same *bed* of audio. An example is the very typical documentary-style story in which (for instance) a teacher is explaining what her day is like. The story starts with a shot of the teacher talking. As she talks, the picture suddenly changes to images of her classroom and the students raising their hands or queuing to leave the room or running around on the playground. All the while, you're listening to the teacher talk. Finally, as the story ends, you return to the shot where you both see and hear the teacher.

That sort of intercut is fairly easy to accomplish with both iMovie and Final Cut. Let's look at iMovie first.

Using Paste Over in iMovie

At the playhead, iMovie has a special command called Paste Over at Playhead that pastes the video from one clip over the video of another. ("Paste over" is iMovie's name for an intercut.)

Here's how it works:

1. In the Timeline, decide which clip is going to include intercut footage. Select that clip, and choose Advanced | Extract Audio Clip. This is an important first step. If you neglect it, the intercut video clip will be added with its audio, which is not what you want.

2. Select the clip that you're going to add as an intercut, and, in the Viewer window, choose the portions that you want to use. Choose Edit | Copy to copy that footage.

3. Place the playhead on the Timeline where you want the footage to be added. Now choose Advanced | Paste Over at Playhead. You've replaced the previous footage with the clip that you just copied, but the audio has been left intact.

Now when you play the footage, the pasted video is shown, but the audio from the original clip plays. It's pretty cool.

Using Intercuts in Final Cut

Final Cut has a completely different—and much more elegant—way of dealing with intercuts. Instead of copy-and-paste-style operations, Final Cut provides multiple video tracks on the Timeline, and you can use those tracks to easily layer video clips over other video clips, while the video on the topmost track remains visible. Because you're not pasting the video, you continue to work with two separate clips. Let's call them the *base clip* and the *intercut clip*.

In Final Cut, you can drag your intercut clip to the moment on the Timeline at which you'd like it to appear. Ideally, your base clip should sit on the Video 1 track and your intercut clip on the Video 2 track. When you drag the intercut clip to the Video 2 track (which is above Video 1), intercut video will automatically be played instead of the base clip video. In the following example an intercut clip has been dropped on the track above a base clip:

6

Picture it: The base clip plays until the playhead reaches the point at which the intercut clip appears on the Timeline. Then, the intercut clip, taking precedence, plays until the playhead reaches the end of the intercut, at which point the base clip picks up again.

The problem with this process is that the audio for the intercut clip is still active in the Timeline, and that audio will play along with the audio from the base clip.

To keep that from happening, you simply delete the audio portion of the intercut clip. Here's how:

1. Select the intercut clip in the Timeline. The audio and video portions both show a selection highlight.

2. Choose Modify | Links.

3. Click the audio portion of the intercut. It should be separately highlighted now, like this:

4. Press DELETE on your keyboard. The audio portion disappears.

That's it. You've now got your intercut clip overlying the base clip while the audio from the base clip plays continuously. Voila!

Adding Transitions Between Scenes

The cuts that you've made so far in iMovie and Final Cut are *straight cuts,* meaning that the clips succeed one another with no special *transition* (which would allow for a more gradual change). Usually, you'll use a transition when the change between two clips is very abrupt, causing it to be difficult to watch. This often happens when the video is moving on to a new topic or the storyline is moving to a different moment in time (perhaps months, or even years, have elapsed). These abrupt changes can be smoothed over with special-effects transitions.

These three basic transition types are commonly used and offered by both iMovie and Final Cut:

■ **Fade**   The clips in a video sequence slowly move from black to full visibility—or vice versa. A fade can be used to start or end a segment, or to suggest that you're moving on to a new idea, a new sequence, or some other change. Fades aren't to be used lightly, because they tend to relax the audience out of (or into) a scene, telling them "this is over" (fade out) or "this is about to begin" (fade in).

■ **Cross-Dissolve**   Two clips seem to melt together, as the video of the first clip slowly breaks up and the video of the second clip emerges. When a change in camera angle or location seems too jarring or abrupt to work in a straight cut, you might consider using a cross-dissolve, which can be used to suggest a change in perspective. A cross-dissolve can take a while to complete, and so you don't want to use them too often in a given project. Still, they're an effective way to smooth a cut between angles or to suggest the passage of time.

■ **Wipe**   A wipe is an abrupt way to get out of a scene and move on to the next. Visually, in a wipe transition, the video image seems to be pushed or cleared off the screen, being replaced by a color, usually black. The type of wipe (left-to-right, top-to-bottom, expanding circles, or one frame of video seeming to be pushed off the screen by another) can be used to suggest a change in perspective. Wipes are a great transition to use for suggesting that the new scene is taking place in a different location—perhaps far away from the preceding scene.

Here's how you add a transition in iMovie:

1. Click Trans. (You'll find this button beneath the Shelf.) The interface changes to show the Transitions panel.

2. In the list, click once to choose the type of transition you'd like to use.

3. Use the speed slider to determine how quickly the transition should take place. You can also use Preview to show in Viewer window how the transition will look.

NOTE   *The speed slider uses the time-code convention. Remember to select the time in seconds:frames. For instance, 1:29 is 1 second and 29 frames. Because video runs at 30 frames per second, that's nearly 2 seconds. (The next increment would be 2:00.)*

4. Drag the transition name from the list to between two clips on the Clip Viewer or the Timeline. When you've positioned the transition between two clips, a little gap opens visually (see Figure 6-7). Drop the transition, which will begin to build between the two clips. Most transitions need to appear between two clips, but a fade can be placed at the beginning (fade in) or end (fade out) of a clip.

In Final Cut, you add transitions by dragging them from the Effects tab of the Browser (on the right-hand side) to the split between two clips in the Timeline. To change the preferences for how a particular transition acts, double-click it. The controls for that particular transition appear in the Viewer window (see Figure 6-8; Figure 6-6 also shows a transition in action).

NOTE   *Transitions in Final Cut are so involved that they're outside the scope of this book. The simple transitions work well at their default settings; however, if you want to attempt more complex transitions, simply dig in and start playing around to see how they work.*

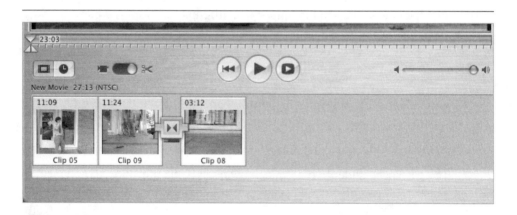

FIGURE 6-7   When you add a transition in iMovie, a slight gap between two clips shows that you've positioned the transition correctly.

Double-click a transition here…   …and you'll see controls for that transition here

FIGURE 6-8   In Final Cut, transitions can become quite complex.

With iMovie, you'll notice that the program goes immediately to work to *render* (paint frame-by-frame) the special transition effect. In Final Cut, you use Special | Render to render the transition. By using a command to control the rendering, Final Cut gives you the opportunity to add multiple edits, transitions, and effects before rendering starts. That way, you don't have to wait to add each change.

Adding Basic Special Effects

iMovie and Final Cut both offer powerful effects—each in its own way. The primary difference is that iMovie effects are easy to add. Effects in Final Cut are extremely powerful, but more difficult to get right. Let's take a look at both.

Adding iMovie Basic Effects

To add effects in iMovie you do pretty much the same thing that you do for transitions, except that you drag the effect directly to a clip instead of between clips. iMovie offers a number of good effects that fit the basic category: Adjust Colors, Black & White, Brightness and Contrast, and Sepia Tone are all designed to change color settings. Other effects create detailed visual changes such as Aged Film, Earthquake, Fairy Dust, and others. As you might imagine, they're all lots of fun to play with.

Here's how to add a basic effect (this example uses Adjust Colors):

1. Select one or more clips on the Timeline, and then click Effects. (You'll find the button on the right-hand side of the iMovie window under the Shelf or the Titles or Transitions panel.)

2. Now, click Adjust Colors at the top of the effects list. Notice that the panel changes slightly, showing different controls. Sliders for Hue Shift, Color, and Lightness now appear at the bottom of the Effects panel (see Figure 6-9).

3. Move the sliders, changing the color settings of the selected clip or clips. You'll see a preview of the color change in the small window at the top of the Effects panel. When you are done making choices, click Apply to apply the effect to the selected clips.

NOTE
iMovie renders all effects, transitions, and titles immediately after you apply them to a clip. In each case, a small status line (red for effects and transitions, green for titles) grows longer as the rendering process progresses. The rendering of special effects can result in a long wait after you click Apply, with the red line that denotes rendering time creeping along in the clip box on the Timeline. You may be able to work with iMovie while it is applying the effect, but you won't be back to full speed until the effect is finished rendering. For that reason, waiting until later in your project to set most of your effects is a good practice.

iMovie has a number of other effects that are designed to alter the overall color of each selected clip. The Black & White effect changes all selected clips to grayscale. Sepia Tone turns the video image a reddish brown, which is meant to suggest an aged black-and-white photo or film. Sepia Tone is also commonly used to give images an American "Old West" appearance.

FIGURE 6-9   As you change the settings for an effect, a small preview in the Effects panel automatically shows the changes.

Varying Effects Over Time

iMovie 3 allows you to set Effect In and Effect Out times for nearly all the special effects that it offers. The effect is then applied as the clip plays. For instance, you might choose to make the clip change gradually from its original color to black and white using the Black & White effect built into iMovie. If you set an Effect In time of three seconds (3:00), the clip will start at its normal level and then gradually fade to black and white until it reaches the full setting at the three-second mark. The rest of the clip will play in black and white until it ends.

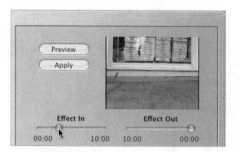

You can use the Effect Out slider to achieve the reverse effect. Set it at two seconds (2:00), for instance, and the clip will revert from black and white to the original color level, so that the video image is back to normal just as the clip ends.

Adding Final Cut Effects

Final Cut puts even more effects at your disposal than iMovie does. The effects are more powerful than the ones found in iMovie, and they are relatively easy to add. They're also considerably more complicated, which is why all but the most basic effects are outside the scope of this book.

Still, let's look at two special cases: a Final Cut fade in/out, and a simple color filter effect.

Creating a Fade Effect

Unlike iMovie, Final Cut Express doesn't offer simple Effect In and Effect Out settings (although Final Cut Pro provides that capability,). However, with Final Cut Express, you can use *keyframes* to establish in and out points for audio and video fades in a way that's very similar to fading audio clips in and out.

In Final Cut, you create fades using *overlay lines*. You display the lines in clips by clicking Clip Overlays (found at the bottom left of the Timeline):

You use the overlay lines to set *levels*. In an audio clip, the line sets the volume level; in a video clip, the line sets the *opacity* of the clip. You can drag one of the lines to change the opacity of a clip from 100, the default, to something lower. The lower the line, the darker the clip:

Because the line is lowered or raised uniformly across the clip when you drag, you need to add keyframes if you want the video to fade up from black or down to black. (A keyframe is simply a point on the video or audio level lines that can be used to change the particular level.)

To add a keyframe, click the Pen in the toolbar or press P. Now when you point at the line, the pointer changes to the Pen tool icon. Click the overlay line to create a keyframe (indicated by the diamond-shaped icon) on the line:

By adding more than one keyframe, you can drag one or both of the keyframes up or down:

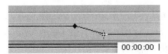

In that way, you can cause the levels in the video clip or the audio clip (or both) to move gradually up or down. To cause a fade to occur quickly, place two keyframes closer together. If you want the effect to occur more gradually, place the keyframes farther apart.

TIP   *To remove a keyframe, right-click it or click and hold the pointer over the Pen tool in the toolbar to choose the pen with a minus sign, which can be used to remove keyframes.*

Creating a Filter Effect

As with transitions, you access effects in Final Cut by clicking the Effects tab in the Browser window and then opening an effects folders (which Final Cut calls a *bin*). For basic effects, open the Video Filters bin, where you'll find a number of subfolders that hold some interesting filter effects. In this example, the Channel bin under Video Filters is selected:

▽ 🔒 Video Filters	Bin
▷ 🔒 Blur	Bin
▷ 🔒 Border	Bin
▷ 🔒 Channel	Bin
▷ 🔒 Color Correction	Bin
▷ 🔒 Distort	Bin

To begin, open the Image Control bin, and find the Color Balance filter. Drag the filter to a clip in the Timeline, and drop it on the clip. Now, double-click the clip to show it in the Viewer window. (By default, that's the window farthest to the left at the top of the screen.) The Viewer window is where you can make changes to a clip's settings once a filter has been applied to it.

> **TIP** *You can also select a clip in the Timeline, and then choose Effects | Video Filters. Next, choose the type of filter and the name of the filter to add it to the Filters tab in the Viewer window.*

When you double-click the clip, the associated video appears in the Viewer window. Click the Filters tab; you should see the controls for the filter that you dragged from the Browser. (In fact, you'll see controls for *all* of the filters that have been added to this clip.) Figure 6-10 shows a clip with the Color Balance filter applied.

Select one of the sliders, and see what moving it around does to the clip. The image in the Canvas window should change to reflect the changes you're making in the filter controls. (If you don't see the image changing, check the playhead on the Timeline to be sure it's over the clip that you're currently editing.)

Note that your changes have been previewed, but they haven't been applied. They still need to be rendered. Until they're rendered, you won't be able to see many of the effects in motion; you may only be able to look at them a frame at a time.

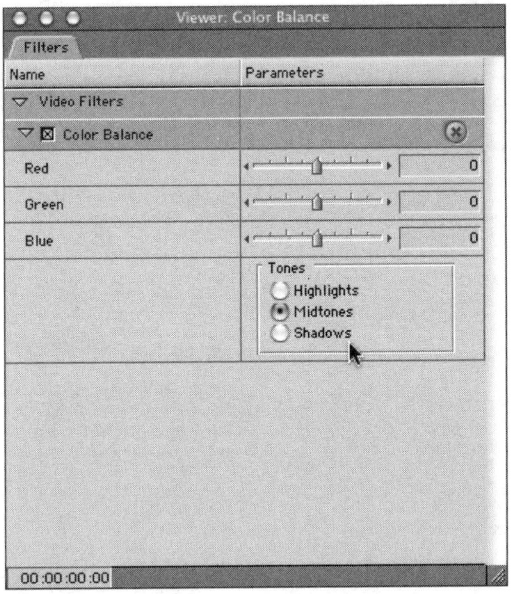

FIGURE 6-10   A clip with the Color Balance filter applied.

Once you've changed the settings to your liking, select Sequence | Render Selection. (You can also choose Sequence | Render All to render other effects or transitions that you may have already added to your project.) When the rendering is done you'll be able to watch the clip with the newly applied filter.

TIP   *It's a good idea to move through the clip frame-by-frame before rendering. Then you can see whether the effect looks good on every frame you've selected. If not, you can improve the look by making changes to the settings for individual frames. This attention to detail may take a little longer, but it will help your finished project look as good as it can.*

Final Cut offers lots of filters to keep you busy. In the Image Control bin alone, you'll find simple effects such as Brightness & Contrast, Tint, and Sepia. Venture outside the Image Control bin, and you'll find a wealth of other filters and effects—unfortunately, the more advanced options are outside the scope of this book.

Where to Find It

Web Site	Address	What's There
Apple Computer	www.apple.com	Logic, DVD Studio Pro, Shake, iLife

Chapter 7

Creating Slideshows

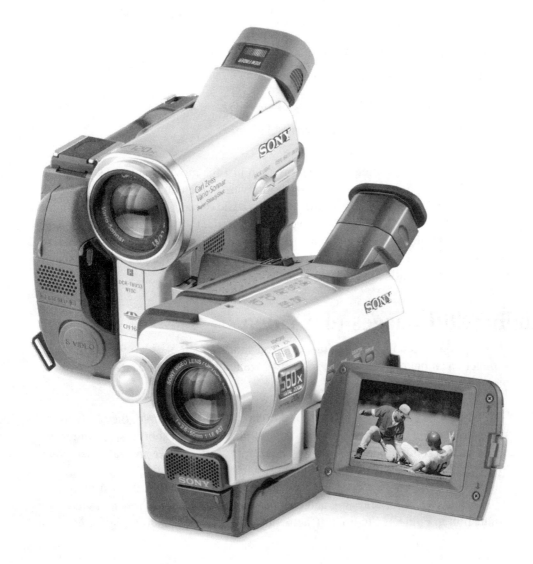

How to...

- Add still images to a video
- Edit the duration for which an image displays
- Match duration to a soundtrack
- Add transitions between images
- Convert image-file formats
- Crop images to DV format
- Grab still frames from video
- Work with automated slideshow generators
- Animate still images with pans and zooms

Video productions often involve more than just the moving pictures you shot with a camcorder. You've surely seen movies—often documentaries—in which the camera examines still images with music or narration taking place in the background. Precisely because still pictures are static, they can have tremendous visual and emotional impact within a motion picture. Documentaries, of course, make frequent use of stills, but so do dramatic films. In this chapter, we discuss how you can use stills in your own videos.

Adding Still Images to a Video

Here's a common home video situation: You shot a bunch of video footage of your summer vacation, but you also took a few dozen photos. You'd like to show off the pictures within the video.

Can it be done? Of course!

Some video editors even make that particular task very simple: they have a slideshow wizard that imports a series of still images, sets a short display duration for each, and combines them with music and transitions. Other programs ask you to do the work manually.

Even without a wizard at your disposal, it's not too hard to make a slideshow; it just involves a lot of dragging and dropping. Let's add a slideshow to a video production in Pinnacle Studio 8. (Check out the subsection "Adding Still Images in iMovie" if you're a Mac user.) Because Studio 8 doesn't have an automatic slideshow generator, you'll first learn what it's like to do everything by hand.

Preparing to Add Images

"So where do digital images come from?" (That's the sort of question digital kids might ask, leading to an awkward silence between their digital parents, Bit and Byte.)

Actually, it's a pretty straightforward issue: images for inclusion in a digital video can generally come from any of three places:

- Your camcorder (see Chapter 2 for a discussion of camcorders that capture video stills)

- A digital camera

- Traditional prints, negatives, or slides

7

The images from your camcorder are easy to pull into your production. Indeed, all you have to do is flip forward to the section called "Grabbing Stills from Video" to get the skinny on that.

What about your other options?

Images from your digital camera are equally easy. You can use the USB cable that came with your digital camera to transfer images to your hard disk. You can then follow the steps in the section "Adding Still Images in Studio 8" to use those images in a slideshow.

But just because your camera came with a serial or USB cable doesn't mean you have to use it. *Memory adapters*—gadgets that let you plug a memory card into your computer and read images from it just as you would from a floppy disk—let you easily transfer images to your computer without having to mess with cables at all.

Using a Memory Card Reader with Your Digital Camera

There are several advantages to using memory adapters on your computer:

- You can conserve camera battery power, because the camera isn't used in the transfer.

- You don't have to access the back of your computer to connect or disconnect cables.

■ Transfers may be faster with an adapter.

■ You can avoid having to use confusing transfer software, because adapters let you drag images directly from the memory card to a folder on your hard disk.

The kind of memory adapter you choose depends largely on the kind of removable memory that your camera uses. In general, all types are more efficient than connecting the camera to your computer with a cable.

■ **Desktop Single-Format Card Readers**   For $15 or $20, you can buy a USB card reader that accepts whatever kind of memory card your digital camera uses. Readers are available for CompactFlash, SmartMedia, SD, and Memory Stick—even xD. The downside? If you ever need to read a different kind of memory card—from a second camera or a digital music player, say—you'll need to buy a second card reader, which will eat up a second USB port and more desk space.

■ **Desktop All-In-One Readers**   Just as digital cameras are starting to accommodate more than one kind of memory card, readers are becoming more flexible as well. Universal readers can accommodate six or more kinds of memory cards, making it easy to read and write to cards for your digital camera, MP3 player, and PDA all using the same device. We use 6-in-1 universal card readers all the time.

■ **Internal Card Readers**   For the ultimate in convenience, you can find card readers that fit into an empty drive bay on your PC. For instance, Y-E Data (www.yedata.com) sells the excellent 7-in-1 Digital Media Reader/ Writer that packs six kinds of memory card slots into a floppy disk drive. Use it to replace your existing floppy disk drive, and you can then have access to any memory card right from your PC.

Using a Scanner

It's a little more complicated, of course, to get prints, negatives, and slides onto your PC. For that task, you'll need some sort of *scanner:* a device resembling a photocopier that takes a snapshot of whatever you lay on the platen (that's fancy talk for the scanning tray). A scanner doesn't just make a copy and print the picture, though. It converts the picture into bits and bytes of data and stores them on your PC in a digital image file, just as if the picture came from a digital camera.

Let's look into this whole scanner issue in a little more detail.

A scanner is kind of like a digital camera that needs to remain stationary. Instead of the grid-like image sensor found in a digital camera, which captures an entire image at once, a scanner uses a sensor with a single row of light-sensitive pixels. This linear charge-coupled device (CCD) registers the light value of the image one "line" or "row" at a time. The resulting information is sent to the computer immediately, and then the scanner head moves along to read the next line.

The *resolution* of the scanner depends partly on the speed and accuracy of the motor that steps the sensor past the document (or the document past the sensor, depending on the kind of scanner you have).

Scanners come in several different types. You're probably already familiar with the most common kind of scanner: the flatbed. It's a good all-around product for most kinds of scanning jobs, but it isn't necessarily the best choice for photo scanning. Here's an overview of scanner types:

- ■ **Flatbed Scanner**   A flatbed is typically a long, narrow tray (usually either 8.5×11 inches or 8.5×14 inches) on which you place a document. The scanning head travels the length of the tray to create a digital image of the document. Flatbeds typically make high-quality images and provide options such as automatic sheet feeders so that you can copy lots of pages at once. They can also scan almost any size of document, from tiny business cards and 35mm slides all the way up to legal-sized pages. On the downside, they have a big "footprint"—meaning that they take up a lot of space on a desk. The major limitation of flatbeds, at least as far as we photographer types are concerned, is that most can't scan slides or negatives without an attachment. If you want to scan only prints, though, most any flatbed will do.

- ■ **Sheet-Feed Scanner**   Sheet-feed scanners do away with the traditional moving optics and flat scanning bed. Instead, sheet-feeds pull documents through the unit, and past the stationary scanning head, to offer a compact scanning solution. You'll have a hard time finding a standalone sheet-feed scanner; they're commonly found as part of a multifunction scanner/fax/ printer device. Of course, you then can't scan thick objects such as books or magazines unless you first separate the individual pages from the source. And some low-grade sheet-feed scanners can introduce imperfections into the scan because of the imprecise motor that pulls the page through. This kind of scanner may be fine for text documents, but we recommend that you avoid it for scanning pictures.

- **Photo Scanner**   Photo scanners are designed specifically to scan pictures—usually 3×5-inch or 4×6-inch prints, although some also can handle prints as large as 5×7 inches. If all you need is the ability to convert 35mm prints into digital images, a dedicated photo scanner is a pretty good solution.

- **Film Scanner**   Want to scan slides or negatives—and want really superb quality images? Film scanners vary dramatically in price. They range anywhere from about $200 at the low end to several thousand dollars at the high end—but they can give you absolutely outstanding results. Film scanners are designed to accommodate slides and negatives and can usually scan at a very high resolution—as much as 8,000 dpi—which gives you rich, detailed digital images that you can print at full enlargement size. On the other hand, it's worth pointing out that film scanners are overkill for video because they capture far more resolution than video is capable of displaying. There's one exception, though: If you want to scan a very small detail from a slide and use it full-frame in video, a film scanner will do the job better than a flatbed scanner.

How to ... Scan an Image with a Typical Scanner

1. Start the scanner software. In most image editors, for instance, you'd choose File | Import | TWAIN | Acquire. The scanner software should open.

2. Make sure the photo is properly positioned on the scanner tray, and then click Preview in the dialog box that controls the scanner. After a few seconds, you should see the image on the screen. It has been quickly scanned in low resolution so that you can adjust the image before the final scan.

3. Crop the image if you don't want to scan the photo in its entirety.

4. Adjust colors and brightness if necessary. Some scanner programs have an auto-adjust tool; in others, you can tweak various color and brightness settings manually.

5. Adjust the scan resolution. You can make do with a very low-resolution scan, because the image doesn't need to be any more than 720×480 pixels. If you plan to crop the image down to a small detail, though, scan at a higher resolution.

6. When you're happy with the result, click Scan.

After the software is done scanning the image, it will either save the result to your hard disk under a filename you specified, or open it for editing in an image program.

Slides, Negatives, or Prints?

Still shooting with film, but want to include your pictures in videos? You might wonder, "Should I use slides, negatives, or prints?"

Here in the How to Do Everything mansion, we firmly believe that you'll get the best results if you start with slides. That's because the slide format is, in the end, the most accurate representation of what you *tried* to photograph in the first place. Negatives and prints are tweaked by the shop that developed them, and they may not reflect what you intended to shoot.

Slides have disadvantages, though. Most importantly, slide film has a fairly narrow exposure range and is less forgiving when shot with an improper exposure setting. A photo that might look just fine when overexposed or underexposed on print film will often look terrible on slide film.

If you don't want to shoot slide film, our recommendation would be to go back to the original negative and scan that instead of scanning a print. That's because the negative has a lot more dynamic range than a print.

That said, switch to digital. It's the twenty-first century, after all; get with the program! You can start by taking a few pictures with your digital camcorder, but you'll get dramatically better results—and be a lot happier in the end—if you shoot with a real digital camera.

Adding Still Images in Studio 8

Let's assume that you've already stored your digital images somewhere on your computer hard disk or on a CD. It doesn't really matter where you put them; you can find the images from within Studio 8. Do this:

1. With your video production open, click Photos and Frame Grabs on the left-hand side of the Album (it's the fourth tab down and looks like a digital camera). The Album changes to show your still digital images (see Figure 7-1). If you've never visited this tab before, you'll see sample photos provided by Pinnacle.

FIGURE 7-1   The Photo and Frame Grabs tab is where you can add still images to your Pinnacle Studio video.

2. Open a folder in which you've stored digital images. You can click the folder icon at the top of the Album and navigate to any memory location available on your computer. Notice that, to open the folder in the Album, you need to select an image. However, don't worry. That image isn't added to the video production, and so you can click any photo. It doesn't matter which one.

3. Now it's time to add an image to the production. Drag an image from the Album and drop it into the video track on the timeline. Repeat the process to add as many still images as you like to the production, and rearrange the pictures if necessary by dragging them to the left or right of their current location in the Timeline (see Figure 7-2).

FIGURE 7-2   Create a slide show by dragging images from the Album into your video track.

Editing Slideshow Runtime

Once you have arranged a number of images in your video, you can preview them in the video Monitor in the same way that you previewed video clips in Chapter 5. Notice that, by default, Studio 8 places each image in the Timeline for 4 seconds.

That's a pretty good starting point, and you might want to leave things that way. But what if you knew before you started that you want all the images to display for 3, 5, or 10 seconds? You can change the default duration very easily:

1. Choose Setup | Edit from the menu.

2. At the Setup Options dialog box, change Titles/Stills to whatever value you prefer (see Figure 7-3).

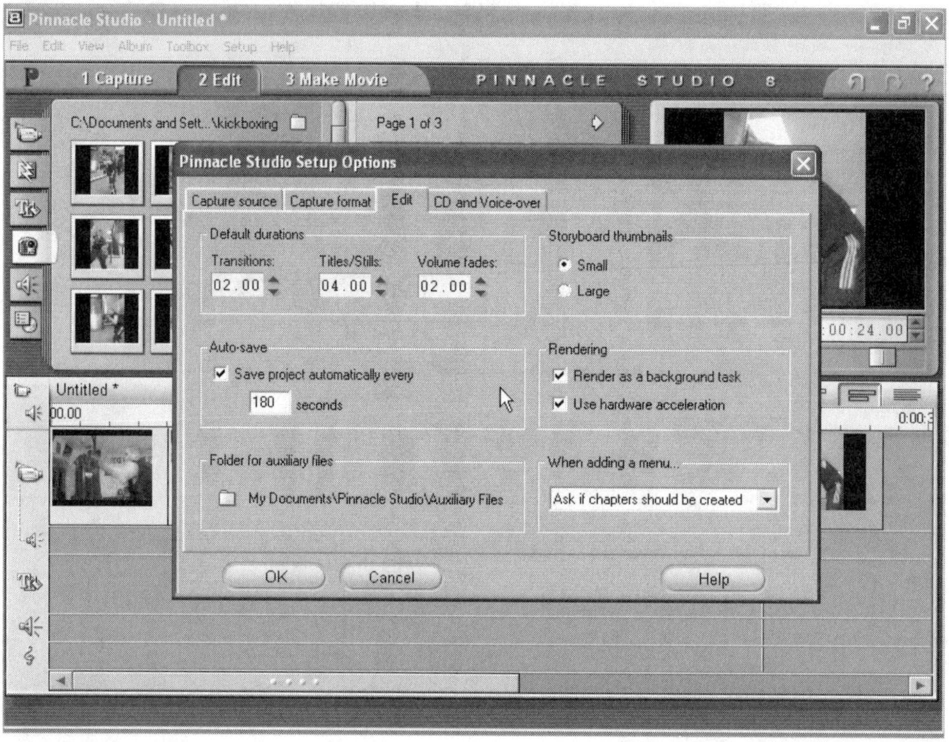

FIGURE 7-3   Use the Setup Options to specify the length of time that each image stays onscreen.

3. Click OK to save your changes.

All of the images that you add to your production after making that change will run for the specified time.

But what if you *don't* want all of the images to display for the same amount of time? For instance, you might want the first image to display just briefly, and the second image to hang onscreen for much longer. That's easy, too. In fact, you can edit the duration of images in the Timeline in the same way that you edited the duration of a video clip in Chapter 5. Drag the right edge of the image to the left to shorten its duration or to the right to extend its duration (see Figure 7-4).

FIGURE 7-4   You can shorten and lengthen still images in the same way that you modify video clips—by dragging the right edge.

Editing a Slideshow to Match a Soundtrack

One of the most common reasons that you might want to edit the length of a series of images is to precisely match the length of the slideshow to the length of the music that you're using as a soundtrack. Using most video editors, you can add a song—usually as an MP3 or WAV file—to the audio track of your production. We'll look at how to do that in the next chapter, but for now, remember that you can finesse the length of still images to end at the same time as a song. In fact, in Studio 8 (as in most programs), when you lengthen the last clip or still to more or less the same time position as the end of the music, the image will "snap" into synchronization and end appropriately.

There's one big difference between editing still images and video clips. When you edit a clip, you can shorten it essentially to zero length, but you can make it only as long as the original video from the Album. You can't add video to the end of a clip that wasn't there to begin with. But when you edit the length of a still image, you can lengthen it indefinitely.

Want the image to play for 30, 40, or 50 seconds? Not a problem. Five minutes? Absolutely. (As long as you have the patience to watch it.) Really long holds on static scenes are not something that most people want to contend with, so be careful that you don't overextend your stills. Even if you're including relevant narration, your movie will progress like a bad Warhol film if you spend more than 10 seconds on an image.

Adding Still Images in iMovie

Using iMovie and your Mac for a slideshow is fairly straightforward. First, you'll need to import the images you're going to use, which you can do using the File | Import command in iMovie or simply by dragging images from the Finder to the Shelf. iMovie can import pretty much any image that QuickTime can deal with: JPEG, GIF, PNG, QuickTime, PICT, and so on. (See more about image types in "Working with Image Files" later in this chapter.)

Once you've imported some images to the Shelf, you can drag them to the Clip Viewer to arrange your slideshow. Just as you did with video clips, you can drag still images from place to place on the Clip Viewer to determine the order in which they will be shown (see Figure 7-5).

By default, every still image that you import into iMovie is set to display for 5 seconds. To change that duration, double-click the icon for the image either on

FIGURE 7-5   Add still frames just as you would video clips to build a slideshow in iMovie.

the Shelf or in the Clip Viewer. In the dialog box that opens, you can use the Duration box to set a new amount of time that the image should stay onscreen. Click OK to accept the change. Remember that the Duration is specified in seconds and *frames*. Standard NTSC (North American) video has 30 frames per second, so that *1:15* equals 1.5 seconds.

NOTE   *iMovie also offers another method for importing images. In the Photos panel, you can directly access your iPhoto library, if you maintain one in iPhoto 2 or later. Locate the image you want, and drag it to the Clip Viewer to add it to your movie or slideshow. You can use the pull-down menu to access your various iPhoto albums, if you have arranged your photos into albums.*

Adding Transitions

If you've already read Chapter 5 (Chapter 6 for Mac users), you know the drill. It's a snap to add video transitions between your still images. Just use the same procedure that you used for adding transitions between video clips.

The easiest way to work with video transitions for still images is to lay out all of the images first: Drag them to the timeline, and set their duration. Then, switch to the transitions. Just as you already did in Chapters 5 and 6, open the tab with the available transitions, and drag the effect you want to the timeline.

You need to keep a couple of things in mind:

■ Try to stick to a single transition effect for all your images—or at least limit the variations. Using too many different effects in a short time makes your video look pretty cheesy. In fact, it might end up looking like a demo disc for a video editor, and that's probably not what you're shooting for. Here at the mansion, we all have a fondness for simple dissolves and fades—especially in a still-image slideshow.

■ In Studio 8, the default image duration is 4 seconds and the default transition duration is 1.5 seconds. When you consider that each image goes through two transitions, that leaves just 2.5 seconds to actually see the picture, and that's not enough time. Try it for yourself: If you build a slideshow in Studio using the defaults, it'll look like someone was running a slide projector while hopped up on Jolt Cola and a bag of jelly beans. When using transitions, you'll need to extend the duration of the still images so that the viewer has time to digest each image. We recommend a value between 6 and 8 seconds. You can see how a slideshow like that looks in the timeline shown in Figure 7-6.

■ In iMovie, the default image duration is 5 seconds, and the default transition length is 2 seconds—a little better than Studio, put pretty much the same problem. Again, increase the duration for the images so that the transitions look smooth and unhurried, and the images remain onscreen long enough for viewers to truly admire them as works of art.

Working with Image Files

The process of creating a slideshow was certainly pretty simple—but what happens if you try to load an image into the video editor and find that you can't? You might see a "file format not supported" message, or something else along

FIGURE 7-6   A completed slide show with transitions in place between each image.

those lines. If you do, it simply means that the image you're trying to insert into your production is saved in a format that your video editor can't read.

Common File Formats

Thankfully, most people use just a few file formats most of the time. So, while you may occasionally hear about formats such as IFF, IMG, and KDC, you can typically ignore all but a very few.

Here's a quick overview of the formats you're most likely to run into and an introduction to what they're used for:

- **JPEG**   Short for Joint Photographic Experts Group (pronounced "jay peg," and stored with the extension ".jpg"), this file format is *lossy*. JPG files are compressed to save storage space, and some data is lost in the process. Why do people put up with a file format that sacrifices image quality? The answer is that the JPEG format does an outstanding job of preserving all the visual information that the human eye can generally see in a picture. Thus, the JPEG format is perhaps the single most common file format in use today for storing digital images, and it is used by virtually all digital cameras as the default format in which to save images. It's worth noting that you can control the amount of compression in your JPEG files. Higher compression means smaller files, but lower visual quality.

- **JPEG2000**   The JPEG2000 format is getting somewhat popular because it offers better image quality at the same compression level as ordinary JPEG. But while many image editors can read and write this format, no digital cameras currently do—and that makes JPEG2000 difficult to use.

- **TIF**   Short for Tagged Image File format, TIF is also very popular, but for exactly the opposite reason that JPEG is popular. TIF files can be saved in two different ways. Using a small amount of compression, they maintain an extremely high degree of image fidelity while slightly reducing file size. Without compression, TIF files are absolutely *lossless:* they preserve 100 percent of the information about every pixel in the original image. TIF files are also popular because they are used on both the Windows and Macintosh platforms. That makes TIF a good choice if you need to share files with someone using a different kind of computer.

- **BMP**   The BMP format is the old standard for Windows bit-mapped files. It can be used for general-purpose storage, for image editing, and as the wallpaper on the Windows desktop, but it isn't generally used by Mac folk. Nor are BMP files used on the Internet. All of which make BMP a relatively unpopular format. Another reason is that BMP tends to be quite large. (The BMP format makes no effort to compress the data at all.) BMP format has been relegated to the "where are they now" file for most modern computer users.

- **GIF**   The Graphics Interchange Format (GIF, pronounced either "giff" or "jiff," depending upon who is doing the talking) was originally developed by CompuServe. GIF-format files are commonly used on the Web, along with files in JPEG format. GIF is different from JPEG and TIF, though, in the sense that it isn't a "true color" format. GIF images store up to 256 colors only (true-color formats can preserve 16.7 million colors).

Those formats are the ones that you'll run into most often. The problem, of course, is that not all video editors recognize all of those formats. Few, if any,

Mac Focus: PICT Format

Another common file format in the Mac world is the PICT format (Macintosh Picture). The popularity of PICT has waned somewhat, particularly because Mac OS X uses TIF and PDF much more extensively. PICT images will import into iMovie with no trouble. PC users will have more difficulty dealing with PICTs unless they have a fairly sophisticated image translation and editing application.

image editors, should have trouble with standard JPEGs. Most will also recognize TIF and BMP files. Beyond that, you may start to run into trouble. Specifically, few image editors recognize JPG2000 or GIF files, and some can't even read TIF files. If a few of your images are in any of these incompatible formats, you'll need to convert them before you can include them in a slideshow.

Preparing Images for Video

If some of your images don't appear in the file list of your video editor—even when you know that you're looking in the right folder—or if an error message appears when you try to load them, you need to convert the files to a different format.

But which formats does your video editor support?

For details, you can check the user guide or online help for the program—or you can just look at the appropriate Files dialog box within the program. In Studio 8, for instance, switch to the still image tab in the Album. Click the folder icon to see the Open dialog box. At the bottom of the dialog box, click the drop arrow for Files of Type. You'll see a list of all the file types that the program can understand, like this:

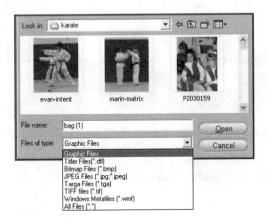

Now you know which file formats you can use. Open the offending file in an image editing program, and use the File | Save As menu item to save the file in a format that your video editor can read.

TIP   *Don't have an image-editing program installed on your PC? Download IrfanView (www.irfanview.com), a surprisingly capable—and free (!)— program that lets you open and save images in a variety of formats. If you have a Mac, check out GraphicConverter (www.lemkesoft.com) for a great shareware option.*

An image being saved in a different format is shown in Figure 7-7. When you're done, you'll have two copies of the image: one in the original file format, and a second copy saved in the new format. You may not want both. If not, it's

FIGURE 7-7   Changing an image's file format is a simple matter of using the File | Save As menu in your image editor.

okay to delete the original file and keep only the more versatile second version. Just remember, though, that the JPEG format is lossy, and you may lose a small amount of detail that can't be recovered if you delete the original file.

> **TIP**   *If your image editor comes with a batch processing feature—and programs such as Paint Shop Pro (Jasc Software), Photoshop and Photoshop Elements (Adobe), and ACDSee (ACD Systems) all do—you can use it to convert a large number of images to a new file format automatically while you step out to lunch.*

Also, keep in mind that digital video has an aspect ratio different from that of many common digital camera files. Most three-megapixel digital cameras, for instance, save images using 2048×1536 pixels. That's an aspect ratio of 1:3. The aspect ratio of the 720×480-pixel frame in DV is 1:5—which is wider than most digital camcorder frames (see Figure 7-8).

We can hear you asking now: So what?

Glad you asked. It's just this: If the framing of your still image is important to you, then you might want to crop the images ahead of time in an image editor. If framing is no big deal for your project, you can just plow on, and your video editor will crop the image for you.

If you want to crop a photo for better video framing, fire up your image editor (Paint Shop Pro, in this example), and follow these steps:

1. Click the Crop tool, which usually looks like a picture frame.

FIGURE 7-8   The aspect ratio of digital pictures and digital video differ. You'll need to crop your stills or be prepared to lose part of the image when you import it into a video.

Mac Focus: iMovie and Final Cut

iMovie is actually a little different: it works better with images that are 640×480 pixels (aspect ratio of 1.3). An image that's 720×480 pixels will be imported in a "letterbox" style, with a black border above and below the image. In most cases, then, images from your digital still camera will work just fine without cropping. For Final Cut, however, images that are 720×480 pixels are recommended.

2. Specify the height and width of the crop as 720 pixels by 480 pixels (see Figure 7-9). If your image editor gives you the option, turn on the feature that keeps the aspect ratio constant while you edit.

3. Now, drag the crop box around the image and resize it as needed until the frame encloses the part of the image that you want to present in the video (see Figure 7-10).

4. Accept the crop, and save the image. You'll probably want to save the cropped image as a new copy. Don't replace the original image unless you expect never to need it again.

Grabbing Stills from Video

Not all of your digital images have to come from a digital camera or a scanner. You can actually nab stills directly out of existing video. Most video editors have this capability. In addition, a few image editing programs can grab still frames from video. (In Photoshop Elements, for instance, choose File | Import | Frame from Video to open a video file and peel off a digital image.)

In Studio 8, you can grab a frame either from the currently open clip or from video that is still on the tape in your camcorder. Here's how to do it:

1. To grab a clip from video you've already captured, drag the clip into the timeline.

2. Double-click the clip to open the clip properties.

FIGURE 7-9   Use the crop box in a program like Paint Shop Pro to change the aspect ratio of your stills to perfectly match the video.

FIGURE 7-10   With the aspect ratio locked, you can resize the crop box without changing the proportions of the crop.

3. Click Frame Grab, which is the fourth icon down the list. (It looks like a hand holding a picture as shown in Figure 7-11).

4. Now click either Movie or Camcorder, depending on which you want.

To grab a clip from the movie, use one of the scrubbers to locate the exact frame. Then, click Grab, and click Save to Disk to save the captured image to your hard disk. You can also click Add to Movie to insert the still frame into the movie timeline.

To capture from the camcorder, make sure that the device is connected, switched on, and set to its VCR or Playback mode. Use the playback controls on the camcorder to find the frame you want, and then click Grab.

The exact method may vary from program to program, but virtually all video editors allow you to grab still frames more or less in this way.

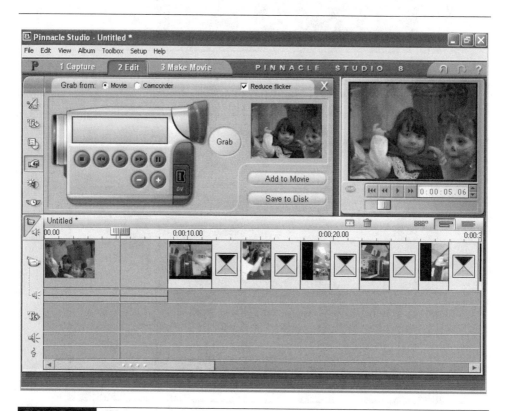

FIGURE 7-11   You can grab moments from video and turn them into still images.

Mac Focus: Creating a Still Within iMovie

In iMovie, to create a still that you can use within your video project, place the playhead at the frame that you want to use as a still. Choose Edit | Create Still Frame. The still frame appears on the Shelf as a 5-second still clip. To export the still image so that you can use it outside iMovie, simply select File | Save Frame As. In the Save dialog box, give the frame grab a name, choose a format from the Format menu, and then click Save.

Using Automated Slideshow Features

Some video editing programs (other than Pinnacle Studio 8) provide an automated wizard-like feature that lets you quickly and easily assemble several images and music into a slideshow. In those programs, you can use the automated feature to quickly select a batch of photos and synchronize them to a musical soundtrack. You can then drop the finished product directly into a video production.

Take a look at MyDVD from Sonic Solutions, for instance. In MyDVD (Figure 7-12), you can create a slideshow in a few easy steps without manually adjusting properties such as slide duration:

1. Click Add Slideshow. (The button is on the left-hand side of MyDVD.) The Create Slideshow window opens, which has its own toolbar as shown in Figure 7-13).

2. Click Get Pictures. At the resulting Open dialog box, you can use SHIFT select or CTRL select to choose multiple images. Click Open to add the images to your slideshow.

3. If you want to add more pictures from a different folder, click Get Pictures again, and repeat step 2.

4. Now that the images are in the slideshow, you can use Rotate to adjust their orientation. That is, if you have portrait-oriented pictures that were taken with the camera positioned sideways, the Rotate button can turn the selected images for you.

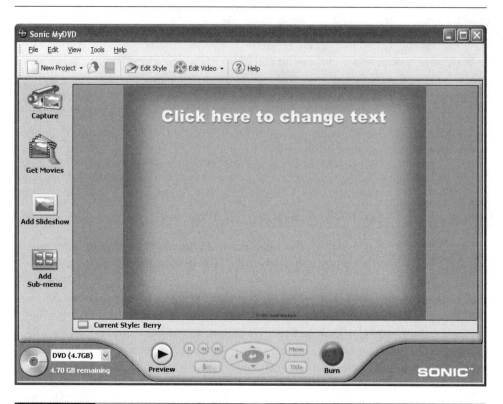

FIGURE 7-12   MyDVD is a simple program that makes it easy to create DVDs of video clips and slideshows, but few of the traditional video editing tools are included.

5. Click Settings to open the Slideshow Settings dialog box as shown in Figure 7-14. Click Advanced to set the slide transitions. By default, MyDVD uses a simple fade effect between the images, but you can turn transitions off or select others from the handful of effects that the program includes.

6. To play a soundtrack with the images, click Basic before leaving the Slideshow Settings dialog box. Click Choose to pick a song from your hard disk. Finally, click Fit Slides to Music at the top of the dialog box as shown in Figure 7-15, and click OK.

7. Click OK to close the Create Slideshow dialog box.

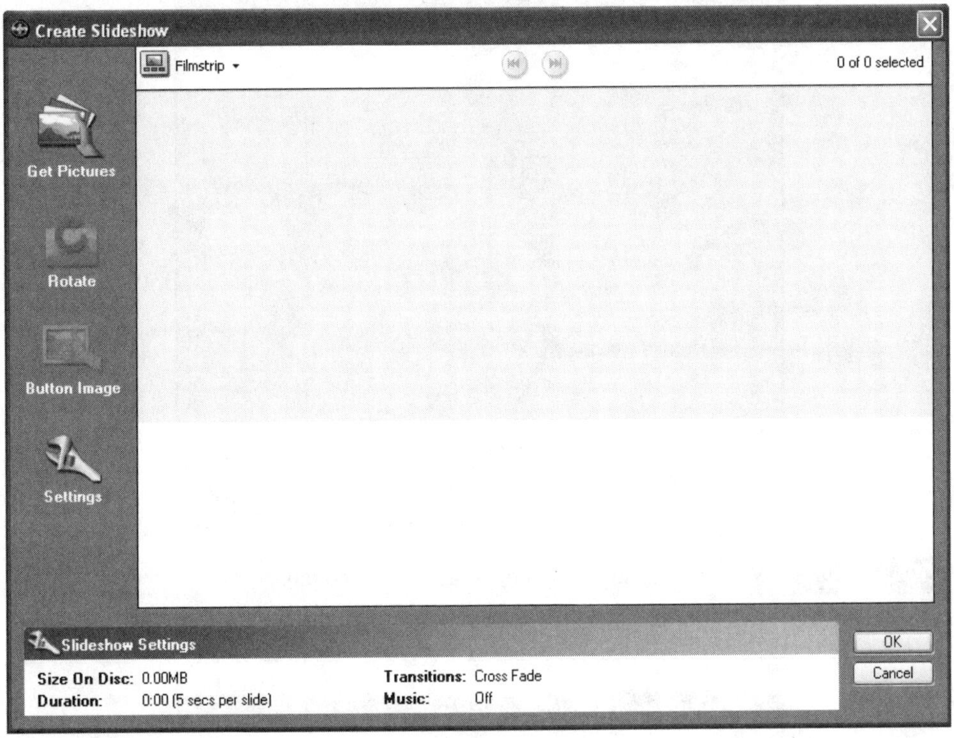

FIGURE 7-13   MyDVD has a complete slideshow wizard built in.

If you want to see the slideshow in action, click the Preview button at the bottom of the MyDVD screen. Click the slideshow button in the display. Sit back and enjoy.

Animating Stills, Documentary Style

If you've ever watched anything on PBS besides *Sesame Street* or *The Electric Company,* you've no doubt been treated to documentaries about Josef Stansilvanmaniski and how he invented the butter churn. Or something like that.

Documentaries of that kind are often littered with dramatic black-and-white still images, complete with "period" music and somber narration. But rarely are those clips totally static. Instead, the camera usually pans slowly across the image

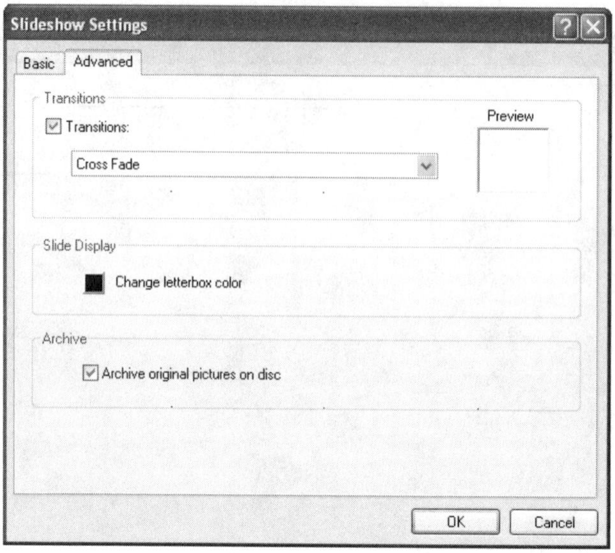

FIGURE 7-14 Vary the transition effects in the Advanced tab.

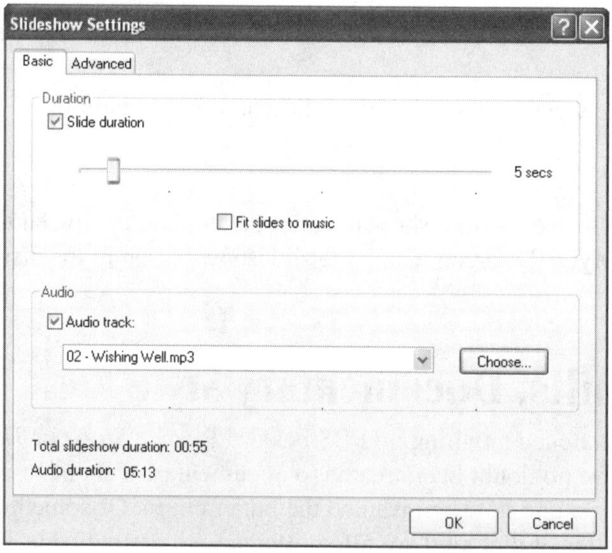

FIGURE 7-15 Want a soundtrack? MyDVD accommodates.

revealing pertinent details. Or it might zoom in for a better look at Josef's dad, who was—no doubt—ill from churning too much butter by hand. And while you may have watched that movie only because your tenth grade social studies teacher made you, the good news is that it's possible to get the same sort of effects in your own movies.

Unfortunately, we haven't found any video editors for the PC that come with this capability built in. Instead, you'll need a second application designed specifically for this job. We've found two excellent solutions: one is inexpensive and somewhat basic in its capabilities; the other is rather expensive, but extremely full-featured. (On Macs, iMovie can animate stills. See "Animating with iMovie" later in this section.)

Animating with Microsoft Plus

The cheapest way to animate still images is to use an inexpensive program from Microsoft called Microsoft Plus! Digital Media Edition. The product costs about $20 and is available in stores or by download from the Microsoft web site. Once you have Digital Media Edition installed, start the component called Plus! Photo Story. Using that application, you can not only create a slideshow of still images, but you can also add narration, music, transitions, and—most importantly—pans and zooms that highlight the narration.

Let's make a short slideshow:

1. On the main screen, click Begin a Story. The slideshow wizard starts up as shown in Figure 7-16.

2. At Import and Arrange Your Pictures, click Import Pictures. You'll see the Open dialog box.

3. Select as many images as you like using SHIFT select or CTRL select. Click Open when you're done. The images automatically arrange themselves into the filmstrip as shown in Figure 7-17.

4. You can rearrange the pictures if you want to by dragging them to new positions in the filmstrip. When you're done, click Next.

5. Now it's time to add narration and control over the movement of the images. There are two ways to do this.

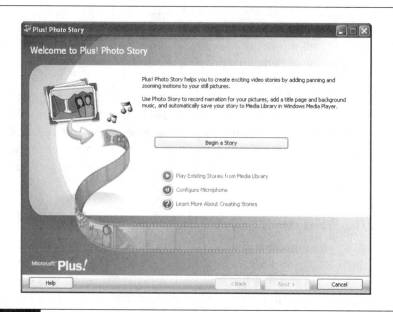

FIGURE 7-16   Microsoft's PhotoStory is a fast and easy way to make slideshows.

FIGURE 7-17   Arrange the images into a slideshow using the filmstrip at the bottom of the screen.

■ **Method 1**   Click Record, and narrate into a microphone while hovering the pointer over the part of the image to which Photo Story should pan or zoom.

■ **Method 2**   First, add narration. Then, click the Advanced button and pan or zoom (or both) manually. Click Control Pans and Zooms Manually, then choose a start and end position for the image (see Figure 7-18). You'll have to set this control for each image in your slideshow.

6. After you set the narration, pan, and zoom controls, click Next.

7. On the Add a Title Page screen, you can do just what it says: add a title to the start of the slideshow. Because we're assuming that you'll eventually insert the slideshow into the middle of a video production, we suggest that you leave this feature switched off. Click Next.

7

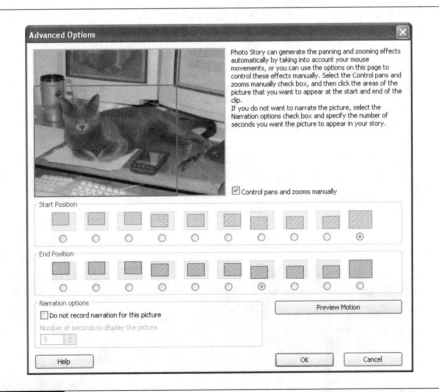

FIGURE 7-18   While you narrate, you can use the pointer to tell the program how to zoom, or you can animate manually using this control panel.

8. Now you can add some music to your slideshow. If you want to, click Browse, and find a song on your hard drive. Click Next (see Figure 7-19).

9. Finally, you reach the stage at which you can save the slideshow. Select the option for High Quality, name the file, and click Next.

When the save is complete, you'll have a complete slideshow on your hard disk. Unfortunately, your slideshow will not be in a format that most video editing programs can read. Instead of using a common format such AVI or MPEG, Plus! Photo Story saves your slideshow in the Microsoft WMV format. Now what?

One more step: You need to convert the WMV file into an AVI video that your video editor can understand. A number of video converter utilities are available for download on the Web, but our favorite is called EO-Video (www.eo-video.com). It's inexpensive ($20 after a 30-day free trial) and supports nearly every file format in the universe. Load your Photo Story file into a program like EO-Video, and save it as an AVI file (see Figure 7-20). Now you can load the video into a program like Studio 8 and treat it like any other video clip.

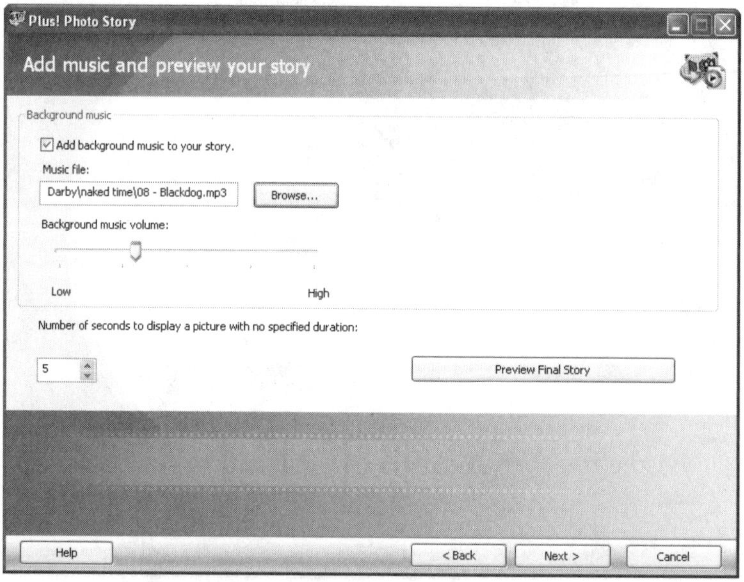

FIGURE 7-19   Photo Story lets you add music to your soundtrack.

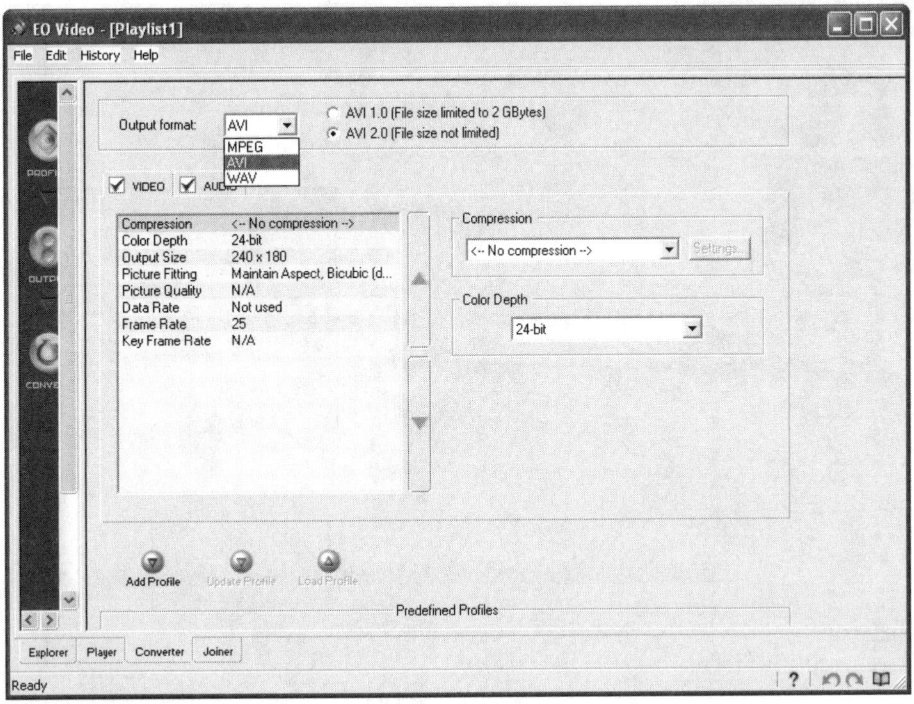

FIGURE 7-20 EO-Video is a great way to covert many kinds of video clips into a format that your video editor can understand.

Animating with Canopus Imaginate

The Photo Story application from Microsoft isn't a bad choice (certainly the price is right), but it is weak in many ways if you're serious about making your own documentary-style videos. The range of pan motion is limited, for instance, and you can't zoom very far into the picture. Also, you can set only a single motion per picture, and so you can't pan across and then down. Finally, the resolution of the finished product doesn't quite match that of a digital video frame.

The alternative? We like a program called Imaginate, from Canopus Corporation (www.canopus.com). Imaginate has incredibly powerful tools for letting you maneuver around a still image, and yet it's extremely easy to use. The program is shown in Figure 7-21.

In Imaginate, you work with one image at a time. You load the image by choosing File | Load Image. Then, you can use the zoom icon in the toolbar on the

FIGURE 7-21   The most powerful, easy to use still image tool for video is, no doubt, Imaginate from Canopus.

left to zoom out and show the entire image in the window. (You can also click Fit to Window, which is the third tool down in the toolbar).

Now you can begin to define *keyframes.* (A keyframe is essentially an important point in your animation.)

As you can see at the bottom of the screen, the timeline is automatically set to the start of the animation. Grab the crop box—which is preset to the appropriate proportion for a DV frame—and move and zoom it. Assume that you want to start with the image filling the frame. Grab the crop box by a corner and expand it to fill the screen. (You will have to move it as well.) It should look something like that shown in Figure 7-22.

The state in which you leave the crop box is the keyframe for the start of the animation.

FIGURE 7-22 Imaginate's scrubber and zoom/pan tools let you precisely move about still images as the video plays.

Now, drag the timeline scrubber to the 5-second point. Assume that you'd like to be zoomed into the subject's face by that point, and so you want to zoom and rearrange the crop box as shown in Figure 7-23.

Finally, at the 10-second point, assume you want to zoom in on someone in the background. Drag the timeline scrubber to the 10-second point, and then move and zoom the crop box appropriately as shown in Figure 7-24.

Now you can drag the scrubber back to the start, press SPACEBAR, and watch a preview of your animation. If necessary, you can adjust the timing and content of your keyframes. When you're happy with the results, you can save the movie in a form that will drop directly into your video editor. Choose File | Render Movie | Microsoft AVI.

FIGURE 7-23   It's a good idea to have high-resolution images available, since Imaginate lets you zoom in for a good look at details in the picture.

Animating with iMovie

In iMovie, you can select any still image clip and add to it what iMovie calls the "Ken Burns Effect": You can slowly pan or zoom in on an image to add some visual interest as the slideshow plays. You can set pan or zoom alone, or both effects together. (We don't recommend setting both for one image, however.)

Here's how zoom works:

1. Select an image in the Clip Viewer.

2. Click Photos in the Shelf/Effects area to switch to the Image tools.

3. At the top of the Photo panel, you'll see a check box next to Ken Burns Effect. Make sure that it's checked.

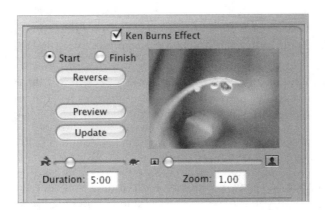

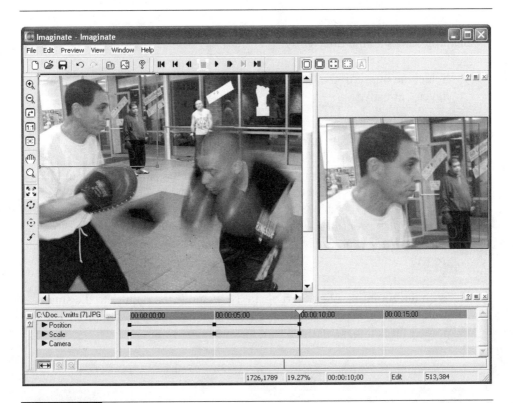

FIGURE 7-24   You can see Imaginate's timeline with several keypoints at the bottom of the screen.

4. Now, you've got a decision to make: Do you want to zoom in or zoom out? Use the Zoom slider, or click in the Zoom box to change the zoom level.

    If you want to zoom in, select Start, and set Zoom to **1.00**. Next, select Finish, and set Zoom to **2.00** or higher (whatever level of zoom you'd like to see the clip end with).

    If you want to zoom out, select Start, and set Zoom to **2.00** or higher. Then, click Finish, and set Zoom to **1.00**.

5. Click Preview to see how the effect will look. (Note that you can change the duration if you'd like the effect to end before the clip does.) When you're happy with the settings, click Update. The clip is updated with the new effects.

Panning works a little differently:

1. Select the image in the Clip Viewer and switch to the Photo panel if you haven't already.

2. Now, select Start, and set Zoom to **1.50**; select Finish, and set Zoom to **1.50**. (You can choose another zoom level, depending on the image, but try this one out for starters.) That bit of zoom gives you some image to pan across, but ensures that no zoom occurs during the pan, which would likely make your viewers seasick.

NOTE   *If you don't zoom in a bit on the image, you won't have any additional image for the pan. Some of your image has to be off-screen for the pan to work.*

3. With the zoom set, click Start again. Now, move the pointer to the small representation of your image, and click and hold the mouse button. The pointer turns into a small fist.

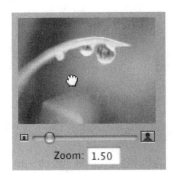

4. Drag the image to exactly where you'd like it to be when it first appears onscreen.

5. Now, click Finish, grab the image again, and drag it to its final location.

6. To see how the pan looks, click Preview. If you like the look, click Update. The image is updated with the new pan effect. (You'll see a render bar appear in the image clip in the Clip Viewer. Fully rendering the effect can take a little while, depending on the duration of the clip.)

Where to Find It

Web site	Address	What's there
ACD Systems	www.acdsee.com	ACDSee
Canopus Corporation	www.canopus.com	Imaginate
IrfanView	www.irfanview.com	IrfanView
Lemke Software	www.lemkesoft.com	GraphicConverter
McGray	www.eo-video.com	EO-Video
Jasc Software	www.jasc.com	Paint Shop Pro
Microsoft	www.microsoft.com	Microsoft Plus! Digital Media Edition

Chapter 8

Working with Sound

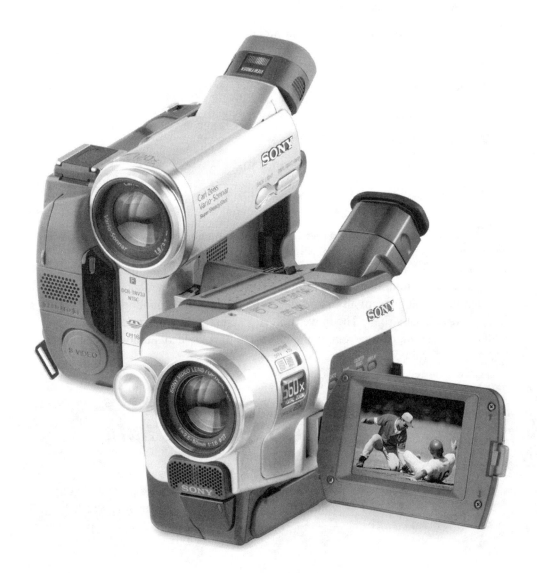

How to...

- Use the audio tools in Studio 8
- Edit an audio track for length or volume
- Ramp and fade volume
- Use J cuts to make audio transitions
- Use L cuts to continue audio through the next scene
- Carry audio through B roll
- Narrate in a video
- Add sound effects to a video
- Add a soundtrack from CD
- Add a soundtrack from MP3 or WAV files
- Use pre-produced, royalty-free music in a video

When people talk about the most important moments in the evolution of cinema, what do they discuss in hushed, reverent tones? The transition from black-and-white to color? The move to widescreen? The introduction of the Steadicam? William Shatner's gripping performance in *The Devil's Rain*? No.

Sure, those things were all important. But not nearly as groundbreaking as the first "talkies." That's right: The move from silent film to the modern era of motion pictures is staggeringly important in the history of film. Indeed, audio has reshaped cinema on several occasions.

Did you know?

More about *The Devil's Rain*

We don't mean to harp on this classic Shatnerfest, but did you know that this movie was also John Travolta's film debut? Rent this movie, and watch Vinnie Barbarino melt!

George Lucas, dismayed at the atrocious sound quality in most local movie theaters, created the THX specification for certifying high-fidelity audio in movie theaters back in the late 1970s. And he was also at the forefront of the movement to bring multichannel surround sound to cinema. And that led, of course, to the 5.1 and 7.1 surround sound systems you can find today in many American living rooms.

Sound is key. In this chapter, we'll look at how you can make the most of the sound track in your video editor.

NOTE   *This chapter focuses on audio in Pinnacle Studio 8 and other topics specific to PCs. If you're using a Macintosh and iMovie or Final cut, see Chapter 9 for specifics.*

Audio Capabilities in Studio 8

This much is true: Every video editor has a different set of audio capabilities. Some elementary video editors only allow a single sound track in a production. Others let you work with two, three, or four layers of audio. Some editors let you add a virtually unlimited array of music, narration, and other sounds.

Pinnacle Studio 8, the program we've used for much of this book, falls somewhere in the middle. In Studio, you can add three layers of sound: the original audio track, which usually comes with the video, direct from your camcorder; a second track for special sound effects; and a third track for music. Figure 8-1 shows the three tracks.

Notice that the volume level in the audio track is represented by a line that runs horizontally through the clip. If the line is high in the clip, the volume is high. If the line is low, the volume is low.

That's not all. Studio 8 also includes a special module called SmartSound. With SmartSound, you can use royalty-free music to create a professional-sounding soundtrack for your movie. You'll find more about SmartSound later in this chapter in "Adding a Soundtrack." For now, let's look at the audio tracks in more detail.

Editing Audio Tracks

Perhaps the single most basic way you can edit the audio in a movie is to vary the volume. For example, you might want to lower the overall volume of the soundtrack. That can be useful, but that trick will really come in handy later when you start adding multiple audio sources to a production.

FIGURE 8-1   Pinnacle Studio has three audio tracks in the Timeline, giving you the ability to use three different layers of sound in your movie.

There are two ways to change the volume in an audio track:

- Use the master volume control
- Use adjustment handles

Using the Change Volume Control

Need to raise or lower the volume of an entire stretch of audio at once? Piece of cake. Do this:

1. Make sure the Timeline contains one or more clips.

2. Choose Toolbox | Change Volume from the menu. The Change Volume panel pops up in the Album area.

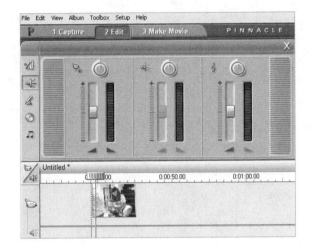

3. In the Change Volume panel, click the round dial for the original audio track (the one furthest to the left) and hold down the left mouse button. Now, by moving the mouse left and right as you continue to hold the mouse button, spin the dial up and down. Notice that the audio level throughout the production moves up and down in sync with the dial movement.

So far so good—but what's the big slider for? Here's where things get just a teensy bit complicated. You use the slider to change the volume in just a section of the movie. Specifically, you use it to change the volume from the current location of the Timeline scrubber forward in the Timeline until the next "break" in the volume setting.

Try this: Load several clips into a new Timeline and then move the scrubber to the far left (the start of the production). Drag the slider up and down. You'll find that the volume changes across the entire production. But now move the scrubber to the right, somewhere in the middle of the movie. Move the slider up and down. What happened?

Notice that Pinnacle Studio added a volume adjustment point at the location of the scrubber. Now you're adjusting the volume only from that point forward into the movie.

One last test: Spin the master volume control. You'll see that the level of the entire production goes up and down, but the volume adjustment points remain.

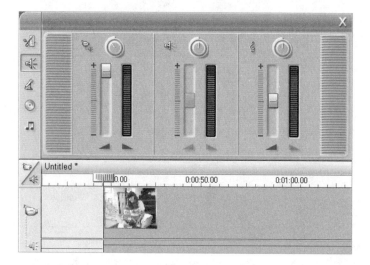

Bottom line is this: The controls in the Change Volume panel are a fast and easy way to make overall changes to the volume of your production. But what (you're no doubt wondering) should you do if you want to gradually change volume? Is there a way to fade volume in and out?

Absolutely.

Ramping and Fading Volume

Not all audio should begin and end abruptly with the start and end of a video clip. Sometimes you might want the volume to *ramp up* from a low level or *fade out* gracefully toward the end of a scene. Both of those options—and much more complex audio controls—are available in your video editor.

In Studio 8, you can control the relative volume within a clip by setting and manipulating volume adjustment points—just like the one that was created automatically back in the previous section. Here's all you need to do:

1. Load a video clip into the Timeline, and stretch the clip so that it fills the entire screen.

2. The volume level should, by default, already be positioned halfway through the clip, meaning that the overall volume level is 50 percent. If the volume isn't at 50 percent, use the controls in the Change Volume panel to set it that way:

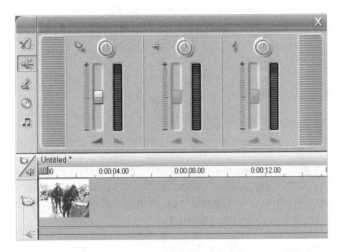

3. Position the pointer over the volume level in the audio track. Hover the pointer directly over the volume level. You'll see the pointer change from a hand to an arrow. Move the pointer about a quarter of the way into the clip. Now click, being careful not to drag. You've just set a volume adjustment point—it's that little square you deposited in the volume level line where you clicked:

4. Position the pointer over the start of the volume level at the left edge of the clip. Drag that point to the bottom of the clip. It should now look like this:

5. Now that you've set a ramp (the volume will gradually increase from silence to full over the first quarter of the clip), let's add a fade. Move the pointer about three-quarters of the way across the audio track, and click the volume level to set a new adjustment point.

6. Finish the fade by dragging the end of the audio track to the bottom:

Obviously, you can use this powerful technique to vary the volume level in complex ways throughout the scene.

TIP   *Don't forget that you can use the master volume dial in the Change Volume screen to raise or lower the entire level without hurting the ramp and fade you've already created.*

Making Audio Transitions

Back in Chapter 5, we talked about how you can use video effects to add transitions to your movie. Fades, cuts, wipes, pushes, and millions of other effects are at your disposal. Those are fine, but some of the coolest effects you can add to cut points in your movie are none other than audio transitions.

What are we talking about? Consider this: Have you ever watched a movie in which a telephone starts ringing—but the telephone isn't even onscreen—it's in the *next* scene? After a ring or two, the film cuts to the telephone. Or have you seen a movie in which a car chase is anticipated by adding police sirens to the tail end of a scene that isn't even on the freeway? After a moment, the scene changes and the video catches up to the audio.

Kinda cool, huh? Well, step right up, folks, because we're about to show you how you can do that for yourself. We're going to explain two common effects:

■ **J Cut**   In this transition, the audio changes before the video.

■ **L Cut**   This effect makes the video changes before the audio ones.

Making a J Cut

The J cut is a very effective transition to use when you're looking for dramatic effect. It's great for introducing elements of the next scene in a subtle way. The trick to a J cut is to edit the audio separately from the video. In Studio 8, the only way to accomplish that is to lock the video track to keep it from changing when you edit the audio (and vice versa).

Let's try it out. Here's what you need to do:

1. Load three video clips into the Timeline. The J cut will happen between the first clip and the second; so, for the middle position, pick a clip that has an interesting sound at the very beginning.

2. Double-click the second clip to open its clip properties. Drag the start time of the clip forward to just past the point at which the interesting sound that you want to place in the first clip occurs. In other words, you want to trim the beginning of the clip to edit out the sound as shown in Figure 8-2.

When you're done, close the Clip Properties window.

FIGURE 8-2 The J-Cut is a clever way to cue audio before you see its matching video onscreen.

3. Now you need to edit the audio without changing the video. To do that, click the camcorder icon to the left of the video track. That locks the track so that you can't edit it. Notice the padlock symbol on the left edge of the track:

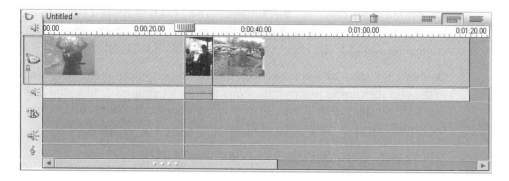

4. Position the pointer over the audio track for the second clip. You'll see arrows pointing in both directions, which means you can lengthen or shorten the audio track. Drag the audio to the left as far as it will go. At the same time, the first audio track shortens. Notice that the video tracks don't move; they're no longer perfectly lined up with each other. But if you scroll to the right, you'll see that the end of the second audio clip is still linked to the video, so that there's no problem with the way it connects to the third clip:

5. Unlock the video clip by clicking the camcorder icon again. The padlock goes away.

That's all there is to it!

Now, play the video in the Monitor, and see what you've wrought. If you don't like the way it came out, you can always fine-tune it.

Making an L Cut

Having already mastered the art of the J cut, you should find an L cut a piece of cake, right? It's pretty simple, in fact. We are going to introduce new video while continuing to play the audio from the previous scene.

The effect is quite different from that of the J cut you just did. An L cut is best used in situations where you want to provide continuity. When you carry the audio over, it's clear that the new scene is a continuation or explanation of the previous scene. This effect occurs often in documentaries: a speaker is onscreen, but then is replaced by location video as the voice carries on, explaining the new onscreen material.

As you can well imagine, the technique is very similar to the one used to make a J cut. Do this:

1. Load three new video clips into the Timeline. The L cut will happen between the first clip and the second.

2. Double-click the first clip to open its clip properties. Drag the end time of the clip backward to just past the point at which you want to begin showing the next clip as shown in Figure 8-3.

   When you're done, close the Clip Properties window.

3. Once again, you need to edit the audio without changing the video. Click the camcorder icon to the left of the video track and make sure that you see the padlock symbol.

4. Grab the end of the first audio clip, and drag it to the right, pushing the audio of the second clip out of the way. What you're doing, in reality, is a rolling edit (which we discussed in Chapter 5) to shorten the second audio without disturbing its end point (Figure 8-4).

5. Finally, unlock the video track, and preview your creation.

Not bad, right?

But what if you want to go one better? You'd like to switch to alternate video (that's often called *B roll,* by the way) while your narrator narrates, then return to the narrator at the very end. How do you do that?

Let's try it next.

FIGURE 8-3   The L-Cut lets you continue the audio from the previous scene over the video.

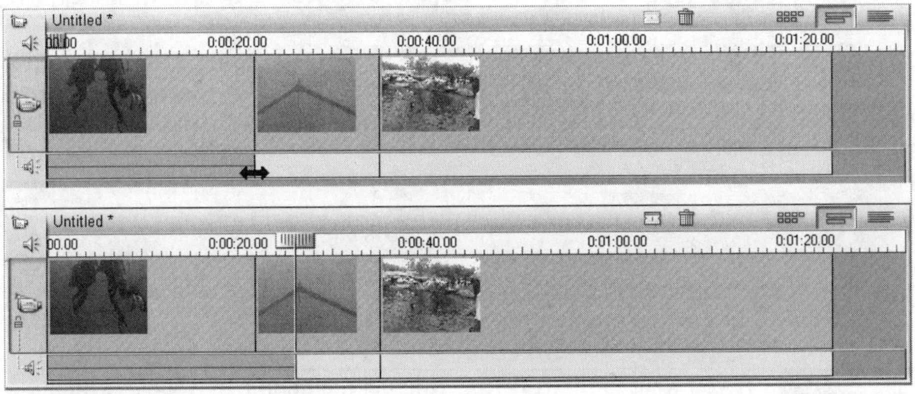

FIGURE 8-4   With the L-Cut in place, you can see that the audio of the second scene starts late, but is still in perfect sync with its video.

Carrying Audio Through B Roll

So here's the deal: You're interviewing your daughter about her recent experiences at summer camp. Rather than keep the camera statically fixed on her for five minutes, you want to cut away to B roll of her actually at camp—without losing the audio of her interview in the first scene. Then you want to come back to her at the very end.

The easiest way to accomplish cutaways to B roll without recording a second narration track (which we'll show you how to do later in this chapter in "Adding Narration to Your Video") is to do a little clip splitting. Try this:

1. Start by loading the interview scene into the Timeline.

2. Find the point in the clip where you want to cut away to the next scene. Place the Timeline scrubber exactly at that location as shown in Figure 8-5.

3. Lock the audio track by clicking the speaker icon to the left of the track. You'll see the padlock symbol.

FIGURE 8-5   If you want to insert B Roll video in the middle of a scene without disturbing the audio, you need to split the scene, as we're preparing to do in this screen.

Did you know?

All About B Roll

Want to sound like a true video geek? Call your secondary video footage "B roll." B roll is the secondary footage that's often interspersed into a movie to provide a different viewpoint. It gets its name from the fact that, in the old days, alternate film of this kind was placed in an actual "B" player and spliced into the finished production between scenes on the "A" player.

In the world of digital, no one works with two different machines any more; however, the name remains.

8

4. Next, right-click the video track, and choose Split Clip from the pop-up menu. If all went well, you should see that the video clip is split in two at the scrubber, but that the audio track has remained intact. In Figure 8-6, we've moved the scrubber out of the way so that you can see the split point better.

5. Your next task is to make some room in the middle of the scene for the B roll video. Click the new clip to the right to select it, and then position the pointer at the cut point. You'll see a dual-headed arrow, which indicates that you can drag the clip in either direction, shortening or lengthening it. Drag it some distance to the right to create a gap in the video track, as shown in Figure 8-7.

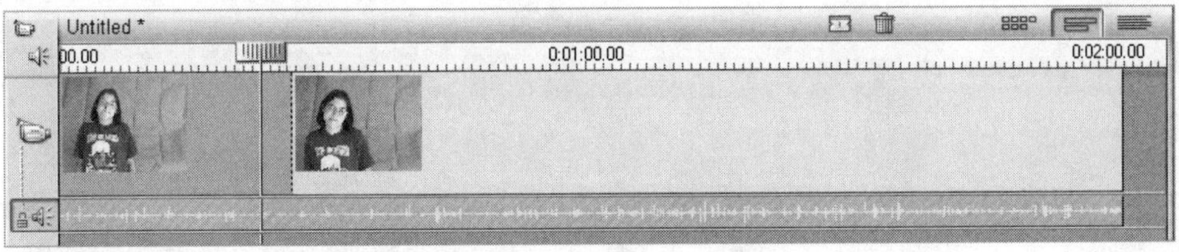

FIGURE 8-6   The image is split and waiting for replacement video.

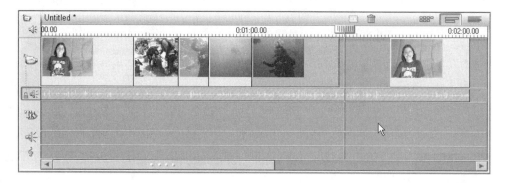

FIGURE 8-7 After dragging the second half of the split scene out of the way, we can now insert the B Roll.

6. Now, drag your B roll clip from the album to the gap and line it up with the end of the first clip. If you have more clips, repeat the process until you have satisfied your need to see other video clips in the middle of the interview.

7. Once all the clips are in place, drag the start of the second half of the first
scene back to meet the end of the B roll footage:

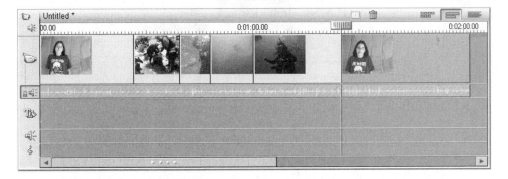

8. Unlock the audio track and test your creation.

Adding a Second Audio Track

The beauty of making your own videos on a PC is that you can add additional
audio tracks—you don't have to be content with whatever sound happens to be on
the camcorder tape. The additional tracks can be used for music, sound effects,
narration—anything you think you need to add to your movie that you couldn't get
"in the camera."

Adding Narration

One hot use for the audio track is narration. A lot of video editors come with
narration tools built right in, and Studio 8 is no exception.

To add narration to your video, first make sure that you indeed have a
microphone connected to the computer sound card and that the audio property
for the mic is enabled.

Whaaa? Simply put: Your microphone must be configured in Windows to
actually record sound.

Not sure that your microphone is hooked up properly? Here's an easy test:
Click Start, and choose All Programs I Accessories I Entertainment I Sound Recorder.
When the Sound Recorder window opens, click the red Record button and talk,
then click the black Stop button. If you can click the Play button and hear what
you just recorded, you're in business.

8

If not, you need to open the mic properties so that you can configure the device properly:

1. Choose Start | Control Panel, and click Speech, Sounds, and Audio Devices. Then, click the Sounds and Audio Devices link. Still with us? Good. Next, on the Sounds and Audio Devices Properties dialog box, click Advanced.

2. You've finally reached the Play Control dialog box, which is where you set audio levels for the many inputs and outputs in Windows. Choose Options | Properties.

3. On the Properties dialog box that opens, choose Recording, and click OK.

Whew! See the Recording Control dialog box? Great. Make sure that Microphone is selected and that the volume is set high as shown in Figure 8-8.

FIGURE 8-8   You need to make sure your hardware is ready for narration.

Now you're ready to narrate. Just do this:

1. Build your production first (save the narration for late in the project). Add your clips, arrange them to taste, add transitions and all that sort of thing. That way, your narration will match the video as the audience sees it, and you won't have to keep changing the narration to reflect new scenes or edited scenes.

2. Position the Timeline scrubber at the point in the video where you'd like your narration to begin.

3. Choose Toolbox | Record Voice-Over from the menu. The Voice-Over panel should appear in the Album area (see Figure 8-9)

4. Take a deep breath, place your script in front of you, and click the Record button.

8

FIGURE 8-9   The Voice-Over controls in Pinnacle Studio.

5. Studio 8 gives you a three-second countdown and then starts recording every bit of sound that the microphone picks up. At the same time, your production plays in the monitor so that you can narrate in time to the finished movie.

6. When you're done narrating, click the Stop button. The narration audio appears in the second audio track at the appropriate point in the production:

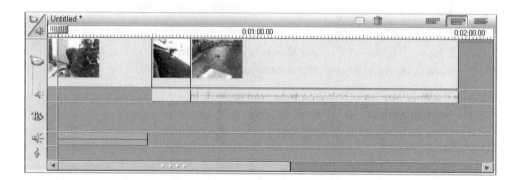

Pretty easy, right? Here are a few tips to help you prepare for your narration:

- You don't have to narrate the entire movie. If just a few spots in your video require voice-over, then do them one at a time instead of creating a huge narration audio file that's filled mostly with dead air.

- Prepare what you'll say ahead of time. Most of the time, if you wing it when you sit down to record a narration, that's how the result will sound. At the very least, outline what you plan to say so that you can do it with a minimum of verbal pauses (um, er) and awkward phrases.

- Don't set the microphone too close to your mouth or it will record a lot of harsh pops as you speak.

Adding Sound Effects

Way back in Chapter 3, we told you about Foley effects—sound effects, in other words—that you can create on your own, download from the Internet, or buy. Here's where you get to incorporate Foley effects into your movie. As long as those sounds exist somewhere on your hard disk in a common audio file format such as MP3 or WAV, you can insert them into your production now.

Adding sounds is very much like adding other multimedia elements to your production. Just do this:

1. Click the fifth tab in the Album (the icon looks like a speaker). The Sound Effects pane opens in the Album area:

2. Navigate to the folder on your hard disk where the sound effects you're interested in are stored. Incidentally, Studio 8 comes with a heap o' sound effects. You can find them in a folder called Sound Effects within the main Pinnacle folder (which, if you used the default install location, is itself stored in the Program Files folder of your computer's hard disk).

3. Drag the appropriate sound from the album to the second audio track and position it where you want it to play in the movie.

Adding a Soundtrack

Think about it: Almost all movies have some kind of soundtrack. Music adds an elegant flourish to your production, and the right music can set the perfect mood for whatever you're trying to convey in pictures and video.

Video editors such as Studio 8 make it easy to add music to your video. Indeed, Studio provides a third audio track designed expressly for music. You can add four different kinds of music files to that track, and we'll talk about each type:

■   Tracks from an audio CD (Studio 8 can "rip" them for you)

■   MP3 or WAV files already stored on your hard disk

- Royalty-free music from the built-in soundtrack generator in Studio 8

- Royalty-free music from an external music creation program

Ripping Tracks from CD

It's entirely possible that you already know how to *rip* (that's slang for "copy") music from audio CDs. You might use a program like Windows Media Player, RealOne, or some other digital music app to do just that. If that's the case, this section is no great revelation to you. But if you're new to the idea of taking a song from a CD and using it in the soundtrack to your film, then you'll appreciate the fact that many video editors have their own CD ripper built right in.

In Studio 8, for instance, it's easy to copy a song from CD and place it directly into your movie:

1. Place a CD into the CD-ROM drive on your computer.

2. When Windows opens a dialog box asking what you'd like to do with the disc, just cancel the dialog:

3. Place the Timeline scrubber at the point in the production that you'd like the music to begin. Note, of course, that you don't have to start the music at the very beginning of the movie.

4. Choose Toolbox | Add CD Music from the menu.

5. Studio will probably report that it doesn't recognize the CD. Type a name into the dialog box, and press ENTER. Later, if you insert the same disc again, Studio will remember the name you gave to that CD and will immediately open the Audio Capture panel in the Album area.

6. Using the Audio Capture panel, you can select a specific song from the CD and preview the music. Use the Track menu to find the song you want, and click Play to hear the music. Notice that you can establish set-in and set-out points for the music as well; but, most of the time, you'll probably want to capture the entire song (see Figure 8-10).

7. When you're ready, click Add to Movie. The music immediately appears in the third audio track... but don't take the CD out of the drive yet, because the music itself hasn't been ripped to the hard disk.

8. Preview your movie in the monitor. Studio will begin by capturing the audio, and then the video will play with the new soundtrack.

Once you've ripped a song or two, remember that you can reposition those songs anywhere in the movie. You can also trim the length of songs, fade and ramp, and change the volume relative to the other audio tracks in the movie—all the stuff we covered earlier in this chapter.

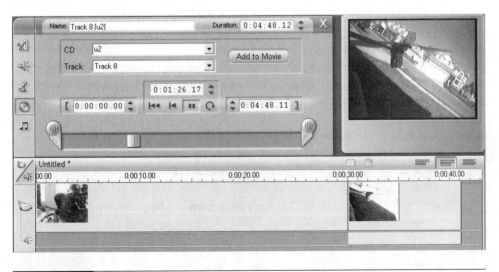

FIGURE 8-10   Capturing a song from CD for playback in your movie.

Ripping Music with Other Audio Software

Even though Studio 8 makes it convenient to rip a song from CD for inclusion in a video, you might want to rip using other software.

Why would you want to do that? Well, using a real audio ripper, you can copy an entire album to your hard disk at once—great if you want to include several songs in your production. Audio rippers also offer more features, higher audio quality, and faster processing speeds. In other words, Studio 8 (or any other video editing software) includes CD ripping as a convenience, but you'll usually do better with software designed specifically for the task.

Best Stand-Alone Rippers Currently Available	
PC	XingMP3encoder (www.xingtech.com)
	Audiograbber (www.audiograbber.com-us.net)
	Easy CD-DA Extractor (www.poikosoft.com)
Macintosh	MPegger (www.proteron.com)
	N2MP3 Pro (www.mp3-mac.com)

All of these programs are compact, efficient rippers that offer a wealth of options for extracting music from CD and saving the result in either WAV or MP3 format.

If you prefer an integrated, all-in-one app, though, you probably want to find a jukebox program. That's what we tend to use most. All the most popular options—RealOne, Windows Media Player, and Musicmatch—are all full-featured players/rippers/encoders. For the most part, you will probably be quite happy with any of those programs.

If you have a CD-RW drive on your PC, it probably came with a program such as Easy CD Creator or Nero. Those two apps are primarily designed to copy data to CD, but they can also rip music from audio CD.

> **TIP**
> *You have one excellent reason to avoid Windows Media Player: it doesn't include MP3 encoding. You can use it to rip music and to store that music in WMA format, but most video editors can't deal with WMA files. They want to see your song in WAV or MP3 format, and the MP3 addition will cost you extra money, because it's an upgrade. Other jukebox programs come with MP3 encoding even in the free trial versions.*

TIP

Some rippers use something called variable bit rates. Smaller, more compact song files may result because the encoder can vary the bit rate based on the dynamic range of the song; however, some video editors can't play music recorded with a variable bit rate. As a result, you might want to stick with a constant bit rate until you know that all your hardware and software support variable bit rates.

When you actually rip music from CD, you might initially be surprised at the speed. Most rippers can read data up to 10 times faster than the ordinary playback speed of the song, and some rippers can work much faster—as much as 16 times ordinary speed, in fact. The maximum ripping speed is a function of several components, including the maximum speed of the CD-ROM drive, the speed of the PC processor, the available memory, the hard drive configuration, and the capabilities of the ripping software itself.

8

How to ...   **Rip Music**

The process of ripping tracks from a CD is pretty straightforward. Here's the rundown:

1. Insert a CD in the CD-ROM drive on your PC.

2. Start the ripper software.

3. If necessary, specify the file format and the bit rate or capture quality for the recording. For use in video, we recommend the MP3 format and a bit rate of either 128 kbps or 160 kbps—anything higher won't make much of a difference when played back through television speakers.

4. Press the Record button in the software, and watch the magic as your computer reads the music from the CD and stores it on your PC in digital form.

NOTE   *It's important to remember than the maximum bit rate and even the speed at which you can rip music is limited in the free trial versions of most ripping software. If you download a program such as Musicmatch and find that the program can't capture the bit rate you need, you can pay the shareware fee and get all of the program's features, including a higher bit rate for the MP3 encoder.*

Using one of the popular jukebox programs to rip music is fast and easy. Before you begin, though, you should make sure that the encoder is set up the way you like. Specifically, set the file format, sound quality, and destination folder for music storage. By default, any songs you rip will be automatically added to your music library. That's a convenient feature.

Ripping with RealOne

Here's how to rip using RealOne:

1. Choose Tools | Preferences, and when the Preferences dialog box opens, click the Audio Quality tab. You'll see a dialog box that you can use to specify exactly how the ripped songs will be saved. You need to do this only once. Your preferences will be used for all subsequent recordings.

2. When your preferences are saved, insert an audio CD into your PC, and click the Record button. RealOne automatically rips the songs and stores them on your hard disk. If you don't want to rip all of the songs from a disc, first click CD in the toolbar. You should see a list of tracks. Deselect any songs you don't want to rip, then click the Record button.

Ripping with Musicmatch

If you're using Musicmatch, here's the rip procedure:

1. To configure the file format and bit rate, choose Options | Settings. When the Settings dialog box opens, click the Recorder tab.

2. Musicmatch divides the recording quality into a number of categories; CD quality is the top section and includes 160 kbps, 128 kbps, and WAV files.

3. Finally, insert the CD and click the central recording button. Musicmatch should open the small Recorder pane. Deselect any songs you don't want to capture, and click the Record button.

Ripping with Windows Media Player

Unlike the other jukeboxes, Windows Media Player doesn't support MP3 recording "right out of the box." Instead, Windows Media Player treats encoders like little plug-in components, and only the WMA file format comes with the basic player. If you want MP3 encoding in this program, you need to upgrade. (For information on how to do that, choose Tools | Options, and click the Copy Music tab. Then click MP3 Information.) Older versions—such as Windows Media Player 7—don't have an MP3 encoding option at all.

That said, if you want to create WMA versions of songs, Windows Media Player can do that for you. The file compression in WMA is similar to that in MP3, and so you don't have to learn anything radically new to use it.

1. To configure the bit rate, choose Tools | Options, and click the Copy Music tab.

2. At the bottom of the dialog box, adjust the slider to reflect your preferred bit rate. Just a reminder: Be sure your video editor can read WMA files before you spend all day ripping songs in that format.

3. Once your WMA file settings are saved for posterity, you need to record songs from your CD. Click Copy from CD (you'll find this button on the toolbar to the left), and deselect any songs you don't want to rip. Then click Copy Music in the top toolbar.

Adding Music from Your Hard Disk

Of course, if you already have music stored on your hard disk, you don't have to rip it all over again from the original CD. Suppose you downloaded *Don't You Forget About Me*, the theme song from *The Breakfast Club*, back in the heyday of Napster. (Yes, we know you don't download music from the Internet any more. It was a youthful indiscretion.)

Anyway, you don't own the *Simple Minds* album, but you have the song in all of its MP3 glory. Getting it into Studio 8 is a snap. Just do this:

1. Click the Show Sound Effects tab—the fifth one down—in the Album.

2. Use the folder icon to locate the song you want to add.

3. Can't tell one song from the other just by the title? Double-click a file in the Album to hear it play.

8

4. When you find the song, drag it to the timeline. Technically, you can place the song in either the second or the third audio track, but it's probably a good idea to put all music in the third track for consistency:

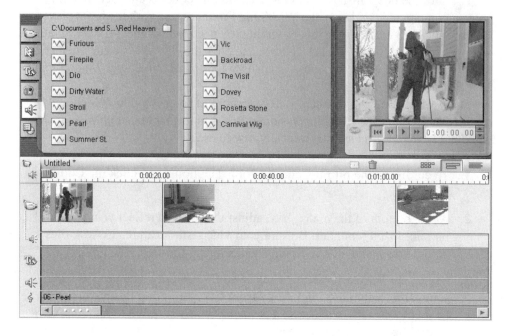

Just as with CD audio, you can manipulate this music any way you like once it's in the Timeline.

NOTE   *Some versions of Studio have trouble recognizing certain digital music files. The program might be able to see some songs, but not others, in a folder full of MP3s—even though all the files are perfectly valid. If you run into this issue, you can rip the song directly from the CD if you have it. Or you can upgrade to the newest version of Studio, which should solve the problem. In a pinch, you can also try to convert the desired MP3 file to the WAV format, which Studio is virtually guaranteed to recognize. Visit Download.com to find dozens of utilities that can perform this conversion.*

Using Pinnacle Studio SmartSound

One of the reasons we really like Pinnacle Studio 8 is the fact that it includes its own royalty-free music generator.

What the heck is that?

Well, commercial music—whether you're talking about the good stuff like Throwing Muses or the Beatles (that would be what Dave listens to) or junk like the Bee Gees, ABBA, and 10cc (Rick's choices)—is all protected by copyright. You have the right to "fair use" under the copyright code. Basically, that means you can make a personal copy of music you buy and use it for personal things— such as home movies that only your family will ever see. But copyright prevents you from publishing commercial music without permission—and it doesn't matter whether your video is headed just for a local audience instead of national distribution, or whether you have no intention of making a commercial gain. So forget about including Bob Mould's *Wishing Well* in a local documentary about the loss of historic sites to commercial expansion.

So, where does that leave you? You could, of course, obtain permission. It's certainly not impossible; Dave has obtained permissions himself, and so it *can* be done. But if you're not up for quite that big a project, you can record your own soundtrack. If you play a musical instrument, you can record music to your PC and add that to the production.

Or, you can use the easiest solution of all: a royalty-free soundtrack. The SmartSound module in Studio 8 lets you create a musical theme of the exact length you need in any of a few dozen musical styles. The output sounds professional, fits perfectly in the video, and takes only a few seconds to generate, with no real musical knowledge required.

Copyright and Fair Use

While we're talking about using commercial music for your movie, it's probably a good time to mention the fact that this practice is marginally illegal.

Actually, let's be specific: Using commercial music that you don't own in an application intended for profit is illegal; don't do it. But if you are making a movie for personal use—for broadcast just to your friends and family, for instance—your soundtrack probably falls under an aspect of the law called "fair use." Just as you're entitled to make a personal copy of music you have purchased, you can include that music in a home movie.

But be careful to use commercial recordings conservatively. In these litigious times—when the RIAA is suing 12-year-old girls for downloading music over the Internet—it's a good idea to play it safe. Use commercial recordings in your videos only when there's clearly no way that anyone could interpret your production as anything other than personal.

Here's what you need to do:

1. Choose Toolbox | Generate Background Music from the menu.

2. In the timeline, select the clip for which you want music to play. If the music should play through several clips, use SHIFT as you select multiple clips.

3. Now cruise through the musical options. Notice that you first need to pick a style, which leads you to several song choices. After you pick a song, you can fine-tune your selection by picking a version. At any point, click Preview to hear what the song will sound like.

4. When you're happy with your selection, click Add to Movie (Figure 8-11).

5. Finally, position the Timeline scrubber, hit Play, and watch your movie in the monitor with the song playing in the background.

TIP *You can add multiple SmartSound audio pieces to your video, and you can intermix SmartSound songs with MP3 or WAV files in the same soundtrack.*

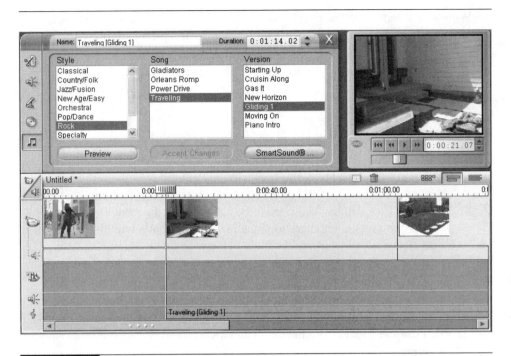

FIGURE 8-11   SmartSound is an auto-music generator that creates music you can use in your video.

The cool thing about SmartSound clips—what makes them "smart," as it were—is that you can shorten and lengthen them without affecting their integrity as songs.

What do we mean?

Try shortening a SmartSound song that you've added to the Timeline. The music doesn't end abruptly, as you might expect. The musical flourish that ends the piece is preserved intact. Likewise, you can lengthen a SmartSound song. In that case, music is dynamically added so that the piece sounds "right" all the way through.

Using an External Music Program

SmartSound is pretty cool, but it's limited: you get only about two dozen songs and a handful of versions to choose from. For a wider selection, you might consider looking at an external music generation program. We highly recommend Sonicfire Pro from SmartSound (www.smartsound.com).

What's confusing—at least at first—is how to combine the video you make in one program with the sound you generate in another. It's pretty simple, actually:

1. Complete all the non-audio aspects of your movie first. Get the clips in position, add transitions and titles, and make sure your project looks completed.

2. Insert any narration that you planned into your movie.

3. Render the movie. Depending on the audio program you're using, you may not have to render a huge, multi-gigabyte DVD-ready copy of the movie; a more modest for-the-Web quality movie may be fine. Be sure to check out Chapter 12 for details. You need to be able to play the movie in Sonicfire Pro, so that you know where to place the music. That's why the video has to be rendered.

4. Open Sonicfire Pro (or whatever other application you're planning to create music in).

5. Load the movie into the external music program. In Sonicfire Pro, choose File | Choose Movie from the menu and locate the rendered movie as shown in Figure 8-12.

6. Now you have to set up your film for audio cues. Where do you want various musical pieces to begin and end? In Sonicfire Pro, you can set markers to indicate major musical events in the video. In the Movie Window, click Play,

FIGURE 8-12　SonicFire Pro is a full-featured version of the SmartSound utility in Pinnacle Studio.

and whenever you reach a point where a new musical piece should begin, click Add Marker in the toolbar atop the screen. In Figure 8-13 you can see a movie with several markers in place.

7. When all of your markers are in position, you can add music. Sonicfire Pro has a wizard that steps you through the process. Click Assistant in the toolbar, and step through the process of selecting a song. When you click Finish, the song will insert into your soundtrack Timeline at the first available marker (see Figure 8-14).

8. From there, it's "lather, rinse, repeat." You can use the Assistant to add songs to the soundtrack until you have as much or as little music as you want in the production.

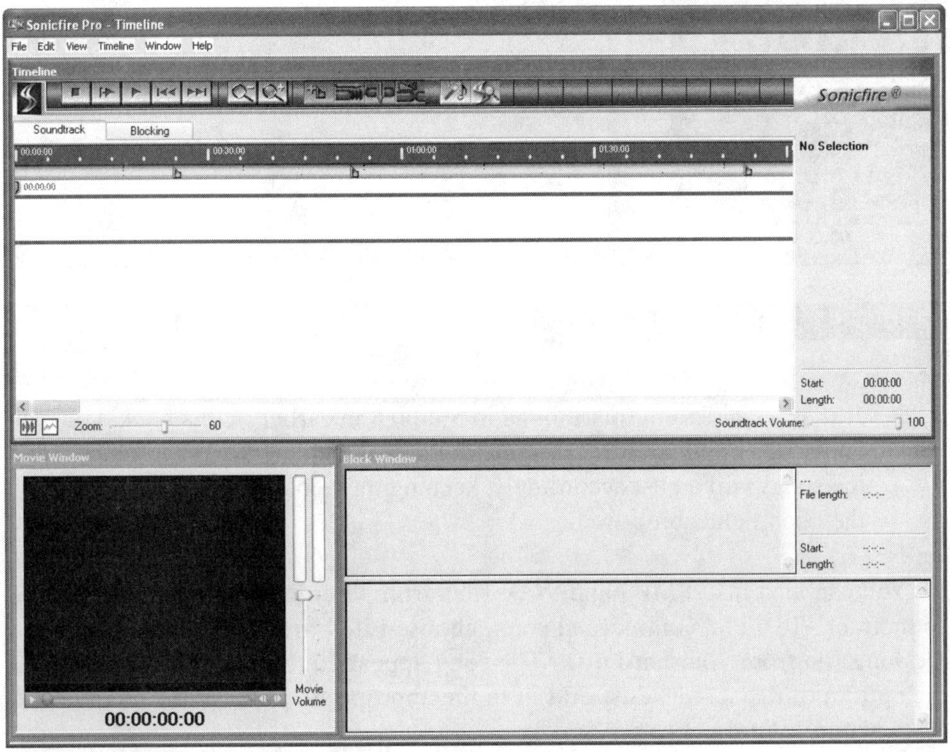

FIGURE 8-13   SonicFire Pro lets you synchronize generated and pre-recorded music to key moments in your movie.

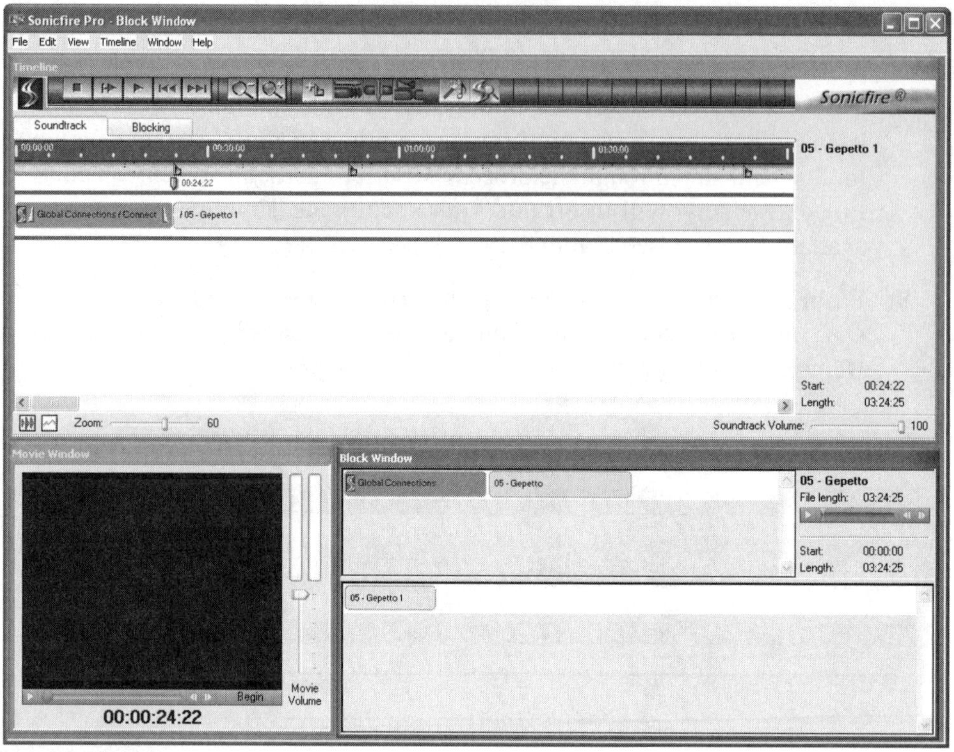

FIGURE 8-14   SonicFire Pro with generated music in place in the Timeline.

9. Just as we did with SmartSound in Studio 8 in earlier in this book, you can edit songs in place. You can shorten and lengthen pieces, for instance, and the songs will adjust accordingly, keeping their ending flourishes so that they don't end abruptly.

You can also insert MP3 and WAV files from your hard disk into the audio soundtrack. To add a commercial song, choose File | Import Audio, and pick the song file from your hard disk. The song appears in the Block Window at the bottom of the screen. Just drag it to the appropriate point in the soundtrack as shown in Figure 8-15.

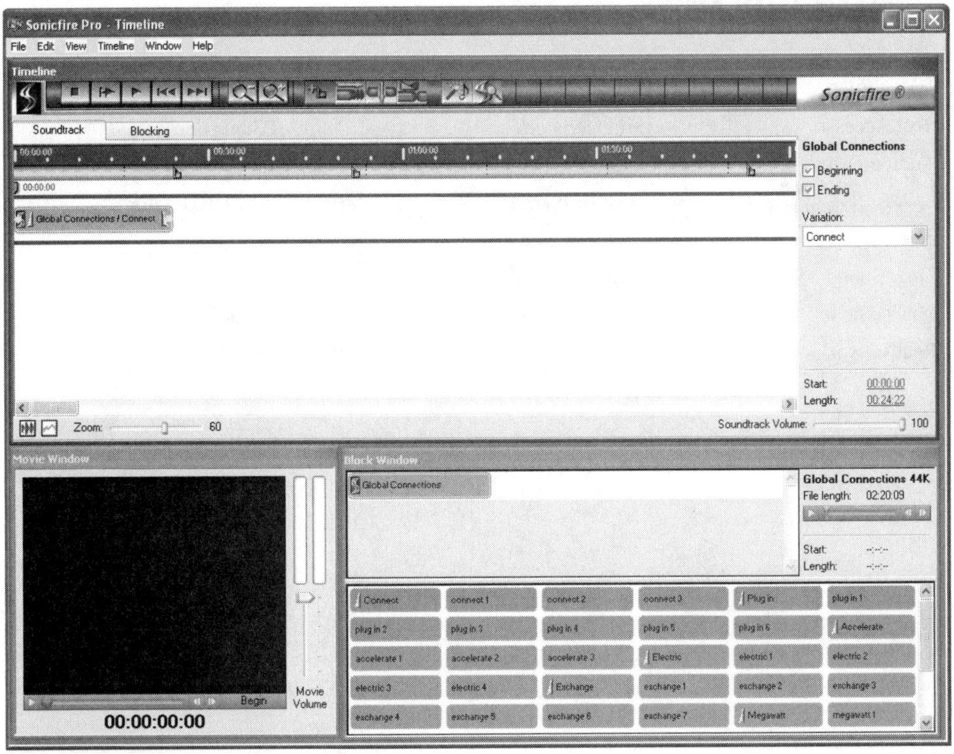

FIGURE 8-15   You can add CD audio and MP3 tunes to your SonicFire Pro soundtrack as well.

When your soundtrack is complete, you need to save it. Some external soundtrack generators require you to save the audio as a sound file, and then paste it into the video editor as an audio file and render the complete movie. Sonicfire Pro allows you to do it that way, but you can also simply attach the audio file to the video file, and output a complete movie, ready for transfer to DVD. Choose File | Export Soundtrack/Movie and select Movie and Soundtrack from the Export menu.

Where to Find It

Web Site	Address	What's There
Real Accessories	www.xingtech.com	XingMP3encoder
Audiograbber	www.audiograbber.com-us.net	Audiograbber
Poikosoft	www.poikosoft.com	Easy CD-DA Extractor
Proteron	www.proteron.com	MPegger
SmartSound	www.smartsound.com	Sonicfire Pro
Musicmatch	www.musicmatch.com	Musicmatch
RealNetworks	www.realone.com	RealOne

Chapter 9

Sound on the Mac

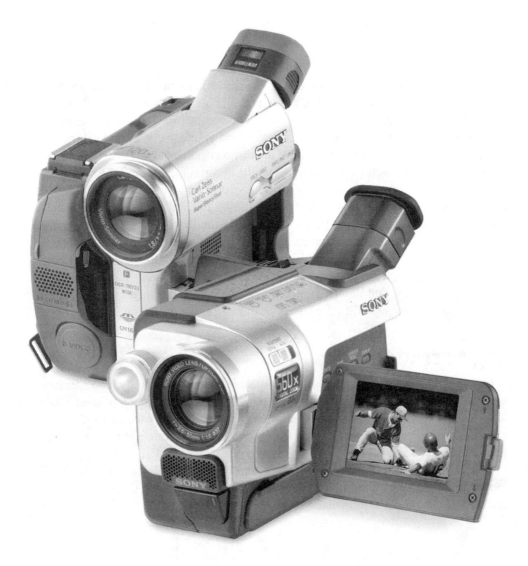

How to...

- Add narration in iMovie

- Use audio from CDs and iTunes in your movie

- Edit sound on the Timeline

- Build audio transitions

- Use Apple SoundTrack

Achieving good sound reproduction in your movies is just as important as shooting good video. In fact, good sound can be even *more* important for making a video watchable. Of course, the key to ending up with good sound is starting with good sound, which means getting the microphone on your camcorder close to the action (or, better yet, plugging an external microphone into your camcorder and getting the mic close to the action, even as you move the camcorder around).

You can do a lot with sound to improve the entertainment and informational quality of a video once it's in digital form on your Mac. iMovie has a number of built-in options to help you achieve that, including the ability to record personal narration, to grab songs from iTunes (creating a soundtrack), and to add sound effects from the built-in sound library. Using Final Cut, you can add CD or digital audio to create a soundtrack, and Final Cut also works with the SoundTrack application from Apple, so that you can create a very sophisticated audio backdrop. Of course, in iMovie and Final Cut alike, you can also trim, change, and transition the audio track, and so we'll take a look at those options in this chapter as well.

Adding Narration

A common reason for adding audio to a project is so that you can include narration or sound recorded separately after the video has been shot and much of the editing has taken place. Narration can be used to establish time and place in a video, to explain things that aren't readily apparent, or even to continue a storyline when your location sound went bad or you had other technical problems.

We'll look at narration for both iMovie and Final Cut. iMovie offers built-in tools; the Final Cut solution involves recording narration using a third-party tool and then placing the resulting audio on the project timeline.

Using Built-In Narration in iMovie

iMovie offers a special feature that allows you to add spoken narration from within the application interface. If you've worked with iMovie to edit your video, then you're already familiar with the Shelf and the associated controls for adding transitions and special effects. Click the Audio tab under the Shelf and that panel changes to yet another set of controls: the audio controls, which you can use to add various types of audio, including narration, sound effects, songs from iTunes, and tracks from an audio CD (see Figure 9-1).

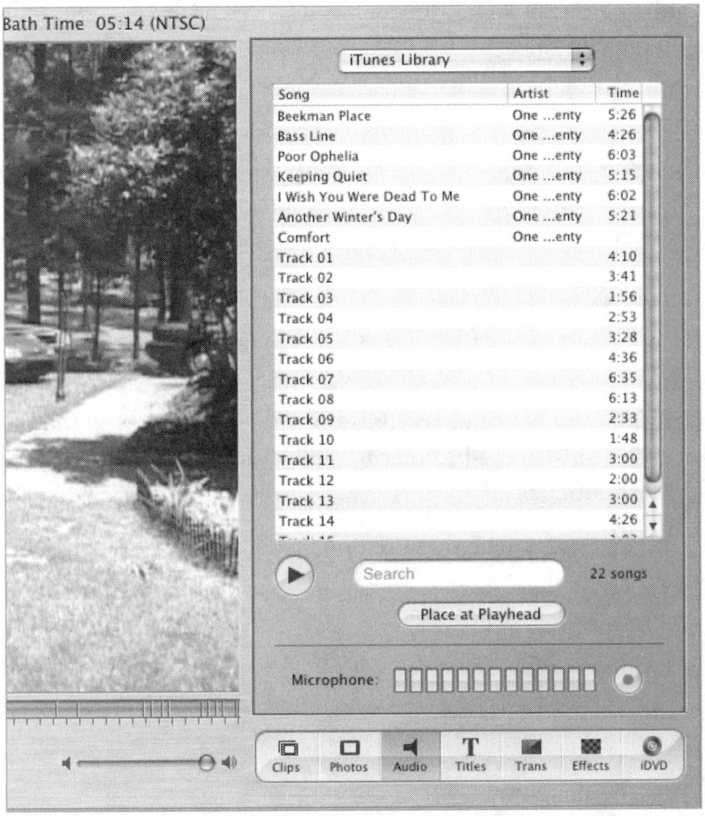

9

FIGURE 9-1   The audio control panel in iMovie opens when you click the Audio tab under the Shelf.

For narration, iMovie includes a control at the bottom of the Audio panel that you can use to record your own voice speaking, singing, whistling, humming… whatever. Here's how to use it:

1. Make sure that you're in Timeline mode for video editing, then place the playhead at the point in your movie where you want the audio to begin.

2. Before proceeding, you should test the recording level. With the Audio control panel showing, speak aloud near the built-in microphone in your Mac. (Alternatively, you could use an external microphone if one is connected.) The audio indicators should react to show reasonable signal strength. You want to see the audio level rise at least about half way, but not too far into the yellow and red indicators (a level that high suggests you're too close to the microphone). Sound that is recorded when levels are into the red can lead to distorted, garbled audio.

3. Now, if you're ready to speak or read, take a deep breath, let it out in a relaxed way, and then, to begin the recording process, click the red circle button (Record) next to the audio indicators:

4. Now, immediately begin speaking or making whatever sound you want to record. You'll see a bar on an audio track in the project lengthen as recording continues.

5. Click Record again when you're done recording. The result should be a new audio clip in the Timeline:

You can move the audio clip, if necessary, or you can trim it or change its volume, as we discussed in Chapter 6. Or, if necessary, you can select the audio clip, delete it, and start over.

NOTE · *In our experience, the microphones built into many Mac models are hit-or-miss for narration. We've had some success using the mic built into a flat-panel iMac G4, partially because it's easier to maneuver close to one's mouth. (The mic pickup on the iMac is on the lower left-hand portion of the flat-panel display.) On many other Macs, the internal mic is much tougher to use. If you're serious about narration and other recording, an external microphone is ideal. For some Mac models, that will mean buying a USB microphone or a USB microphone adapter; many newer Macs lack an audio-in port for typical computer-compatible microphones.*

Using Voiceover in Final Cut

Final Cut offers a tool similar to the audio recording capability of iMovie, but the interface is a bit more complex and offers additional options.

To record your voiceover, choose File | Voice Over. The Tool Bench panel with the Voice Over tools opens (see Figure 9-2).

9

FIGURE 9-2   Final Cut is ready to record voiceover.

What's clever about the approach in Final Cut is that you can watch the project video as you record your voiceover or narration. That way, you can work to get the timing right so that your narration matches perfectly with the changing scenes.

Another thing that's handy is that, in Final Cut, you have unlimited opportunity to practice and test your script, your reading, or your sound effects to see what works and sounds best with the video. With the Voice Over tools enabled, all you have to do is place the playhead where you would like to begin the voiceover recording in your project, and then click the Record button (that circle with the red dot in the middle) to begin the process. The Voice Over tool counts down from 5 to 0 to allow you to prepare to begin speaking. (You can use the Sound Cues option to toggle the beeps that you hear by default as the Voice Over tool counts down.)

When you're told that Final Cut is recording, start speaking.

As you record, you'll notice something else helpful: the video track plays along with you to show you exactly what is happening in the video as you narrate. Likewise, the recording indicator shows when you've reached the end of the available video, showing how many seconds you have left when you're down to 15 seconds or fewer (indeed, by default, you'll be cut off when the video ends).

When you're done speaking, click the Record button again. Recording stops, and you'll see the voiceover track appear on one of the audio tracks at the bottom of the Final Cut Timeline. You can now move that audio track around and edit it as you would any audio track, or you can delete it and try again.

Besides performing just basic recording, the Voice Over toolbox gives you a variety of other options. You can select the Source and Input devices for your recording (if you have multiple sources), and you can use the Offset menu to compensate for any syncing problems you have with the microphone. (Sometimes when you use a digital recording device—such as a USB mic—you'll have problems where the recording is a frame or two behind the voiceover.) You can also choose a recording rate: 44,100 Hz is CD-quality; lower rates take up less storage space but offer lesser degrees of quality. A Gain control is also available to raise or lower the level of the clip as it's being recorded. (More gain can make the clip louder, but may also introduce distortion.)

Once you've gotten your voiceover clip into the project, you can click the Close box on the Tool Bench to get it out of the way if you need to return to the Viewer and Canvas windows for editing.

Using Third-Party Audio Recording

If you want to use third-party tools to add narration in Final Cut or iMovie, you can. Some of those tools will give you finer control over the quality of the recording, enabling you to edit and "sweeten" it (improve the recording after the fact). If you're a recording pro, you may already have your favorites.

For instance, Peak from Bias (www.bias-inc.com) is a high-end professional waveform editor that comes in a variety of prices and toolsets. Using it, you can edit sound recordings with tools whose caliber is similar to that of the video tools in Final Cut.

Pro Tools by Digidesign (www.digidesign.com) is another popular pro-level option.

If your needs are a bit more modest—you simply want to record some narration or dialog using your Mac—then a good option is Sound Studio (see Figure 9-3) from Felt Tip Software (www.felttip.com). At the time of writing, it was $49.99

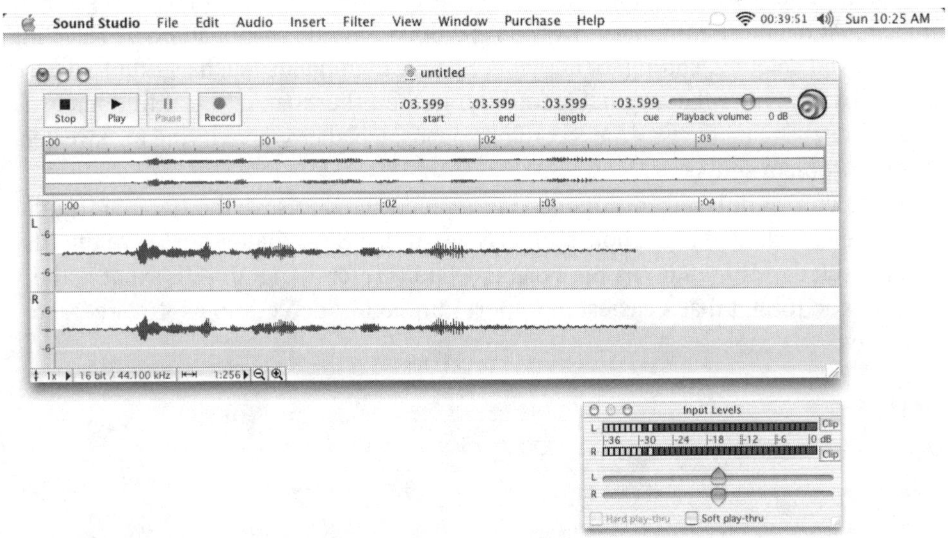

FIGURE 9-3 Sound Studio is a great, inexpensive sound-editing application that's handy for narration, singing, or recording from line-in devices.

and offered a downloadable demo. In Sound Studio, you can use the built-in microphone in your Mac or an external microphone (or a line-in connection, if you're recording from other audio equipment) to record audio files, which you can then save and use in Final Cut.

Using Sound Studio is pretty straightforward: Click the Record button to begin recording. Sound levels show in the Input Levels palette so that you can adjust the audio level with the L and R slider controls. (You can also adjust the level by changing the distance between your mouth and the microphone.) When you're done, just click the Stop button to stop recording. The result is a left and right *waveform* visual that enables you to "see" the recording.

NOTE

If, for some reason, the correct audio input device isn't selected in Sound Studio, choose Audio | Input/Output Setup to open a dialog box in which you can select various audio devices for recording. Also note the Soft Play-Thru option in the Input Levels palette. That option can be handy if you'd like to hear the recording through speakers or headphones as it happens. (We recommend using headphones. If you play the live recording through your speakers, the mic may pick it up, potentially causing feedback or an echo effect, or both.)

Sound Studio's editing tools are outside the scope of this book, but it's got a lot of them. At the most basic level, you can use Sound Studio to edit audio by selecting portions and deleting, cutting, or copying. Special commands (such as Edit | Silence) are available to alter the original recording. In the Filter menu, you'll find many options for changing the way the recording sounds, whether you're trying to "sweeten" it or fix problem spots.

Once you've finished editing the audio, you'll need to save the file in a format that Final Cut can handle. Choose File | Save. In the Save dialog box, give the file a name, select AIFF audio as the Format (Audio Interchange File Format is the default Mac format that's easiest to import into your video editing software), and click Save.

Sound Studio: Save	
Save As:	narration
Format:	AIFF
Where:	Documents
	Cancel Save

You can also choose File | Export With QuickTime if you'd like to save the audio file as a QuickTime movie that has only audio tracks. That choice gives you finer control over the compression options that QuickTime offers.

To add the audio in iMovie, first switch to the Timeline mode. Next, place the playhead at the spot where you'd like the imported audio to appear. Then, choose File | Import, and locate the file. When you've found the file, click the Open button. The audio file is added to the movie starting at the point where you placed the playhead.

You can also drag certain types of audio files from the Finder directly to the Timeline, where you can drop the files in the locations at which you want the audio to start playing. (Drag-and-drop is handy, but can be a bit less than precise; the playhead method lets you choose the exact frame where the audio should start.)

To add audio in Final Cut, you can also do one of two things. First, you can choose File | Import and locate the saved audio; that adds the audio as a file in the Final Cut Browser. You can then drag the audio file to an audio track.

The second option is similar to the second option in iMovie: Simply drag the file from the Finder to the Timeline in Final Cut. Choose an audio file, and drop that file on the track. When you do, the audio file is added just as if it were any other audio or video clip.

9

Using Audio from CDs and iTunes in Your Movie

One of the most effective ways to boost the entertainment value of a home video, business video, or a fiction film is to add some music. Of course, iMovie, with its home-movie focus, makes that easy by integrating closely with iTunes, the digital music library application from Apple. You can easily grab digital songs from your iTunes library or from an audio CD in your CD drive, and drop them into iMovie. The tools in Final Cut aren't quite as friendly, but adding music is still a simple import or drag-and-drop operation.

NOTE *One problem with grabbing audio from CDs and iTunes is that you're likely using copyrighted music. That can be okay in home movies, but it will be a problem if you want to distribute your videos for business purposes or at such venues as film festivals. Apple has a couple of ways to help out. If you have a .Mac account (www.mac.com), you can access royalty-free music on iDisk by opening the Software folder, opening Extras, and then opening FreePlay Music. There, you'll find a ton of royalty-free sound clips. For a more sophisticated approach to royalty-free music, the solution is SoundTrack, discussed in the section "Meet Apple SoundTrack" later in this chapter.*

Adding Music in iMovie

Using iTunes, you can build and manage a library of digital music files—songs or spoken recordings that have been translated into MP3 or AAC computer files—which can then be played back by applications that understand those formats, including iTunes and iMovie. You get those MP3 files by translating them from audio CD tracks (using CDs that you own) or by acquiring them online, such as through the iTunes Music Store. Once those music files are in the iTunes software, you have lots of choice about what to do with them: you can arrange them, create playlists, burn them to CDs, and so on.

Another thing you can easily do with those music files is add them to your iMovie projects. iMovie 3 has a direct line to iTunes from within the Shelf and the Effects panel interface. Click the Audio button in iMovie, then choose the iTunes library from the menu at the top of the panel (see Figure 9-4). You now have direct access to the songs that you've previously ripped or imported into iTunes.

FIGURE 9-4   iMovie offers direct access to your iTunes library of music files.

Not only can you access the entire library, but you can also access individual playlists that you've created within iTunes as well. Simply select one of the playlists from the menu in iMovie:

When you find a song you like, you can easily place it in your movie:

1. First, make sure you're in Timeline mode. Place the playhead at the point in your project where you'd like to add the song.

2. Now, select the song in the Audio panel. Note the small Play button to the left of the Place at Playhead button. You can use the Play button to preview songs before placing them.

3. When you're ready, click Place at Playhead to add the currently selected song to your iMovie project. The song appears on an audio track:

One common problem is that you may not need the entire song on your soundtrack. It may be too long for the movie or you may want more than one song snippet in your video. As we discussed in Chapter 6, you can use iMovie tools to edit an imported song just as you can edit an audio track that's been extracted from a video clip. The nondestructive method is to grab the Out handle of the audio clip and drag it to the point at which you'd like the song to stop playing (see Figure 9-5).

Otherwise, if you'd like to remove unused portions of the audio, you can choose Edit I Crop once you've placed the In and Out handles where you want them in the clip. Remember, too, that you can edit the overall audio volume, and

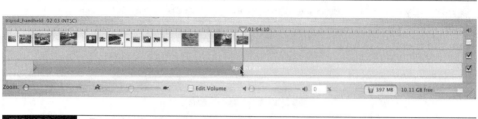

FIGURE 9-5 Drag the Out handle of the audio clip to where you want the song to end.

you can use iMovie tools to create "fade in" and "fade out" transitions for the audio. (We'll discuss those in the section "Building Audio Transitions.")

Adding Music in Final Cut

Final Cut doesn't offer the same clever hooks into iTunes that iMovie does. To add a song or other digital audio file, you'll need either to import it or to drag it into the interface from the Finder. Final Cut can import nearly any digital audio file that is QuickTime-compatible, which means MP3, AAC, AIFF, WAV, and other popular audio formats including audio-only QuickTime movies.

If you'd like the audio clip to appear in your project Browser window as part of the current sequence, then you should choose File | Import and use the Import dialog box to locate the file. You can also import audio CD tracks directly off an audio CD in the optical drive on your Mac:

An alternative is to drag audio files from the Finder—including those stored on CDs or in your iTunes library. You'll have to dig a bit to get at songs that have been stored in iTunes. You'll find them, by default, in your home folder, inside the Music folder, inside the iTunes folder. There, you can dig through the various artists and albums that have been stored and cataloged by iTunes. When you find the song you want to work with, you can drag it from the Finder to an audio track in Final Cut (see Figure 9-6).

Actually, it might not be quite that simple. It all depends on how your Timeline is set up. To add the music file where you'd like it to be, you may need to do some clicking in the Timeline.

First, check the small green bar at the far left of each audio track. If it's off, you won't be able to drag your song file to the associated track. Click the bar to toggle it on and off, as required.

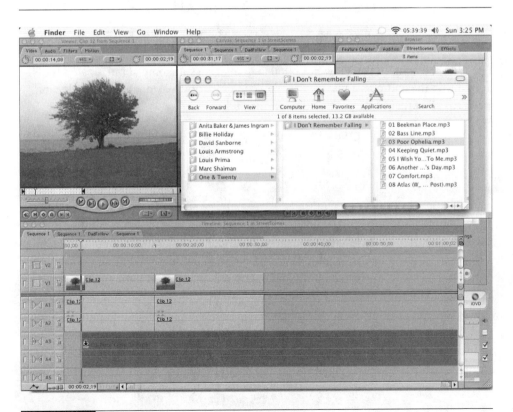

FIGURE 9-6   Importing an MP3 into Final Cut can be as easy as drag-and-drop.

Second, the small speaker icons indicate which track is the target for the left audio channel of a stereo song and which is the target for the right channel. You can click to choose which track accepts which channel. (In Figure 9-5, you can see the small "1" for left channel and "2" for right channel.) If you can highlight the tracks that you want to target when you're dragging to them, check those little indicators to make sure that they are correctly set.

Once the song is imported, you can drag the right-hand edge of the tracks right and left to change the duration of the song. You can also double-click the song to bring it up in the Viewer window, where you can edit it as you would a video clip, setting in and out points:

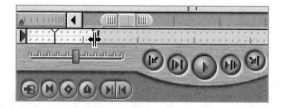

With the song in the Viewer, you also gain access to some sophisticated tools for editing the audio as a waveform. You can cut, copy, paste, change levels, and perform all sorts of interesting edits on the audio:

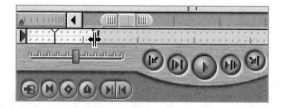

Editing of that sort is a little outside the scope of this chapter, but we will discuss how to use audio transitions—fade in and out, and others—in the next section.

Adding Audio Transitions and Effects

Like video clips, audio clips in your movies can be altered with special transition effects. However, unlike video transitions, audio transitions are generally limited to a basic set: fade in, fade out, and volume level. In this section, we look at how to set those transitions, including some special transitions that Final Cut makes available.

Creating Fades in iMovie

To create audio fades in iMovie, you first need to switch to Timeline mode. Next, you check the Edit Volume box beneath the Timeline. When you do, you'll see thin horizontal lines appear in each Timeline track that has audio—and that includes the original video clips if their audio hasn't been extracted:

Those horizontal lines represent the volume level for the audio on each track. If you click to select a particular clip in the Timeline, you can then use the Volume slider to move that line up and down:

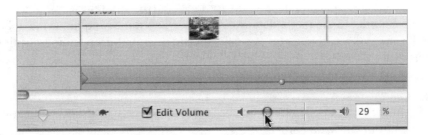

But the really cool part is that you can click the line to create an audio keyframe. When you do, you can then change the volume for *part* of the clip, instead of changing the volume uniformly. Click the line to insert the keyframe marker. Then, when you drag up or down on the keyframe marker, you change the volume level beyond that point in the clip:

Now you can see how to fade a particular audio clip in and out. Select the clip and set its volume to **0**. Next, click a little way along the audio line, and drag the marker to fade the audio up so that you can hear it. At the end of the clip, you can click to set another marker that you can drag down to move the audio back down to **0** again.

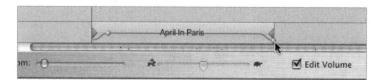

Play with dragging keyframes on the audio line to get a sense of how you can make volume changes more gradual or more abrupt. Remember, too, that you can add more keyframes to the line just by clicking. Extra keyframes can be handy if you're looking to change the volume in steps over time or if you want to make quick volume changes as the clip progresses.

Creating Fades in Final Cut

In Final Cut, you can edit audio tracks for fades in two different ways: you can use a method similar to the method in iMovie (place keyframes and move the volume level up and down within a clip), or you can add drag-and-drop audio transition effects that are similar to the transitions used for video clips.

Let's start with the keyframe approach:

1. In the Final Cut Timeline, locate and click the Clip Overlays button (at the bottom left-hand corner):

Clip Overlays causes overlay lines to appear. You can then use those lines to set volume levels in your audio clips. In fact, you can drag an audio line within the Timeline to change the volume level:

2. To create a fade effect, you need to create a keyframe on the overlay line. You do that by clicking Pen in the Tools palette:

Now you can use the Pen to create a keyframe on the overlay line.

3. Once you've created one or more keyframes, you need to switch back to the Pointer tool. Then, you can drag the keyframes up and down to create fade-in and fade-out effects. As you can see in the example, you generally need more than one keyframe to create a fade, which is a little different from the way fades work in iMovie. You can also see in the example that two linked stereo tracks will both fade in and out when you change the lines and settings for just one of those tracks:

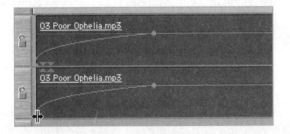

Adding an audio transition is even easier:

1. In the Browser, click the Effects tab, and then click the disclosure triangle next to Audio Transitions. (If you don't see a disclosure triangle, you may need to choose View | Browser Items | As List to make it visible.)

2. When you reveal the Audio Transitions, you'll see some icons:

(Note: the Browser window shows:)

Name	Type	Length
▷ ☐ Favorites	Bin	
▷ 🔒 Video Transitions	Bin	
▷ 🔒 Video Filters	Bin	
▷ 🔒 Video Generators	Bin	
▽ 🔒 Audio Transitions	Bin	
▱ Cross Fade (0dB)	Audio Transition	00:00:01
▱ Cross Fade (+3dB)	Audio Transition	00:00:01
▷ 🔒 Audio Filters	Bin	

3. To use one of the fade transitions—which offer a more automatic way of accomplishing the fades you've already practiced—simply drag them from the Browser window to the beginning or end of the audio clip. The fade transition automatically figures out if it's supposed to fade a clip up or down (depending on whether you placed it on the left or the right side of the clip, respectively).

4. To change the length of a clip, you can drag one of its edges to make it longer:

002 | Cross Fade (+3dE
002 | Cross Fade (+3dE

NOTE *Fade transitions are especially useful when you're transitioning between two different sound clips. They can make the transition sound more professional by "crossing" the audio between the two clips, pulling the first audio clip down gradually while bringing the second clip up gradually. Use the "(0dB)" option for clips that are very different-sounding (they have different background levels, for example) and the "(+3dB)" option for clips that are relatively similar (they have approximately the same background noises, volume levels, and so on).*

Meet Apple SoundTrack

In this final section, we take a quick look at an application that Apple Computer has just recently made available at the time of writing. This new application promises to be exciting for Mac-based moviemakers—that is, if they're willing to pay the price.

SoundTrack is a professional-level royalty-free music generator. Using this software, you can take various instrument *samples*—audio segments that are made by recording individual instruments digitally—and mix them to create songs that can be used for a movie soundtrack. The approach works because the samples are almost infinitely malleable and interchangeable. For example, you can take a guitar sound and change the speed, key, rhythm, and so on. (Unfortunately, software like this doesn't come cheap. Apple is charging $299 for SoundTrack as of this writing. Of course, that's not terribly pricey compared to the cost of having a royalty-free soundtrack produced by professional musicians.)

To work with SoundTrack, you begin by creating a video project in Final Cut. SoundTrack can then load that video project and display it within the SoundTrack interface. You can then create the music while watching the video, with the result that you can watch and compose simultaneously so that the music works as well as possible with the rhythm and timing of your video project.

Here's an example:

1.   After creating your video project, launch SoundTrack.

2.   On the left-hand side of the screen, you'll see the Media Manager. You begin in that window. Locate your Final Cut video project at the File Browser tab by digging into the folders on your hard disk until you find the project you want to work with:

3.   Once you've found the project, drag it over to the Untitled project window, which adds it to the SoundTrack Timeline. It will serve as the foundation

9

for the musical soundtrack you're going to create. From here what you'll be doing is adding tracks of instruments that work together to create a song. That song—with its drums, guitars, pianos, wind instruments... whatever you're using—will serve as your soundtrack.

4. To begin adding instruments, return to the Media Manager, and click the Search tab. (That is one way to do it, but you can also go directly to the instrument files with the File Browser—that's a bit more manual, however.) When the Media Manager switches to Search mode, you'll see something like this:

5. Click one of the labeled buttons to see some of the options that appear in the list below the search box. You can scroll through and click each one to get a sense of what they sound like and to get information about the selection as shown in Figure 9-7.

6. When you find an instrument sound that you like, drag it to the first audio track on the Timeline. Once it's there, you can drag it from the right-hand side to stretch it as shown here:

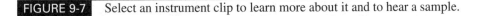

♪ Live Edgy Drum Kit	80	none	8
♪ Live Edgy Drum Kit	80	none	8
♪ Live Edgy Drum Kit	80	none	8

1–50 of 901   Add Favorite

Path

Mac OS X:Documents:Apple Loops for Soundtrack:PowerFX
Loops:Drums:Acoustic Drum Kits:Live Edgy Drum Kit 41.aiff

▼ Additional Info

	Tempo: 80 BPM
	Key: none
	Scale Type: Neither Key
Sample Rate: 44.1 kHz	Beats: 8
Bit Depth: 16 Bit	Time Signature: 4/4
Channels: stereo	Looping file: Yes
Genre: Rock/Blues	Size: 1.01 MB
Instrument: Drum Kit	Hints:
Author: PowerFX.com	
Copyright: PowerFX Systems AB	

–6 dB

FIGURE 9-7 Select an instrument clip to learn more about it and to hear a sample.

Most of the clips are between 4 and 16 beats, with some being longer and a few being shorter. The more beats a clip has, the longer it plays before repeating.

Now, even though you haven't done a lot to the "song" so far, you can press SPACEBAR or click Play at the top of the project window to play your current choices and see how they sound together.

The point with SoundTrack is to build up a song from the separate instruments and samples. Most of what you'll do is simply find samples that you like—a guitar, a bass, a drum line—and then let them play together. SoundTrack automatically matches the beats per minute and the key of each clip so that they sound as if they're supposed to be played together. To add more tracks, choose Project | Add Track or press COMMAND+T. Now you can drag more instruments to the Timeline, place them at different points, and so on.

> **TIP**
> *Each track has a slider that can be used to set that track's volume relative to the entire project. At the top of the project window are other important controls, including menu items that you use to choose the musical key for the entire project and to change the beats per minute or overall volume.*

Eventually, you'll have a number of instruments on the timeline that, together, make up your song for the project (see Figure 9-8).

At this point you should probably save your project (if you haven't already). Choose File | Save to save a SoundTrack project. But you're not done: Now you need to take the movie out of SoundTrack and get it into its final format.

There are really two ways to get your music out of SoundTrack. First, you can export the music as an audio file that you can pull into Final Cut, where you can

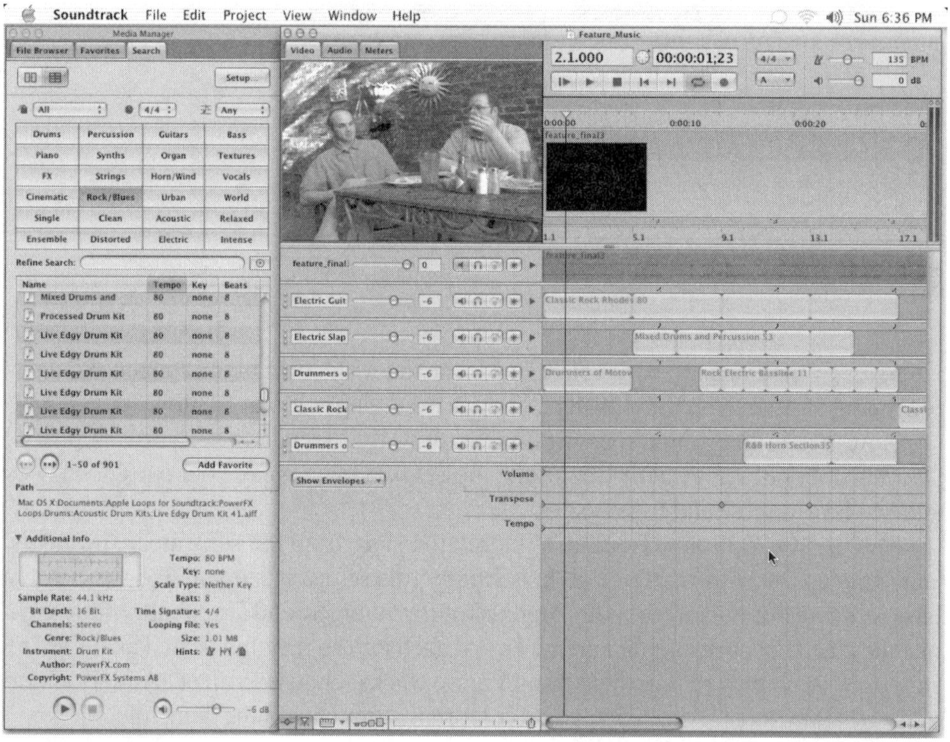

FIGURE 9-8 Here's an example of how SoundTrack looks once you've put together a complete song.

export the entire project. That approach might be handy if you're planning to export the final video project to your camcorder. To export the music, choose File | Export Mix. In the Export Mix dialog box, switch on the Mute Audio Track From Video option if it isn't already on. Click Export. The result is an AIFF file that you can then bring back into Final Cut.

If you'd like to export your entire project to QuickTime (video, the audio tracks from the video, and the music you've created), choose File | Export to QuickTime. In the resulting dialog box, give the movie a name, switch on the Make Movie Self-Contained option, and click Export. The video and audio are exported together as a new QuickTime movie that includes the video at the same size and quality as originally shot. (If you want a smaller or more compressed movie, you'll need to import the QuickTime file into iMovie, Final Cut, or a third-party tool to perform the desired compression.)

Of course, there's a lot more that you can do in SoundTrack, including transpose the song midway through, change instruments, and edit individual clips. (For some hints, CTRL-click a clip to see some of the options.) Remember, SoundTrack is an advanced program designed for people who are fairly serious about building, customizing, and adding music to their movies. If that's you, consider buying a copy and learning more about how SoundTrack works (and plays!).

Where to Find It

Web Site	Address	What's There
Apple Computer	www.mac.com	.Mac
Bias	www.bias-inc.com	Peak
Digidesign	www.digidesign.com	Pro Tools
Felt Tip Software	www.felttip.com	Sound Studio

Chapter 10

Titling Your Movie

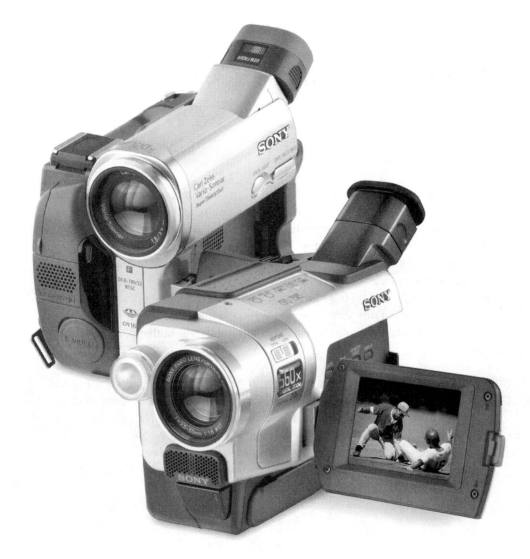

How to...

- Work with titles in Studio 8
- Add canned titles to a movie
- Create titles from scratch
- Make full-screen titles
- Make overlay titles
- Spice up your titles
- Add transitions to titles
- Make titles roll
- Create titles on the Mac
- Use titles effectively in a movie

As any fan of *Monty Python and the Holy Grail* will tell you, titles can be very important to a movie. That's true whether you're introducing the cast (and various kinds of llamas) or just revealing that the viewer is about to see your Vegas vacation. Titles can be as simple as text that appears over your video or as sophisticated as a full set of opening credits, complete with a soundtrack and animation.

It pays to give a little advance thought to your title plans, because how you use them can have an impact on the music you choose (it might be a perfect fit for the video, but too short to run during credits), the overall length of your production (adding just a minute or two of titles could put you "over budget," so to speak), and so on.

> **TIP**
>
> *If the whole idea of titles is foreign to you, or if you're just not sure how you want them to look in your product, just turn on the television. You probably barely notice titles when you're watching television shows, movies, and news programs. However, if you pay close attention, you'll immediately start to see how and when titles are used and what looks best. You can then take that knowledge and apply it to your own titling efforts.*

When you're done with this chapter, you'll know everything you need to about adding, inventing, editing, and enhancing titles for your production.

First up: Titles for PC (Windows) users.

Creating Titles in Studio 8

Pinnacle Studio 8 makes it blissfully easy to add titles to a project—and we don't mean just stark, 1970s-style newscast captions, either. You can whip up titles that look professional, fancy, fun, or all of the above. Check out some of the options shown in Figure 10-1 (and, um, imagine them in color).

Titles come in two basic types, and Studio provides both kinds:

Overlays   Titles that appear over the video—much as a reporter's name appears along the bottom of the screen during a newscast—are called *overlays.* You add overlay titles to the Title track of the movie (see Figure 10-2). Overlay titles are transparent, meaning they let the video show through and appear to "float" over the video.

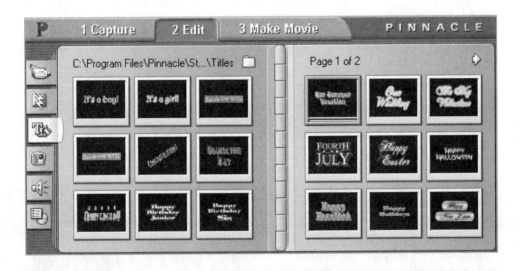

FIGURE 10-1   As you can see, the built-in titles in Pinnacle Studio 8 can be plain or flashy, serious or wacky.

10

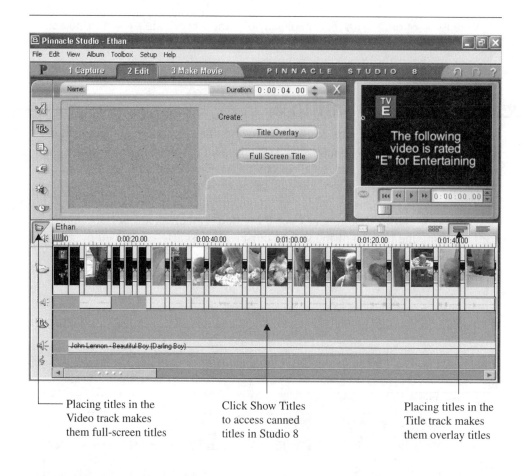

Placing titles in the Video track makes them full-screen titles

Click Show Titles to access canned titles in Studio 8

Placing titles in the Title track makes them overlay titles

FIGURE 10-2   You add titles to a production by dragging them to either the Video track or the Title track.

Full-Screen   Titles that resemble the opening credits of a movie are called *full-screen titles.* The title text or images (or a combination) can appear on a background of your choosing. Full-screen titles go right into the Video track alongside your clips (see Figure 10-2). That's because they appear in a linear fashion rather than "on top" of video, as with overlays.

You can mix and match these titling options as you please—adding, say, full-screen titles to the beginning and end of your project, and overlays throughout the middle.

So, how do you actually add overlays and full-screen titles? Studio provides two methods:

- ■ Drag one of 36 canned title designs to the Video or Title track.

- ■ Create a title from scratch in the Title Editor.

Adding Canned Titles to a Project

If you're looking for a quick-and-dirty way to add some nice-looking titles to your movie, Studio supplies three dozen options. These canned titles cover a general range of holidays and occasions, and all can be used as either full-screen titles or overlays. To access them, do this:

1. Make sure you're in Edit mode (click the Edit tab if you're not), then click the Show Titles tab at the left-hand side of the Album (see Figure 10-2).

2. The Album now shows half of the 36 canned titles. Click any one of them to see it in the preview window, or click the arrow in the top right-hand corner of the Album to flip to the second page of titles.

3. Pick a title you like, then drag it from the Album to the Storyboard or Timeline (either view is fine). The process works in exactly the same way as dragging video clips and transitions from the Album; see Chapter 5 if you need a refresher.

That's all there is to it! You can now modify the duration of the title, surround it with transitions, and so on. In other words, the title is now a movie element like any other, and you can work with it accordingly.

Editing Canned Titles

Like the look of the canned titles, but want to change the text?

No problem. Most of the pre-designed titles in Studio can be modified using the Title Editor. Once you've dragged the title to the Storyboard or Timeline, just double-click it to open the Title Editor. You'll see the title in a new window surrounded by the various editing tools—all of them explained in the very next section.

Creating Titles in Title Editor

The Title Editor in Studio provides a robust set of tools for designing exactly the kind of title you want—be it for an overlay or the entire screen. You have three ways to access the Title Editor:

- From the pull-down menus in Studio, choose Toolbox | Create Title. Notice that the Album now looks like Figure 10-3.

    Click the button associated with either a full-screen title or an overlay.

- In the Movie window, position the scrubber where you want the title to appear. (Remember, you can always move it later.) Right-click, then choose Go To Title/Menu Editor. If you right-click in the Video track, the Title Editor loads in full-screen mode. If you right-click in the Title track, the Title Editor loads in overlay mode.

- Double-click a title that's already in the Video or Title track.

    Regardless of whether you start the Title Editor in full-screen or overlay mode, it looks and functions in more or less the same way. (Actually, in overlay mode you're likely also to see whatever video is already in the corresponding position on the Video track. In full-screen mode, you usually start with a blank black background.)

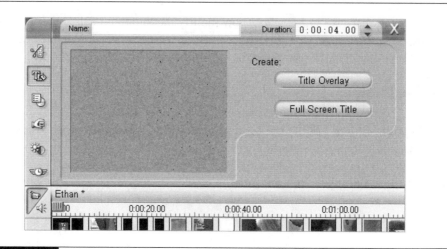

FIGURE 10-3   Use this menu to choose between a full-screen title and title overlay. Of course, you can always switch it later.

Essentially, you're given a blank slate on which to design your title. You can add basic shapes such as circles and squares, choose from a variety of fonts and styles, and even make your titles roll (from bottom to top like credits in a movie) or crawl (from left to right like in… um, a movie). Figure 10-4 identifies some of the key areas in the Title Editor.

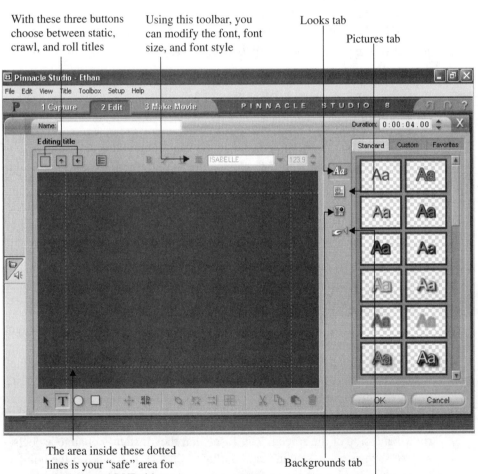

With these three buttons choose between static, crawl, and roll titles

Using this toolbar, you can modify the font, font size, and font style

Looks tab

Pictures tab

The area inside these dotted lines is your "safe" area for television and DVD titles

Backgrounds tab

Buttons tab

FIGURE 10-4　The Title Editor in Studio 8 provides a wide variety of tools for creating full-screen and overlay titles.

NOTE *In the Title Editor, you can also create menus and add buttons, which can be helpful if you're getting ready to produce a DVD. See Chapter 11 for more information on DVD titling.*

Let's walk through the process of creating a full-screen title from scratch.

Creating a Full-Screen Title

Suppose you want a title at the beginning of your movie that says "Our Honeymoon." Sure, there's already a canned title that says "Our Wedding," and you know that you could just load it into the Title Editor and make the appropriate edit. But you want something new. Something original. Something with… lots of funky colors.
Let's get to it.

NOTE *The procedure given here is just one way to go about creating personalized titles. If you're experienced with, say, desktop publishing or image editing software, you may prefer to do things in a slightly different order. That's fine. Our goal here is simply to introduce you to the operation and some of the basic tools of the Title Editor.*

1. From the pull-down menus, choose Toolbox | Create Title, and then click Full Screen Title.

2. By default, the Add Text Field tool is selected. Click anywhere in the work area. A small box appears. Start typing the words "Our Honeymoon." Don't worry if the words don't look the way you want, or even if they don't fit properly in the box. We'll fix that later.

3. Press CTRL-A to select all the text you just typed. Now you can make changes to the font, size, style, or look of the text. For example, click the drop arrow next to the font name. A list opens of all the available fonts—and what they look like. Use the up/down arrows to change the size of the text—or just type a number into the size field and press ENTER. Experiment!

4. When you're ready to get fancy, click a few of the Looks options along the right-hand side of the screen. You'll see that they instantly change aspects of text, such as color, shading, and outlining. In fact, if you hover the pointer over one of the Looks boxes for a couple seconds, another box appears,

giving you various color and style choices within the current look. Again, experimenting is the best way to learn what's available to you. Nothing you do here is permanent.

5. When you've settled on the size and look of your text, you can then modify its location on the page. Click Select in the lower left-hand toolbar (the icon is a black arrow), and then click the text you just created. A thick box appears around the text. Move the pointer to any side of the box; when the pointer becomes a four-headed arrow, click and hold the left mouse button, and then drag the box to the desired location.

6. When you're done, click OK. You'll be returned to the main screen. Your new title appears in the Video track, where you can now preview it alongside your video, add transitions, modify the duration, and so on. You can also move the title to another spot in the Timeline, just as you can with any other component.

TIP

If you plan to use a similar title style throughout your movie, be it for credits, captions, or whatever, there's an easy way to make duplicate titles. In fact, it's nothing more than the old copy-and-paste trick. Right-click the title you want to duplicate, and choose Copy from the pop-up menu. Left-click the Timeline where you want the duplicate to appear, and then right-click in the same spot without moving the pointer. Choose Paste. Presto: An exact duplicate of your original title appears, styles and text locations intact. You can now open the duplicate in the Title Editor to make whatever changes are needed in the text. Copy-and-paste is ideal if you're making a documentary-style video, and you need to flash people's names on the screen. Instead of recreating each overlay from scratch, you simply copy, paste, and edit.

More Tools to Spice Up a Title   In the preceding example, you did nothing more than create some text and sample a few of the available Looks that Studio supplies. But that's just the tip of the title iceberg. As shown in Figure 10-4, the Looks, Pictures, and Background tabs open the door to a lot more titling options. Here's an overview:

- **Looks**   With the Looks tab selected, you can choose Custom, and gain access to some way-cool text-modification tools. First, make sure that the box containing the text is selected (or that the text itself is selected using CTRL-A). Now, fiddle with the Face, Edge, and Shadow sliders and see what happens. As you'll quickly see, those controls can add some very neat effects to your text.

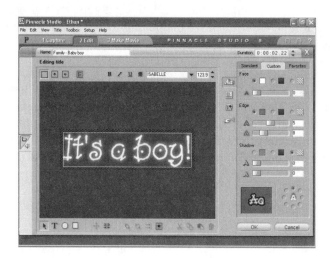

■ **Backgrounds**   A title background can be a solid color, a gradient (meaning that it blends from one color to another), or transparent (the very definition of an overlay—more on that later). Click the Backgrounds tab to see the choices that are built into Studio (it comes with a couple dozen very nice ones). Click the little white folder: You can import any image on your hard disk to use as a background. See Figure 10-5.

TIP   *Went looking on your hard disk for other background images and lost track of the built-ins in Studio? You can find them again by navigating to Program Files | Pinnacle | Studio 8 | Backgrounds.*

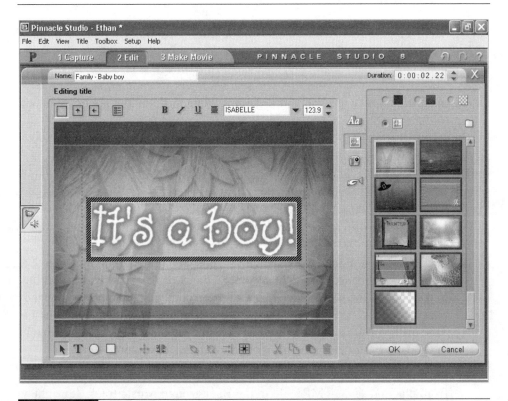

FIGURE 10-5   Studio 8 includes a variety of cool-looking backgrounds for your titles, but you can also import images stored on your hard disk.

■ **Pictures**   Just as you can use any image on your hard disk for a background, so too can you add any image to the foreground of your title. You might want, say, a baby photo to go with a baby movie. Or a wedding photo to go with… aw, you get the idea. Just click the little folder, then navigate to the location on your hard disk that contains the images. Once they appear in the Title Editor, drag the one you want to the work area. You can then resize it by moving any of the eight yellow handles around its border.

Creating an Overlay Title

An overlay is exactly what its name suggests: a title that lies over your video. Overlays have transparent backgrounds, thus allowing you to see both the title and the video at the same time. Whenever you watch a newscast or a Ken Burns documentary and see a person's name appear in the lower left-hand corner of the screen, that's an overlay.

TIP   *Here's an old reporter's trick: If you're filming people you don't know, and you plan to flash their names onscreen during the movie, ask them to state their name—and spell it (!)—on camera before you move on to shoot whatever you want them to do or say. That way, when the time comes to add titles, you won't find yourself scrambling to figure out the names of all these strangers.*

Surprise! Creating an overlay is 97.8 percent the same process as creating a full-screen title. In fact, go back to step 1 of "Creating a Full-Screen Title," but instead of clicking Full Screen Title, click Title Overlay instead. Everything from that point on is exactly the same.

Well, almost. The differing 2.2 percent can be summed up thusly:

1. By default, you're now working with a transparent background instead of a solid one. Although you might see only a black background while working in the Title Editor, rest assured that the background will be transparent when matched up with your video. On the other hand, depending on where in the Title track you create the new overlay, you may see the "background video" in the Title Editor as you work. For an example, see Figure 10-6.

2. Placing your newly created overlay in the Title track is not much different from placing, say, an MP3 file in the Background Music track. It might seem a little odd that the "overlay" goes on the Title track that's "under" the Video track, but that's how it works. You can move the overlay around

Editing title

B   *I*   U   ≣   GENUINE   ▼   76.

What a cutie!

T O □

FIGURE 10-6   You may see the video behind the Title Editor as you work.

a bit so that it appears exactly when you want it—perhaps a few seconds after a new clip appears rather than right at the same time.

Adding Transitions to Titles

Just as you can add transitions (fades, wipes, slides, and other special effects) between video clips, you can also add them to titles—regardless of whether they're full-screen titles or overlays. Transitions can be great for opening credits—for instance, if you want each title to fade slowly in and out rather than jump sharply from one to the next.

Adding transitions to titles is handled in exactly the same way as adding transitions to video clips. Therefore, see Chapter 5 for all the handy how-to information.

Creating Titles on the Mac

The theory behind adding titles in Mac applications is, of course, very similar to that in PC applications. The implementation is just a little different. We'll start by discussing titles in iMovie, and then we'll take a look at the tools in Final Cut—

which are more involved and powerful, with the result that we'll be able only to touch on their possibilities.

Adding Titles in iMovie

You add titles in iMovie the same way that you do just about anything in iMovie: First you switch the Effects panel of the iMovie window over to titles by clicking Titles, and then you make choices about those titles. Once you've made your choices, you drag the title effect to the Clip Viewer to add it to your video. Figure 10-7 shows the Titles panel.

Using the Titles panel in iMovie is very straightforward. Here's a quick look:

1. First, select the style of title that you'd like to use. (When you select one of the styles, you'll see a quick sample in the small window at the top.) The list contains options such as Bounce Across and Centered Title. The names

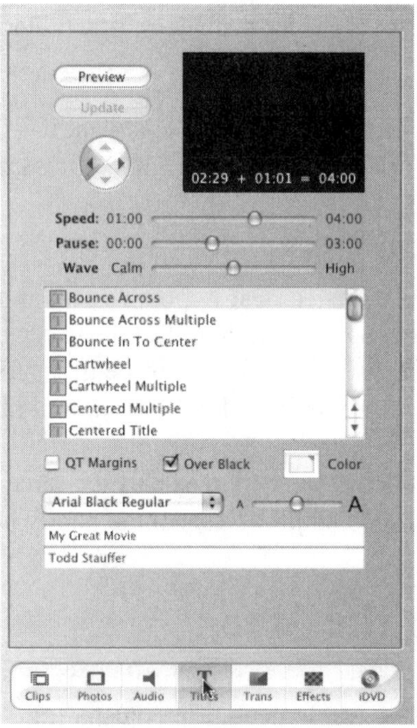

FIGURE 10-7   In iMovie, you make your titling decisions in the Titles panel.

give you clues to the ways you can use the titles. With "Multiple" titles, for instance, you can add more than one screen's worth of text; "Scroll" titles are the type used for credits at the end of a movie.

2. With a title style selected, type the title text into the text area near the bottom of the Titles panel. Notice that the number of spaces available changes depending on the type of title you're creating.

3. Now you can set some other options, depending on the title. Immediately above the text area are controls for font and font size, which you can change to your liking. Similarly, just above the font controls you'll see the Color option, which you can use to choose a color for your title font.

> NOTE *Another important option—QT Margins—is available in the vicinity of the font controls. Select QT Margins if you're creating titles for a video that will be used exclusively for computer-based playback because, with this option selected, iMovie can ignore the "television safe" area that is necessary for video playback.*

4. Once you've entered text and formatted it, you need to make an important decision—whether to switch Over Black on. If the Over Black option is switched on, the title that you create will actually be added as a new video clip; if Over Black is switched off, the title will overlay existing video when you add it to your project. Figure 10-8 shows examples of each choice.

5. Now you can set the timing for the title effect. Toward the top of the Titles panel you'll find some sliders that determine how quickly a title's visual effect occurs (the fade in and out, or the "bounce" in, and so on) and how long the text stays onscreen before the "out" effect takes place. Use the Speed slider to determine the length of each effect, and the Pause slider to decide how long the text will remain on the screen without any effect happening.

10

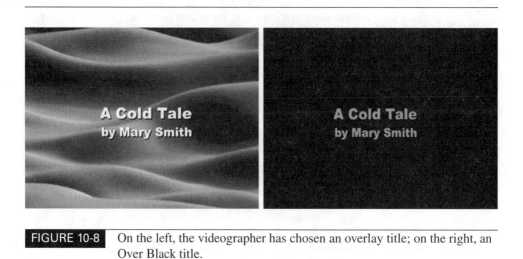

On the left, the videographer has chosen an overlay title; on the right, an Over Black title.

6. Next, if the title effect has a "direction" (it enters from one side of the screen, for instance), you can make choices about that direction by clicking one of the small arrows at the top of the panel. If the arrows are inactive, then you're using a title effect that doesn't let you choose direction.

7. Finally you're ready to add this title to your project. To add the title, you drag its icon (located next to the title style in the list) to the Clip Viewer. For an overlay title (one in which Over Black is deselected, so that it will appear over existing video), drag the icon to the beginning of the clip in question. For an Over Black title, drag the icon to the point where you would like the title to appear in your movie.

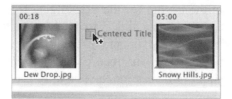

If you like, you can add transitions either between clips that have titling or to Over Black titling clips. You can also move titled clips around in your project in just the same way you would other clips. You can also update the title effect if you find a typo or decide to change your wording. Simply select the titled clip, make the necessary changes in the Titles panel, and then click the Update button at the top of that panel. The title effect is immediately updated.

Adding Titles in Final Cut

Final Cut offers titling tools that are considerably more sophisticated than those in iMovie. Putting them into action can therefore be a bit more difficult, but of course the final product can be quite a bit more professional.

Here's a look at how to create titles in Final Cut:

1. Start in the Browser window by selecting Effects. Scroll through the effects to find the Text bin, and open the bin to see some of the *video generators* that can be used to create text—and hence titles and credits—for the current editing project. ("Video generators" are effects that create new video clips instead of altering existing ones.) Additional video generators—for example, Title 3D and Title Crawl—can be found outside the Text bin.

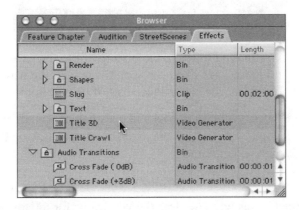

2. To generate titles for your project, drag one of the text generators to the Timeline and place the clip on a Video track. In the window that then pops up, you can enter text for the title. Choose the fonts, font sizes, and other options that you want to set for this title, then click Apply.

Once the title is in the Timeline, you can change it easily:

■ You can change the length of the title clip by dragging it in the Timeline.

■ To make other changes, start by double-clicking the clip, which places it in the Viewer window. Next, click Controls to see the controls for the associated video generator. Click Text Entry & Style to see a text-entry window such as the one you used to create the title initially. Experiment with the other controls to see how they affect the appearance of your title.

To put your titles in motion, you can use the Image+Wireframe control in the Canvas window. Here's how:

1. Begin by moving the playhead to the beginning of the title clip in the Timeline. (Use the arrow keys to make sure that you get to the very first frame.)

2. In the Canvas window, switch on the Image+Wireframe option.

3. Drag the image in the Canvas to the bottom of the screen so that it's barely visible, as in Figure 10-9. (You can send the text all the way off the screen if desired, as long as you can still see part of its wireframe.)

4. Click the Keyframe button (it looks like a small diamond) at the bottom of the Canvas window, below the playback controls. Clicking that button sets the first frame as a keyframe.

5. Move the playhead to the end of the clip.

6. Back at the Canvas window, drag the wireframe for the text up to the top of the window. Notice the line that appears, showing you the path the title is going to take (Figure 10-10).

7. Click the Keyframe button again.

8. Choose Sequence | Render to render the clip. Afterward, select the clip and watch it play back. The text will scroll up the screen for the duration of the clip. The longer the clip, the slower the scroll will be.

FIGURE 10-9 To begin the title sequence, drag the title graphic to the bottom of the screen.

10

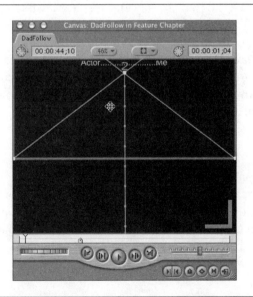

FIGURE 10-10 Now set the ending position for the animation in the clip by dragging the title graphic to the top of the screen.

How to ...   Make Credits Roll

Want to add a little Hollywood luster to your movie? One way is to make "The End" roll up from the bottom of the screen and stop in the middle. (You can make it a full-screen title or an overlay—works the same either way.) Here's how:

1. Fire up the Title Editor, then create a text box and type **The End**.

2. Click the Roll button in the upper left-hand corner (it's a small upward-pointing arrow).

3. Position the box containing the text wherever you want it to end up on the screen.

4. Click OK, and then preview the title in the main screen. It will roll up from the bottom of the screen and stop wherever you placed the text box in the Title Editor.

Keep in mind that the rolled-in text disappears once the title clip has run its course. If you want "The End" to stay onscreen for a while longer, make a copy of the title, paste it into the Timeline right after the roll version, then open the copy in the Title Editor and change it to a static title.

By the way, crawls work almost exactly the same way, except that the text moves from right to left and scrolls all the way across the screen—it doesn't stop at a predetermined point. The only effect your placement of the text box has on a crawl is its height on the screen.

This technique probably isn't the most ideal for scrolling—after all, that can be done more automatically using the Title Crawl video generator. But, you can use the preceding technique to invent creative motion effects or even to generate titles that include rotation (grab one of the corners of the frame in the Canvas window and drag) and other motion effects.

Using Titles Effectively

It's easy to get carried away with the titling capabilities in your video editing application, what with all the fancy fonts, effects, and transitions. However, as with the video itself, less is usually more. All the spinning, flashing, and jumping may strike you as really cool, but the end result can be a movie that looks silly and amateurish rather than polished and professional. Of course, if silly is what you're after, then feel free to go nuts with splashy colors and wacky effects. We're not so dull that we can't appreciate that kind of thing. (Well... Dave is, a little.)

Anyway, here are some good guidelines to follow when creating and using titles:

- **Don't Go Overboard with Credits**   Where credits are concerned, the shorter, the better. Let's face it: they're boring. People don't go to movies to read, they go to watch. Rick once made a movie with 3 minutes' worth of opening credits—and the movie itself was only 10 minutes long. Not good.

- **Pick a Style and Stick with It**   Don't use lots of different fonts, colors, and styles—and this holds true whether you're talking about a single title page or lots of them. Look at any movie, television show, infomercial, or what have you, and you'll see that there's probably no more than a single font style. There's a reason for that.

- **Choose Thick Fonts for Overlays**   Thin fonts can be very hard to read when placed over live video, so always choose a medium or heavy font for overlay text.

- **Dress Overlays with Drop Shadows**   To make your overlay text even more readable, add a black drop shadow. The shadowing will give it some contrast, regardless of the color of the video underneath.

- **Don't Overdress Overlays**   Remember that overlays have transparent backgrounds, and so any fancy effects you apply—gradient colors, blurred edges, and so on—may not look too hot on top of your video. Certainly you can experiment to see what works, but the best bet is to keep it simple.

10

Part III

Deliver Digital Video

Chapter 11

Making DVD Titles on a PC

How to...

- Understand and use the parts of a DVD menu

- Plan a menu

- Create a new DVD menu

- Preview your menu before creating the DVD

- Create motion menus

- Change the look of a menu

- Animate the background of a menu

- Manually set chapter points for a menu

- Tell a menu to play a single chapter and return to the menu

- Create submenus for special movie features

In the old days of video production, "making a movie" usually meant dumping the finished product to videotape. But the advent of affordable DVD burners means that videomakers can easily transfer finished movies to the all-digital wonder disc known as DVD. Not only do DVDs offer twice the resolution of VHS tapes, they also never degrade through repeated playing; they offer random, instant access to any scene on the disc; and they have a clever interactive menu system for navigating around the video.

And you never have to rewind a DVD!

It's those characteristics of random access through interactive menus that concern us in this chapter. If you're making DVDs, you'll surely want to add a menu at the beginning so that your viewers can choose where to go in your production. Nearly all video editing programs let you build such menus, and Pinnacle Studio 8 is no exception. In this chapter, we'll look at how you can add interactive menus to your productions.

NOTE *Working on a Mac? See Chapter 13 for the specifics of using iDVD to create DVD movies from your iMovie and Final Cut projects.*

Menus Work on CDs, Too

Even if you don't have a DVD writer installed on your PC, you can still make videos with DVD-style menus. Video CDs (VCDs) or Super Video CDs (S-VCDs) are videos burned onto CD-R discs using any standard CD-RW drive. They contain low-resolution, VHS-like video that plays in many (but not all) standard DVD players.

So, if you want to give people a DVD experience without the DVD, make an S-VCD with DVD menus in Studio 8 or another video editor. And when you eventually buy a DVD writer, you'll already be an expert at making DVD menus!

Making Sense of DVD Menus

Unless you happen to be one of the historical figures brought back from the past when Bill and Ted used George Carlin's time machine to help complete a report for their high-school history class, then you have almost certainly used a DVD player. In other words, we really don't need to explain the basic concept of DVD navigation to you.

However, you may never have considered all the parts of a DVD menu. Consider Figure 11-1.

11

Planning Your Menus

Before you sit down and start creating menus, it might help to sketch them out on paper. To make good menus, you need to answer a number of questions in advance:

- **Background**   What will the menu background look like? It can be a solid color, a digital still, or a frame grab; it may even feature some sort of animated effect.

- **Buttons**   Will the buttons be large or small? Animated or still? How will they be captioned? You can name them by chapter or use a more descriptive title. Animated buttons (often called *motion menus*) show a looping clip of video from the related scenes. Done well, the effect can look great. But, like most things in video, a loop can also look clichéd or silly.

- **Pages**   How many pages (or screens) of menus do you plan to have? It pays to keep some sense of perspective about this choice. If you have 30

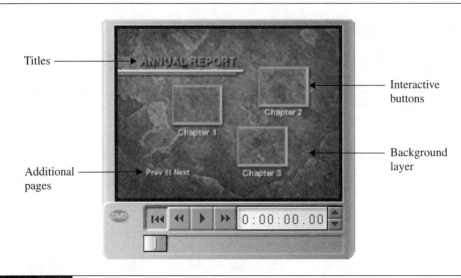

Titles

Interactive
buttons

Background
layer

Additional
pages

FIGURE 11-1　DVD menus are generally composed from a standard list of virtual parts.

scenes in your video, for instance, you probably don't want a button for each one—you'd have 10 pages of menus to browse! Try to keep your menu to just a few screens.

- **Menu Organization**　When you navigate the menu in a commercial DVD, you sometimes run across buttons that don't launch a scene from the disc. Instead, they take you to another page with nested buttons. Many video editors allow you to create these same sort of nested buttons, ideal for opening pages of "special features" or other elements that won't play with the normal movie. And that takes us to the last menu characteristic…

- **Menu Behavior**　How will the DVD respond to menu selections? Think of a movie: When you start it, it plays all the way through no matter how many scenes it includes. But special features, such as deleted scenes and interviews, return to the menu after each individual segment. In most video editors, you have that same level of control over your menus.

You can adjust all those elements in Pinnacle Studio 8, so let's move on to actually design a DVD menu.

Creating a DVD Menu

Ready to add menus to your video project? Great! You can use a video you've already made or, for the sake of this chapter, feel free to make a "simulated" video by dragging a half-dozen clips into the video track of the Timeline.

When you have a handful of video clips ready, click the Menus tab in the Album (it's the very bottom icon). Now do this:

1. The Album should now show a wide variety of predesigned menu templates. The templates have various style attributes—for example, casual or professional, seasonal or topical. They also vary in important ways such as how many buttons appear on each page. To preview a menu, click a template, and review the image in the Monitor.

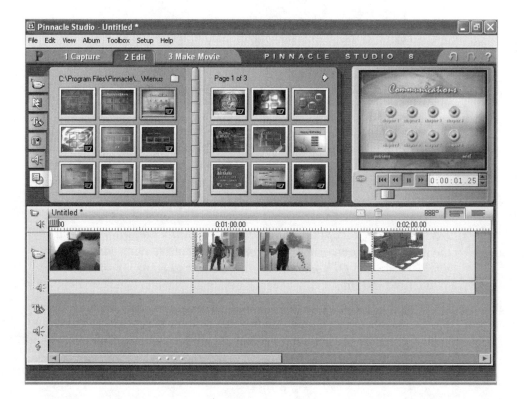

2. When you find a menu type that you want to use in your DVD, drag it from the Album to the video track of the Timeline. Notice that a new track appears

atop the Video track, and that this new menu track can't be locked like the other tracks in your production.

3. Studio 8 next asks if you want to create chapters at the start of each scene. Typically, you'll want to do this—they're just like the chapters in commercial DVD menus. Studio also asks if you want to automatically return to the menu after each scene finishes playing. Usually, you'll want to play straight through the movie and return to the menu only at the very end. So leave that checkbox blank for now, and click Yes to automatically make chapters.

Adding Menu to Movie

Would you like Studio to create chapters at the start of each scene?

☐ Automatically return to menu after scene finishes playing

(Yes)   (No)

☐ Don't ask me this again

4. The Menu Properties window for the menu opens over the Album. You can now fine-tune the menu (see Figure 11-2). To change the caption under a chapter button, click the button in the Menu Properties window, and then select the chapter caption in the edit area to the right. Type the new button text, and press ENTER.

NOTE   *You can't leave a caption blank, but you can label a button with just the chapter number: Erase the word "Chapter," leaving just the number sign (#). Or you can create specialized captions—for example, "Baby's First Bath."*

5. If your video has more than one page of chapter buttons, you can change pages by pressing the page arrow in the lower left-hand corner of the Monitor.

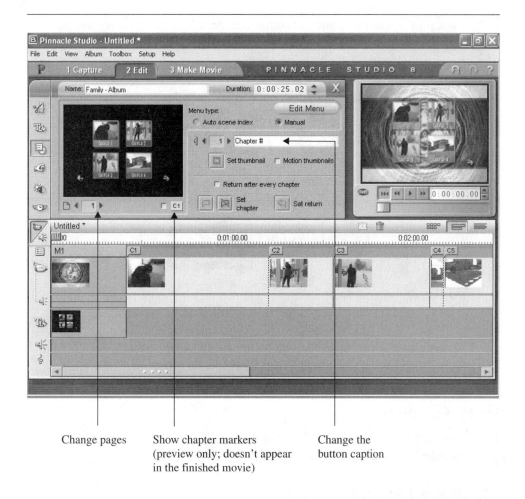

Change pages | Show chapter markers (preview only; doesn't appear in the finished movie) | Change the button caption

FIGURE 11-2   Using the Menu Properties, you can customize DVD menus in Studio 8.

Previewing Your Menu

Now that you've made a very simple menu, let's see what it will look like.

All video editors with menu controls let you preview the menu to see if it works the way you expect. In Studio 8, just click the DVD icon in the Monitor and then click Play.

If the scrubber wasn't positioned somewhere in the menu when you pressed
Play, the movie might start playing. To get back to the menu, just click Main
Menu, as shown here:

Start or stop DVD
preview mode

Previous Menu button

DVD remote control

Main Menu button

Just as in a real DVD, the menu loops indefinitely until you select a specific
chapter.

And that's a basic menu. There's much more you can do with menus, though.
Let's move on and see some other choices that you can make.

Editing a Menu

Like most video editors, Studio 8 lets you tweak all sorts of elements in menus,
from the titles to the buttons and even the background.

Tweaking Chapter Buttons

What if you don't like the picture in the launch button associated with a given
chapter? (Your video editing software typically grabs the first frame of the
chapter and uses it for the thumbnail that represents the scene.) You can usually
adjust that choice.

Suppose the first frame of the video is boring—perhaps even totally black. To
pick a more representative frame of video, do this:

1. In the Menu Properties window, click the chapter button that you want
    to modify.

2. Use one of the scrubbers to select from the associated scene the specific frame that you want to use as a thumbnail.

3. Click Set Thumbnail in the Menu Properties window:

And there's more where that came from.

One of the most popular tricks in menus these days is something called "motion menus." Here's the deal: Instead of showing a static thumbnail like the one you just made, how about showing looping footage containing a bit of the action from the associated chapter? It's really easy to do: just click the Motion Thumbnails button in the Menu Properties window. That's all there is to it.

Here are a few notes about the technique:

■ If you're previewing the menu in the Monitor, motion menus won't occur the instant you select them. As is the case with the movie itself, the motion menu needs to be rendered in advance (see Chapter 12 for details). Rendering takes a minute or two, and you can see the status of the rendering process as a colored bar that creeps across the menu track after you enable motion menus.

However, once the thumbnails are rendered, you can switch the DVD preview on and see them in action. We'll discuss that step shortly.

■ You can control which portion of the scene appears as a motion clip in the button. By default, the very beginning of the scene is chosen for the motion thumbnail, but you can use the Set Thumbnail control discussed earlier to set the starting point. How long will the motion thumbnail run? For however long all the motion menus are set to run. You can change the clip length by lengthening or shortening the menu sequence in the Timeline.

Editing the Template

Studio offers you a lot of menu templates, but you need not use them exactly as is. You can modify them to your heart's content. The menu templates are really just title screens, and so you can use the Edit Title window that you learned about in Chapter 10 to make changes. To do that, follow these steps:

1. Open the Menu Properties by double-clicking the Menu track or the menu in the Title track.

2. Click Edit Menu in the upper right-hand corner of the window. The Edit Menu window opens.

3. At the Edit Menu window, you can make any changes you like: you can change the text on the screen, the fonts, the styles, and the colors. Notice that you can use the panel on the right-hand side of the screen to add buttons divided into categories. There are page control buttons—Next and Previous—as well as thumbnail (chapter) buttons.

4. When you are happy with the changes, click the Close box to return to the Timeline and Album view.

Animating the Background

If you've experimented with some of the menu templates in Studio, you may have noticed that some have animated backgrounds while others are static. The choice of which to use is personal—some of the animated backgrounds that Studio provides look pretty snazzy. But what if you wanted personalized animated backgrounds? Could you do it?

Would we ask the question if you couldn't?

Before we actually show you how to do it, though, you need to understand the various parts of a menu. Check out a menu, like the one in Figure 11-3. It has three parts:

- **Menu Track**   This Menu track represents all the components of the menu. If you double-click it, you open the Menu Properties. If you select it and press DELETE, the entire menu (with all of its parts) is deleted from the project. The Menu track has no physical presence in the video project; it just represents the other parts.

- **Video Track**   If you added a menu with a static background to your project, then the menu appears in this track. But, if you added a menu with an animated background, then the video clip that serves as the background occupies this space.

FIGURE 11-3   The first Timeline shows a static menu; the second shows a menu with an animated background.

■ **Title Track**   If the menu background is animated, look for the menu here in the Title track. This track isn't used if you select a static menu.

Let's put an animated menu in the movie:

1. If your practice movie already has a menu, select it in the Menu track, and press DELETE. Gone!

2. Now, drag a static Menu template to the Video track. The very first template in the Album is static, and so you could start with that one, if you like.

3. Grab a video clip from the Album or from later in the Timeline and drop it in front of the menu. The clip should now be the first thing in the Timeline (Figure 11-4).

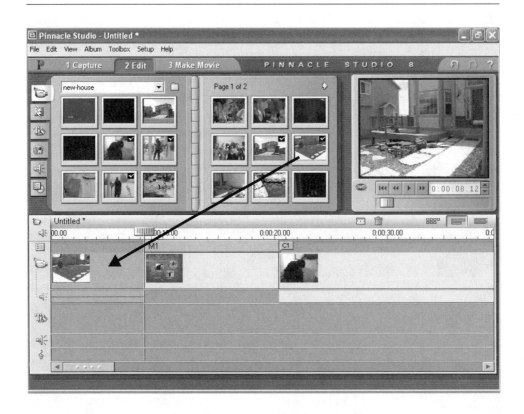

FIGURE 11-4   To start building an animated background into a menu, drop the animation clip in front of a static menu in the Video track of the Timeline.

4. Grab the menu itself from the Video track, and drag it down to the Title track, lining it up at the start of the project (Figure 11-5).

5. If the ends of the animation video and the menu don't line up (end at the same time), adjust one or the other so that they do.

Preview your menu in the monitor. Note that, unless you carefully chose your background video with an animated menu in mind, a glitch will occur in the Matrix—er, I mean in the menu—at the moment when the menu loops back to the starting point. In the supplied templates, most of the animated backgrounds loop pretty well; however, if you're using actual video from your movie in the menu, the clip will probably glitch at the loop point. That may not be a big deal to you; play with it and see for yourself.

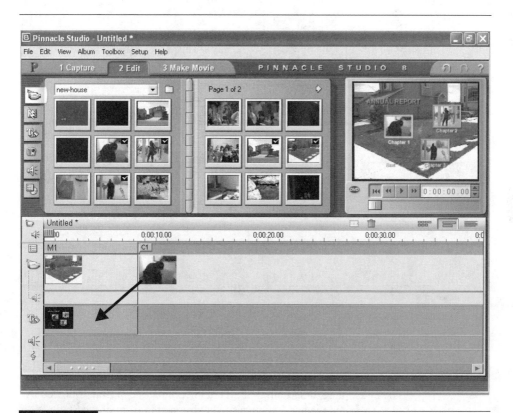

FIGURE 11-5   Now that the animation clip is in the Video track, move the menu itself to the Title track.

Also, it's worth noting that you can mix and match menu templates and animated backgrounds to suit your needs. Do you like the animated video background from Family – Album 1, but want to combine it with the overall look of Corporate – Business Ideas?

No problem. Here's how:

1. Add the Static menu to the Timeline first.

2. Next, drag the menu with the animated background to the Timeline and drop it in front of the Static menu, right at the start of the movie (Figure 11-6).

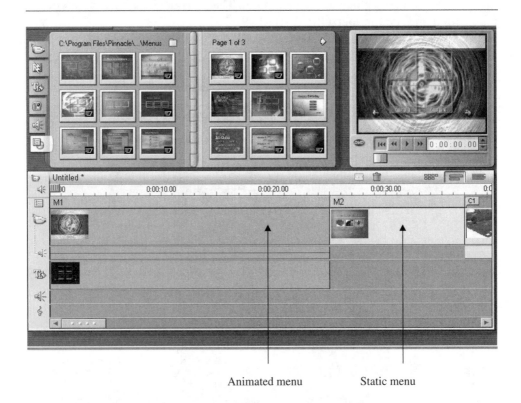

Animated menu   Static menu

FIGURE 11-6   To build the animated background from one menu template into a Static menu template, drag both to the Timeline: Static menu first, followed by the Animated menu—which has to be dropped in front of the Static menu, right at the start of the movie.

3. Select the Animated menu in the Title track (under the animated background), and delete it.

4. Drag the Static menu from its place at the right-hand side of the animation video and place it in the Title track:

5. If the two components of the menu don't perfectly align, fix that now.

You're done! Preview your menu.

Creating Chapters Manually

Up till now in this chapter, we've been advising you to let Studio 8 assign chapter marks automatically. In essence, we've let the video editor decide how many chapters the movie will have. Because Studio chooses chapters based on scene breaks, automatic assignment might make sense a lot of the time. But what if you have two dozen or more scenes in a movie? Do you really want that many buttons? That many menu pages?

Menus can get out of control and become hard to navigate. If you'd rather pick your own chapter marks, that's easy enough to do. You can also use the same technique to make certain chapters return to the menu after playing—ideal for special features you might want to add to your DVD.

Here's how to do it, starting from scratch without a menu already loaded in the Timeline:

1. Pick a menu template, and drag it from the Album to the start of the Video track.

2. When the Adding Menu To Movie dialog box appears and asks if you want to create chapters automatically, click No.

3. Now you have a menu template, but all of the thumbnails are blank. The first button is already selected; use one of the scrubbers to scroll to the point in the movie that you want the first chapter to start (Figure 11-7). Your chapter start does not have to occur at a normal scene break—it can happen at any point in the movie.

4. When you have settled on the start point for your first chapter, click Create a Chapter Link in the Properties window. A chapter marker should appear in the Menu track:

FIGURE 11-7   Use the scrubber to manually mark chapter starts. You can start a chapter anywhere in your movie; it's not necessary to start a chapter at a scene break.

5. Select the next menu button: Click in the menu preview, or click Select Next in the Properties window.

6. Use the scrubber to find the start of the next chapter. Set the chapter mark.

Repeat steps 5 and 6 until you have assigned all of the chapters you want. Don't forget that you can have multiple pages of menus.

If you want to undo a chapter assignment at any point, you have two choices:

- To change the location of a chapter in the movie, select the chapter button and then move the scrubber to the new location for the chapter. Click Create a Chapter Link. The chapter mark automatically moves from the old location to the new one.

- To simply erase a chapter mark without creating a new one, select the chapter button, and click Delete the Current Chapter.

Setting Return Marks

Now imagine that you're going to add special features to your video—for example, a still image slideshow or extra video footage that didn't really fit into the movie. For those chapter sequences, you can set *return marks,* so that when the chapter is done playing, the DVD returns to the menu without playing subsequent sequences.

Adding return marks is very easy to do:

1. Set the chapter mark using the technique that you just learned in "Creating Chapters Manually."

2. In the Menu Properties window, click the Set Return button. A return mark should appear at the very end of your video footage.

3. Drag the return mark to the position that marks the end of the chapter sequence:

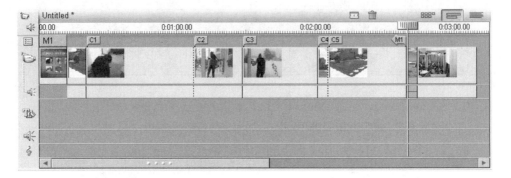

When the chapter plays, the viewer will be returned to the menu when the video player encounters the return mark.

Making Submenus

You've seen the director's cut of *Logan's Run*, right? So, you know the drill: The main menu has buttons for playing the movie, *and for selecting other menus.* Those other menus have chapter buttons, special features, and so on.

Can you create your own submenus using your favorite video editing software? Probably. You can certainly do it in Studio 8.

Suppose you want to make two menus: a main menu with chapter buttons, and a second menu filled with buttons for special features. Here's how to make that masterpiece of menu engineering:

1. Start with a video that contains a handful of clips, but no menus. (You'll add those in a moment.)

2. Drag a menu template from the Album to the start of the Video track.

3. Let Studio create chapters at all of the scene breaks in the production.

4. Assume that the last two scenes are "special features" that shouldn't play along with the rest of the movie. Scroll to those scenes, and delete the chapter marks that sit in the Menu track above the video track. You can

select them and press DELETE, or you can use Delete The Current Chapter in the Menu Properties window—your choice.

5. Because you don't want those last two scenes to play after the end of the movie, you need to add a return mark to the menu track. Click Set Return, and position the return mark immediately before the start of the special-feature scenes.

If you stopped there, you'd have a complete movie and menu system. And, even though the special-feature scenes would be copied to the DVD when you render the movie (see Chapter 12), they would forever remain totally inaccessible to the viewer. You'll fix that next.

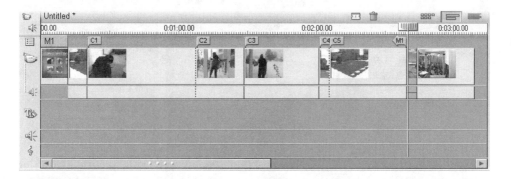

6. Drag another menu template to the Video track, placing it after the main menu, but before the first scene in the movie.

7. When Studio asks if it should automatically add chapter marks, click No.

8. Double-click the Menu track for the first menu, and find the first unused chapter button (it might be on a subsequent page).

9. Select that button, and use the scrubber to find the very start of the second menu.

10. Click Create A Chapter Link. Now when viewers click that chapter button, they will be taken to the submenu (Figure 11-8).

11. Double-click the Menu track for the submenu.

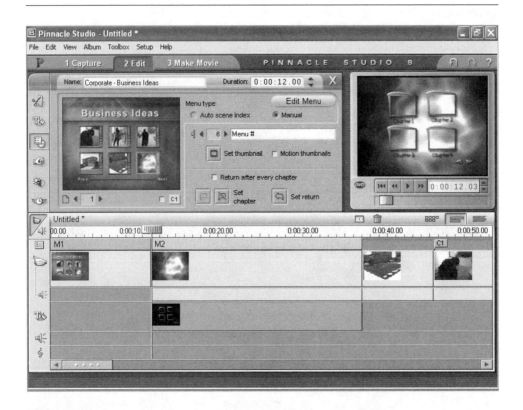

FIGURE 11-8   In the main menu, use the scrubber and Create A Chapter Link to create a chapter button that points to a second (sub) menu.

12. Assign chapter and return marks for the buttons in the submenu, using the techniques discussed in "Creating Chapters Manually". When you're done, the Timeline will look something like Figure 11-9.

Now you're ready to render your movie and copy it to DVD. See you at Chapter 12.

11

FIGURE 11-9   A DVD with submenus can have all the fun factor of a commercial movie. Here, you see a movie that uses submenus to access "special features" outside the main production.

Chapter 12

Sharing Your PC-Based Movies

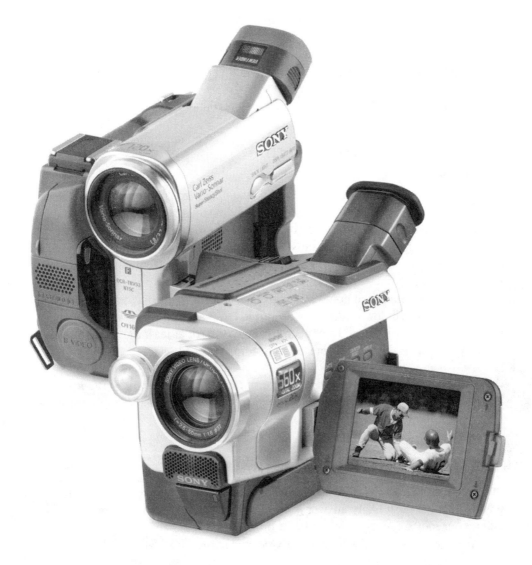

How to...

- Select an output format for your movie
- Output movies to tape
- Output movies in digital formats
- Output movies for Internet viewing
- Upload your movies to StudioOnline
- Use StudioOnline to invite others to view your movies
- Output movies to DVD
- Choose DVD media
- Modify DVD settings
- Decide if you should use VideoCD

Two of the sweetest words in the English language are "all done." (We're also partial to "royalty check"—which is our way of saying that, if you enjoyed this book, you should recommend it to 50 or 60 of your closest friends and neighbors.)

There's nothing quite like the satisfaction of finishing a movie project, one that you've toiled to make just right (or even slapped together in 10 minutes). Now for the fun part: You get to show it off.

Ah, but how? Sure, you could invite all your friends over to watch the movie in the little preview window in Pinnacle Studio 8, but that would just be cruel. Your movie needs to get *out there,* to be seen by the world (or at least the grandparents). For that, we turn to the third main step in Studio: Make Movie.

NOTE   *In case the title didn't make it clear, this chapter is just for PC users. Mac users will find the same treasure trove of movie-sharing wisdom in Chapters 13 and 14.*

Making Your Movie into... a Movie

The big question now is where do you want your movie to end up? We'd venture to guess that the most likely answer is on a DVD. But Studio makes it possible to render your movie (generate the finished product in a watchable format) in a variety of ways. In fact, if you've already peeked at the Make Movie tab in Studio (hey, it's okay, you were curious—we forgive you), you've seen the six different options listed there.

Let's take a quick look at those options, how to use them, and why you'd want to:

- **Tape** You can output your finished movie to a VCR tape—or even back to your camcorder tape, if you like. Why would you want to do that? Find out in "Outputting Movies to Tape."

- **AVI** AVI is one of three available formats for producing your movies digitally in Studio—that is, as a computer file that can be viewed on a computer or distributed on a CD-ROM or over the Web.

- **MPEG** MPEG is like AVI, only better. It's another digital format that sets up movies for viewing on a PC or distribution on a CD or over the Web.

- **Stream** If you've ever visited a web site with streaming video (iFilm.com is one of our favorite destinations), you know it can be pretty neat. Studio can render your movie in a format suitable for streaming, so that you can make it viewable to others from your own web site.

- **Share** There's nothing like instant gratification. Your purchase of Studio 8 also includes access to StudioOnline (www.studioonline.com), where you can upload movies for subsequent viewing by others.

- **Disc** Last, but definitely not least, the Disc option is where you turn your movie into one of those shiny little DVDs, suitable for viewing on just about any home-theater DVD player.

Outputting Movies to Tape

Most, if not all, of the source material for your movie came from tape—why would you want to put it back there again?

Allow us to answer your question with a question: Do you want to play your movies on a VCR? If so, tape is the way to go, and you have two basic options:

- Output the movie directly to a VCR.

- Output the movie to your digital camcorder, then copy it from there to your VCR.

Believe it or not, the second option usually makes more sense than the first. Although it may seem odd to send your footage back to the digital camcorder from whence it came, there are several good reasons to do so.

First, you end up with a digital backup copy of your movie—a good thing to have if your computer's hard drive goes kerflooie (that's a technical term—feel free to look it up). The video will be as pristine as when you shot it, because no quality was lost in transferring it to the computer and back again.

Second, your camcorder is already connected to your PC—chances are good that your VCR is not. It's often a lot more convenient simply to output the movie to a fresh MiniDV tape, and then to take the camcorder to the VCR and make a copy.

> NOTE   *Obviously connecting your digital camcorder to your VCR requires that the camcorder have RCA outputs—one for video (the yellow one), two for audio (the red and white ones). If your camcorder doesn't have those connectors, you may have no choice but to connect a VCR directly to your PC. But that requires a bit of doing, as is discussed next.*

Finally, just as connecting an analog camcorder to your PC for capturing video requires special hardware (see Chapter 4), so does connecting a VCR for recording video. In other words, if you want to output your movie straight from your PC to a VCR, the PC needs RCA video-out jacks. (Sorry for the alphabet soup in that last sentence.) Many of the video-capture products described in Chapter 4 have video-in jacks only. If you're looking for a device that has both, check out the ADS Tech Instant DVD+DV.

Outputting from PC to Digital Camcorder

Let's assume that you're going to output your movie to your digital camcorder, the most common (and logical) tape destination. Here's the process:

1. Making sure your project is loaded into Studio, click the Make Movie tab, and then click the Tape option.

2. Load a blank tape into your DV camcorder, and then connect the camcorder to the PC using the process described in Chapter 4. (Nothing complicated—just connect the FireWire cable.)

3. Switch the camcorder on and into Play or VCR mode. (You may also want to plug in its power supply, as it will be switched on for an extended period.)

4. Click the Settings button, and then select the box labeled Automatically Start And Stop Recording (Figure 12-1). Click OK.

5. Click the Create button.

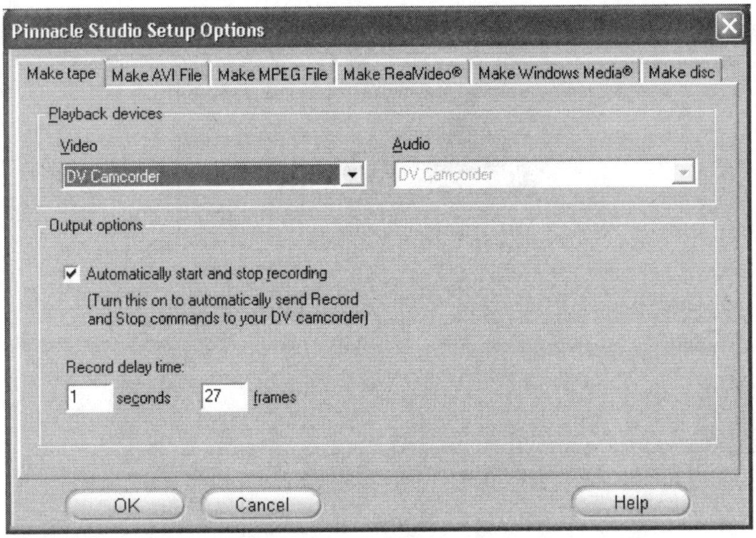

FIGURE 12-1   To prepare to output a movie to tape in Studio 8, complete the Make Tape tab in the Setup Options dialog box.

The movie will take some time to render. Could be a few minutes, could be an hour; it depends on the length of your movie and the speed of your computer. When the rendering process is finished, Studio instructs you to click the Play button on the Player window (Figure 12-2). From there, Studio automatically starts your camcorder recording, streams the movie to it, and stops the recording when it's done. Easy-peasy.

NOTE   *What happens if you've outfitted your project with DVD menus? Studio will treat the menus as ordinary images, resulting in a perfectly functional—if a bit odd-looking—videotape. If you don't want DVD-menu images at the beginning of your video, simply delete them from the Timeline, then save the project with a new name—something like "My Movie – No Menus."*

Outputting Movies to AVI or MPEG

Studio 8 is nothing if not versatile. It can output your movie in a variety of digital formats, suitable for viewing on a computer or copying to a CD or the Web for easy distribution. In fact, Web distribution is often a great way to share your creations with friends, relatives, clients, and other interested parties.

12

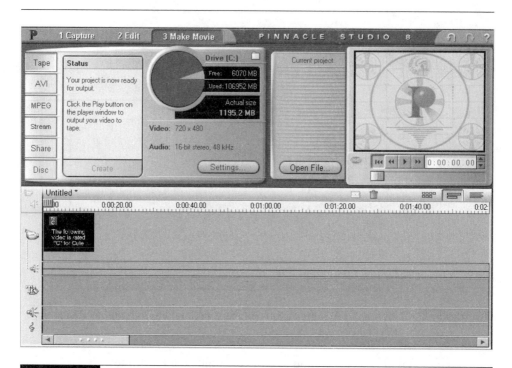

FIGURE 12-2 Once your movie has been rendered, Studio prompts you to click the Play button to start the process of recording the rendered movie onto tape.

Why not just hand out DVDs? Well, not everyone has a DVD player, or even a computer with a DVD-ROM drive. (You need one or the other to view DVDs made in Studio.) What's more, you need to have a DVD burner on your computer if you want to create DVDs (see Chapter 2), and those are still pricey, complicated propositions for many users. Finally, blank DVDs are expensive, and so you don't want to be handing them out willy-nilly.

On the other hand, chances are good you have a CD burner. Moreover, blank CDs are dirt cheap. But wait—we're getting ahead of ourselves. First we need to take a quick look at the differences between AVI and MPEG, and then discuss the output options for each. *Then* we can talk about CD distribution.

What Is AVI?

AVI stands for Audio Video Interleave, a fact you are now permitted to forget. Without going into too much detail or putting too fine a point on it, AVI used to be the standard for watching video clips on PCs, but it has long since given way to

MPEG. That's because the latter format is capable of higher resolutions (meaning sharper video) and higher frame rates (meaning smoother video).

Unless you have a very specific reason for wanting to output your movie in an AVI format (and we're hard-pressed to think of one), we highly recommend that you stick with MPEG.

What Is MPEG?

MPEG can be plenty confusing in its own right, so we'll try to keep it simple. MPEG is a compressed digital video format that has more or less become the standard for playing video on PCs. There are two varieties floating around out there—MPEG-1 and MPEG-2—and Studio enables you to work with both varieties.

As a point of interest, MPEG-2 (the successor the MPEG-1) is the format used in DVDs. But that doesn't necessarily mean you should output to MPEG-2 if you're planning on creating a DVD.

Hey, we told you that this was confusing!

> **NOTE** *A new variant, MPEG-4, is starting to catch on for mobile devices such as personal digital assistants (PDAs). MPEG-4 creates files that consume much less memory, yet still deliver high-quality video.*

A bit of explanation and then a few examples will simplify things.

First, the key thing to understand is resolution: the sharpness and clarity of an image. The higher the resolution of an image, the more dots (or pixels, in this case) are packed into it, and the sharper it will look. MPEG-1 delivers a maximum resolution of 384×288 pixels, while MPEG-2 tops out at 720×576 pixels.

But the issue isn't just about resolution—there's also the issue of space. Assuming you're planning to put your movie on a CD so that you can share it with others, you have to consider how much space will be required to hold the movie in the desired format (MPEG-1 or MPEG-2). A CD can hold only 650MB or 700MB of data. Fortunately, based on the settings you choose, Studio tells you roughly how large the resulting file will be (see Figure 12-3).

Speaking very generally, you can fit about an hour's worth of MPEG-1–formatted video on a CD, but only about 15 minutes of MPEG-2 video. Needless to say, if you have a feature-length film you want to distribute, a CD isn't the answer. But a tightly edited vacation movie or basic business promo should fit just fine.

Okay, what does all that have to do with sending a birthday video to grandma?

Let's assume that grandma has a computer that's a couple of years old—one that she uses primarily for e-mail. Windows Media Player, which is found in every version of Windows (except perhaps Windows 3.0—we can't remember that far

12

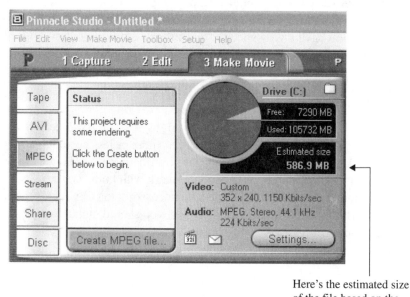

Here's the estimated size
of the file based on the
selected output settings

FIGURE 12-3   You can use the size estimate provided by Studio to determine if your
MPEG file will fit onto a CD.

back), can play all MPEG-1 files. However, unless grandma has spent a few bucks
on DVD player software for her computer, she probably won't be able to view
MPEG-2 files. Thus, you'll want to send her a CD containing an MPEG-1 version
of your movie.

NOTE   *Even Windows XP doesn't include the necessary "DVD decoding" software
to view MPEG-2 files. However, many newer computers come with DVD-
ROM drives, and those drives are usually bundled with DVD software. That
software should be able to play MPEG-2 files, even though they're stored on
a CD and not a DVD. That's because the file itself can be recognized by the
software—the delivery vehicle doesn't matter.*

In short, use MPEG-2 if your movie is short enough to fit on a CD, and if you
know that the intended recipient has the necessary DVD player software. Otherwise,
stick with MPEG-1.

Now let's translate that into Studio terms.

Creating an MPEG File

Now that you know what kind of MPEG file to create and why, let's look at how.

The only tricky part here is understanding the various Studio settings, which you can access by clicking Settings in the Diskometer. In the resulting window, the Make MPEG File tab is already selected, and the first option is a Presets menu:

Of the eight options listed, three are important for your purposes:

■ **DVD Compatible**   Select the DVD Compatible option if you want to produce an MPEG-2 file.

■ **VHS**   Select the VHS option to create an MPEG-1 file. (We know that this is confusing, because you're not intending to create a VHS tape, but just trust us on this one.)

■ **Custom**   Use the Custom option when you want to modify various audio and video settings for your MPEG-1 and MPEG-2 files. You'll rarely need to tinker with the latter, however—DVD Compatible usually includes optimal settings for an MPEG-2. However, if you're a somewhat advanced user and want to fiddle with MPEG-1 settings, choose Custom instead of VHS.

12

Once you've made your choice, click OK. Then, check the estimated size of the movie (see Figure 12-3) to make sure that it is under 700MB (or 650MB if you're using a 650MB CD). If the output will fit on a CD, you're good to go: Click the Create MPEG File button. Otherwise, you may have to return to Settings and make some changes. If you started with DVD Compatible, try switching to VHS. If you started with VHS, try switching to VideoCD. It's virtually identical, but uses a lower data rate.

> NOTE
> *What's "data rate"? Put simply, it's the amount of data packed into a second of video. More data per second means better-quality video, but also a larger file size. If you're having trouble getting your video to fit on a CD, you can try switching to Custom mode and lowering the data rate to see if the estimated file size will decrease sufficiently.*

When you eventually click Create MPEG File, you'll need to choose the folder where the file is to be stored (we recommend someplace easy to find, such as My Documents) and to give the movie a file name. Once you've provided that information, click OK and be prepared for (potentially) a long wait. Depending on your chosen settings, the length of the movie, the speed of your processor, and so on, output could take upwards of an hour or two.

Outputting a Web-Compatible File

The fourth Make Movie option in Studio is called Stream, and it serves a single purpose: to produce a digital file that you can place on a web site, thereby allowing others to view it. It's called Stream because it refers to *streaming video,* which is not the same thing as downloading a video clip.

A perfect example is iFilm.com, a nifty site that you can visit to watch short films, movie clips and trailers, and other bits of cinema. However, you don't download iFilm content to your PC and then view it, much in the same way as you would, say, download an MP3 file and then listen to it. Instead, all iFilm content is streaming video, meaning that it starts playing almost immediately after you click Play. That's because the video data *streams* into your PC, a little at a time, but fast enough that you can watch it as though it were live.

How to ...   Show Your Movie on the Big Screen (or Wall)

Rick once made a faux documentary to celebrate his sister's 40th birthday. The plan was to show this story of her life at her party, where a few dozen friends and relatives would be gathered. The problem was, the party was at her house, where the largest television was a mere 13 inches—not exactly ideal for a group showing. In fact, at the time she didn't even have a DVD player. (Rick really isn't sure how she got into the family.)

The answer? An ordinary laptop, an ordinary business projector, and a big open chunk of wall. (A painting had to come down, but that was easy enough.)

Rick used Studio 8 to output the movie in the highest-quality format (MPEG-2, the equivalent of DVD), copied the resulting file to the laptop, then played the movie on the laptop. He positioned the projector so that the image was about six feet across on the wall—not bad for a jury-rigged home theater.

We're not advising that you go out and spend $1000 or more on a projector, but you may be able to rent one or borrow one from work—or you may even have sufficient need for one that you can justify the purchase. Either way, a projector and notebook computer are the ideal combo for showing movies just about anywhere—and showing them big, too.

12

NOTE   *Using the Stream option in Studio, you can also send video files by e-mail. We haven't discussed that option previously because, for the most part, e-mail is an impractical distribution method. A 3.5-minute movie (with an MP3 audio track) at 320×240-pixel resolution (anything smaller is barely worth watching) results in a 3MB file. Many mail servers won't accept attachments that large, and anyone with a dial-up Internet connection won't appreciate having to download it. (It could take half an hour or more.) That said, if you have a really short movie, and you want an e-mail–friendly version of it, click the envelope in the Diskometer (after you've rendered the movie, that is). You can see the envelope in Figure 12-4.*

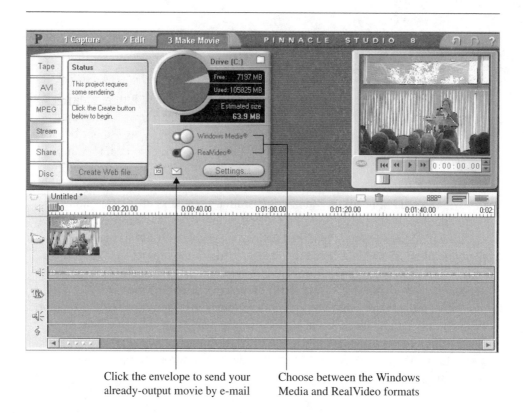

Click the envelope to send your
already-output movie by e-mail

Choose between the Windows
Media and RealVideo formats

FIGURE 12-4 The Stream option is where you generate movies in a file format suitable for web streaming or for sending by e-mail.

Streaming format is an ideal solution for videographers who want to share their movies with the world while still maintaining control over the files. Anyone who visits your web site can view the movie, but they can't actually download or redistribute it themselves.

The downside is that the video generally plays in a smallish window at a low resolution, and so it's not going to look its best. What's more, unless your audience has a broadband (that is, high-speed) Internet connection, the video playback might be a bit jerky.

Creating a Streaming Video File

You need to make two decisions before you let Studio get to work rendering your movie. First, do you want the file to be in RealVideo or in Windows Media format (see Figure 12-4)? Second, which resolution should you use?

RealVideo and Windows Media (WM) are simply two different formats for streaming video. The big difference is that RealVideo requires watchers to have one of the Real players from RealNetworks installed on their PC. WM, on the other hand, requires only Windows Media Player, which is part of the Windows operating system.

Ultimately, your choice depends on what kind of web site you're hosting and what your needs are. That said, if you're planning on working with RealVideo, you might be better off with the free encoding tools from RealNetworks, which offer features that are more advanced than Studio can provide.

As for resolution, after you've clicked either RealVideo or WM, click the Settings button in the Diskometer. Here's an example of what the WM window looks like:

Click the Playback Quality menu, and you'll see four choices—low, medium, high, and custom. Video and audio information appear for whichever option you select. Studio also tells you the Internet connection speed that each setting is optimized for—which can be helpful if you're not sure how resolution translates to performance. Low (176×144), for instance, works best for dial-up connections (traditionally, 56 Kbps modems). Of course, the result is a video window about the size of a postage stamp; streaming video and dial-up connections aren't the world's most wonderful pairing.

That said, if you like the idea of making your video available for viewing online, but don't have a web site or the know-how to host video, you're in luck: Studio 8 does. Read on.

12

Sharing Your Video at StudioOnline

Your purchase of Studio 8 includes 10MB of storage space at StudioOnline, Pinnacle's web site for hosting and sharing videos. This solution is really neat and effective, because Studio can automatically upload your movie in the correct format, and then send e-mails to friends and family inviting them to view it. But before we show you how to do this, you should be aware of two important limitations:

■ That 10MB of storage isn't much, and at press time you weren't able to upgrade (although Pinnacle was reportedly working on changes to the site that might include an upgrade option). On the other hand, our 3.5-minute sample movie consumed just under 2MB of the available space. By that reasoning, you should be able to share a movie that's as long as 20 minutes, right? Wrong. StudioOnline limits you to movies of 4 minutes or less.

■ When you upload your movie from Studio, StudioOnline converts it to a relatively low resolution and data rate, and so it's going to look a bit choppy to the viewer. The price is right, sure—but you'll have more control over how your movie looks if you host it on your own web site.

Uploading a movie to StudioOnline is blissfully easy. Here's how:

1. With the Make Movie tab selected, click the Share tab on the left-hand side of the screen.

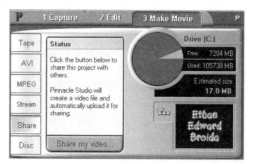

2. Notice the thumbnail image that appears just below the Diskometer (it may be just a black square). Whatever's in that box will appear as the preview image that represents your movie at StudioOnline. To change it, drag the scrubber in the Movie window to a desirable frame (something like the

opening title or a close-up shot of one of your stars), and then click the Set Thumbnail icon next to the image.

3. Make sure your computer is online, and then click Share My Video. As with all the other rendering procedures, this one will take a little time.

4. A web browser window then opens and directs you to StudioOnline, where you'll need to complete a short registration process. (On subsequent occasions, you'll be taken to a screen where you log in to the service.)

5. Even after rendering is complete, it can take a fair chunk of time for Studio to upload the movie to StudioOnline. In fact, it might look as if Studio has stopped working altogether. However, if you look below the Preview window, you'll see status bars slowly creeping to the right. (Best bet here is to go get a cup of coffee or call a friend to talk about this great book you've been reading on digital video.)

When your movie has been uploaded, StudioOnline takes you to a page where you can select a kind of "video postcard" to accompany your movie. Then you enter the e-mail address of the intended recipient, who will receive an e-mail with a link to the site for watching the movie. You can return to StudioOnline at any time (without using Studio) to send invitations to other viewers.

Outputting Movies to DVD

Last, but certainly not least, we come to the big one: DVD. Now that burners and blank media have become affordable, it's only natural to make DVD your movie destination of choice. Assuming you already have a burner installed in or connected to your PC (see Chapter 2 for more information), Studio can produce professional-looking DVDs, complete with fancy menus and animated buttons, that are ready for viewing on almost any DVD player.

NOTE *To learn everything you need to know about creating those fancy menus and animated buttons, flip back to Chapter 11. Here, we assume that your movie is all set up and ready for output.*

But before we delve into Studio's DVD-creation process, we need to talk about the kind of DVD media—the blank discs—you're going to use.

12

Choosing DVD Media

As we discussed briefly in Chapter 2, DVD media comes in five different flavors: DVD-R, DVD-RW, DVD+R, DVD+RW, and DVD-RAM. (For detailed explanations of those formats, visit www.idvd.ca/dvd-formats-explained.htm.) Yes, we're mad at the DVD industry too.

Fortunately, you can save yourself a fair bit of time and trouble by remembering this: stick with DVD-R. Here's why:

- **Compatibility**   Most DVD burners support the DVD-R format (a few limit you to DVD+R and DVD+RW), and so do most set-top DVD players. Newer players and burners support more formats, but older models are likely to be limited to DVD-R. Compatibility is important if you're planning to give DVDs to friends, relatives, clients, or whomever, because you want them to be able to watch your movie—not stare at a DVD that won't play.

- **Price**   At press time, DVD-R discs were among the least expensive of all DVD media, selling for as little as $1.25 each in quantities of 50. (That said, DVD+R discs were selling for about the same price—but remember, they're not as widely compatible as DVD-R.) DVD-RW discs, which are rewritable (unlike DVD-Rs, to which you can write just once), cost about three times as much.

- **Speed**   If you're willing to spend a little extra, you can buy 2× and 4× DVD-R media—but, at press time, other formats were still stuck at 1×. (This situation will no doubt change with time, but DVD-R is likely to maintain the lead.) You see, your DVD burner may be capable of recording DVDs at a certain speed (such as 2× or 4×), but that doesn't do you much good unless you have media that's rated for that speed. A 4× DVD can be recorded four times faster than a 1× DVD. But fear not: the rated speed of the media has nothing to do with playback. A DVD-R is still a DVD-R when it comes to set-top players.

TIP

Watch your Sunday newspaper for deals on blank DVDs and rebates at superstores such as CompUSA and Best Buy. Check web sites such as Techbargains.com, too. We recently scored a 10-pack of blank DVDs—with cases—for $10. Remember, too, that you'll always get a better deal on a 25- or 50-pack than on a box of 3 or 10 discs.

What About VideoCD?

Wouldn't it be great if you could record your movies on dirt-cheap CDs using the CD burner you already own, and then play those CDs in set-top DVD players? Well, you can—thanks to a format known as VideoCD (VCD) and its offshoot, Super VCD (S-VCD).

A VCD is very much like a DVD, only it stores MPEG-1 video instead of MPEG-2, and therefore produces a duller, lower-resolution picture. However, that lower resolution isn't too bad when viewed on a television (it's about on par with VHS tape), and S-VCD is better still.

A VCD can hold upwards of 70 minutes' worth of video at 352×240 pixels; an S-VCD can hold close to 40 minutes of video at 480×480 pixels. So, unless you're dealing with a feature-length project, you may want to consider distributing your movie on VCD or S-VCD. Indeed, if you have a movie that's just 5 or 10 minutes long, it may seem wasteful to bother with a DVD at all, because so much of the available space will go unused.

However, there's a fairly major caveat here: compatibility. While the VCD format is quite popular in Asia, where you can actually buy standalone VCD players, it's more of a hobbyist format in the United States. Some DVD players can read VCDs; some can't. The recipient of your movie probably won't know until the disc is fed into the player. For the record, Rick has owned four different DVD players over the years, and only one could read a VCD.

Studio 8 can generate both VCDs and S-VCDs, and the process is nearly identical to that for producing DVDs (see the next section). Thus, our advice to you is to experiment. You probably already have a CD burner on your PC, and blank CD-R media is very inexpensive. Try creating a VCD, then see if it works in your DVD player. See Figure 12-5 for an example.

If so, try again with S-VCD. The only major cost is a bit of time, and you may discover that one of those two options suits your needs quite nicely.

12

TIP   *To find out more about the VCD and S-VCD formats, visit VCDhelp.com. The site is packed with information, how-to guides, links to relevant software, and more.*

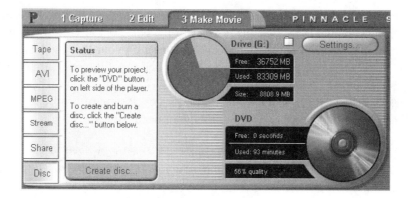

FIGURE 12-5 Try creating a VCD and see if you can play it on your DVD player.

Creating a DVD

Ready to make your DVD? Click Studio's Make Movie tab, and then click Disc. Notice that the Diskometer is now a double-Diskometer:

The top portion reflects your hard disk: the amount of free and used space, and the projected size of the rendered movie. Studio requires a chunk of hard disk space to render the movie before copying it to DVD, and so you need to make sure your disk has room. If not, delete unnecessary files (but *not* the video files captured from your camcorder—Studio still needs those) or choose a different drive to use during the rendering process. Click the little folder icon if you need to choose a different drive.

The bottom portion of the Diskometer shows the type of disc you're going to create (VCD, S-VCD, or DVD) and the amount of free and used space. It also tells you if your movie is going to run too long to fit the available space (which can be helpful in determining the kind of media to use). If everything's ready to go (you have a blank DVD loaded, and the available space is sufficient to hold your movie), click Create Disc.

Before you do, however, you might want to peek at the DVD settings.

Modifying DVD Settings

The Settings menu (Figure 12-6) is divided into four sections:

- **Output Format** The Output Format frame is where you choose between VideoCD, S-VCD, and DVD.

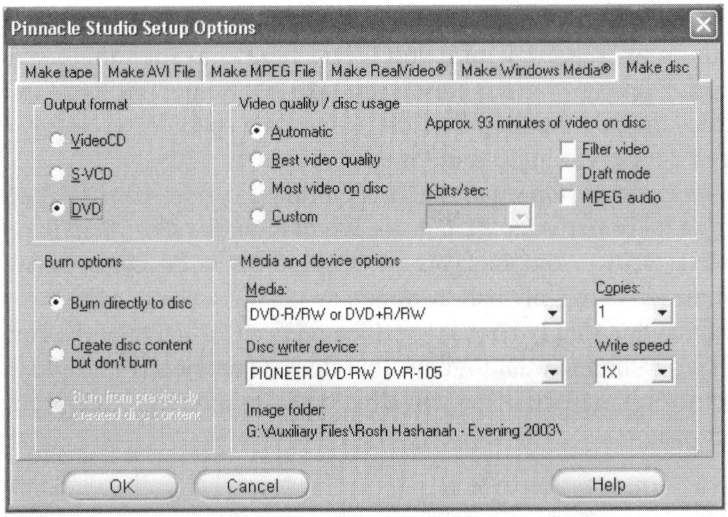

FIGURE 12-6   The default DVD settings should be fine for most users, but if you want to make some changes, this is the place.

■ **Burn Options**   When you choose Burn Directly To Disc in the Burn Options frame, Studio renders the movie, then burns it to the blank DVD—no input required on your part. If, at a later time, you want to burn another copy of the movie, select Burn From Previously Created Disc Content. That option saves you having to wait through the rendering process again.

■ **Video Quality/Disc Usage**   Automatic is almost always the best choice in the Video Quality/Disc Usage frame, because it gives you best possible video and audio quality given the available space on the DVD. Select Filter Video only if your source material is of poor quality. Select Draft mode only if you're in a hurry—that selection renders the movie more quickly, but at a somewhat lower quality. Selecting MPEG audio allows you to fit a bit more video on the disc, but with slightly reduced audio quality, and your DVD is less likely to work in set-top DVD players.

■ **Media and Device Options**   In the Media And Device Options frame, the default settings are usually fine. But, if you like, this is where you can select the type of media, the drive to use, the number of copies to make, and the write speed (which won't be adjustable if you're using 1× media).

DVDs Take Time

When it comes to creating your own DVDs, there's no such thing as instant gratification. Even a 5-minute movie can take 30 minutes or more to complete. The variables include the length of the movie, the speed of your processor, and the speed of your DVD burner and media.

Here's an example: On our 1.5 GHz Pentium 4 system with 1GB of RAM, it took about six hours to render 90 minutes' worth of video. After that, it took another hour or so to actually record the DVD (at 1× speed—a 2× DVD would have finished that part of the job in roughly half the time).

We mention this simply so that you'll be prepared when the time comes to burn your DVD. It's natural to want to show your finished movie to the world the moment it's done, but you'll have to be patient a bit longer to turn your masterpiece into a shiny silver platter.

Where to Find It

Web site	Address	What's there
ADS Tech	www.adstech.com	Instant DVD+DV
RealNetworks	www.real.com	RealVideo player and encoding tools
VCDhelp.com	www.vcdhelp.com	Information on VCD, S-VCD, and other video formats

12

Chapter 13

Making Tapes and DVDs with Your Mac

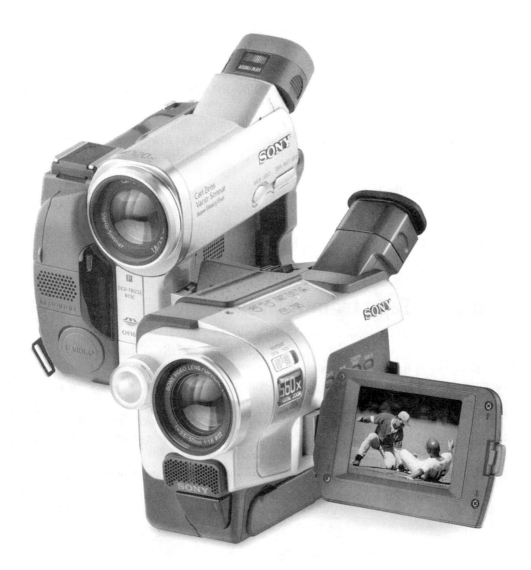

How To...

- Export to tape on the Mac

- Create a DVD-compatible project

- Import to iDVD

- Edit in iDVD

- Save and burn (record to disc) your DVD project

Now that your Mac-based project has been shot, imported, and edited, you probably have one of two desires—to output the video either for playback on a television using VHS tape or DVD, or for playback on a computer. In Chapter 14, we'll look at the computer playback—specifically, how to turn your project into a QuickTime movie (or how to export it to other digital movie formats) so that it can be shown on a computer screen, transmitted over the Internet, or posted for viewing in a web browser.

In this chapter, we'll begin by taking a look at how you can export to analog media (tape) for playback from your camcorder or a VCR. Then you'll see how to use iDVD (the application from Apple Computer for creating DVD movies) to create, edit, and save a DVD project. Finally, we'll discuss some other Mac-based options for video output.

Exporting to Tape from the Mac

Once your video has been edited, there's a good chance you'll want to see it played back on a television or recorded to analog tape (usually VHS). If that's the case, your plan will be to export the video to a tape in your camcorder. With the video in your camcorder, you can hook the camcorder up to a television for playback, or you can connect it to a VCR to transfer the video to an analog tape.

Exporting from your computer to a DV camcorder is pretty easy. You've already seen how both iMovie and Final Cut communicate directly with your camcorder. The process works pretty much as easily in reverse.

Here are the first steps to take regardless of the program you're using:

1. Make sure that the camcorder contains a good tape, and cue the tape to the point where you want to begin recording.

2. Check to make sure the safety tab on the tape is set so that you can record onto the tape. (And if the tab is set so that you *can't* record, then ask yourself why before you change it. Did you or someone else already record something to this tape that you want to keep?)

3. Use a FireWire cable to connect the camcorder to your Mac if they aren't already connected.

At this point, the steps change a bit depending on the software you're using. We'll look at both iMovie and Final Cut.

Exporting from iMovie

Here's how to export to a camcorder from within iMovie:

1. With iMovie in Edit mode, choose File | Export to open the Export dialog box.

2. In the dialog box, choose To Camera from the Export menu (see Figure 13-1).

3. Now, enter the amount of time that iMovie should wait before beginning to export the movie so that the camcorder can start rolling. (This setting really depends on how quickly your camcorder can get "up to speed" after you press the Record button. In most cases, the default setting provided by iMovie will work fine, but if you notice that iMovie gets rolling before the

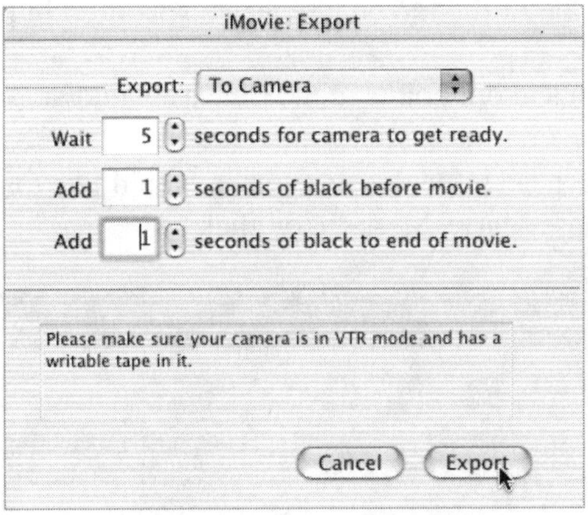

FIGURE 13-1 Completing the Export dialog box in iMovie.

camcorder does, you might add a few extra seconds.) You can also change the number of seconds worth of black that you want at the beginning and end of your movie when it's sent to tape.

4. Click OK to begin the export.

NOTE   *If you don't have a tape in the camcorder or if the tape is write-protected, a dialog box opens to warn you that the export may not complete successfully.*

Clicking OK sets both iMovie and the camcorder in motion. The Export dialog box opens. It contains a progress bar that shows how the export is going. If you need to stop the export, click Cancel. Otherwise, you can sit back and allow the movie to play through to the camcorder.

Using Print to Video in Final Cut

In Final Cut, a good first step before you export to tape is to render any titles, effects, or transitions that you've added to the movie. If you don't, you'll be prompted to render when you attempt to export. Rendering can take a while—although the faster your Mac, the faster Final Cut will finish rendering.

To render the various elements, choose Sequence | Render All, and wait for Final Cut to complete the rendering.

Setting In and Out Points

Final Cut is designed to export either the entire movie as you've arranged it in the Timeline or the portion of the movie between a specified in point and a specified out point.

You can set the in and out points in the Canvas window:

1. Move the playhead to the location where you'd like to place the in point, and then choose Mark | Mark In, or click Mark In:

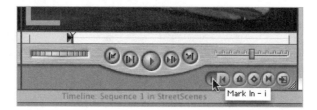

2. Next, move the playhead to the location where you'd like to place the out point, and choose Mark | Mark Out or click Mark Out (that button is just to the right of the Mark In button).

By setting in and out points, you've limited the portion of the movie that will be played back in the Canvas window—and you've limited the portion that will be sent to tape.

Printing to Video

Once rendering is accomplished, and you've set your in and out points (if you elect to use them), you're ready to *print* (another term for "record") to tape. Interesting, the approach used in Final Cut is actually a bit more manual in nature than the approach used in iMovie. Here's how to export to tape:

1. Chose File | Print to Video, which opens the special Print to Video dialog box (see Figure 13-2).

2. The Print to Video dialog box gives you choices for many different variables, such as what the movie *leader* will look like (the leader is video

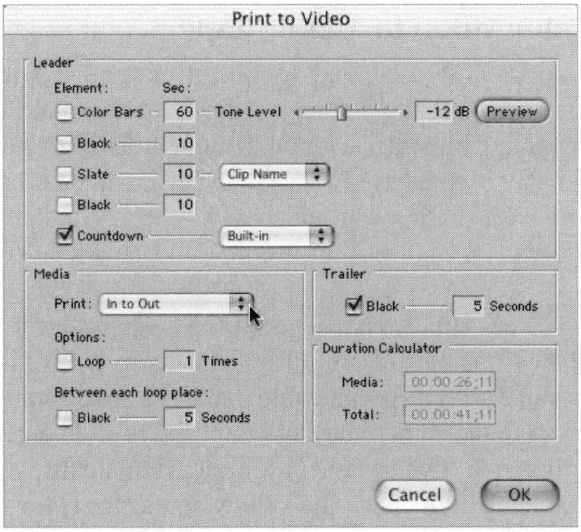

FIGURE 13-2   Complete the Print to Video dialog box to set all the variables associated with printing your production to a camcorder tape.

that appears before the movie starts) and whether the movie has a trailer (a portion of video that appears after the movie ends). Make those selections.

3. In the Media section, you can use the Print menu to select the portion of your project that you want to export to tape. By default, the selection is In to Out, which is the correct selection if you've opted to set in and out points. If you just want to export the entire edited movie, choose Entire Media instead. You can also choose to have the movie loop (meaning repeat from the beginning a given number of times).

4. When you've made all those selections, click OK. Final Cut then writes your video project to tape. As part of that process, Final Cut renders any effects, titles, or transitions if necessary.

5. When the rendered movie is ready, Final Cut tells you to begin recording on your camcorder. Once again, after you make sure that the tape is cued to the correct place, press Record on the camcorder, and click OK in the dialog box.

That's it. Now you can sit back and watch as the movie plays on the screen and, if all goes well, records to your camcorder. When the recording is done, press Stop on your camcorder. Your movie is now recorded on DV tape.

Transferring Your Video to Analog Tape

With your movie now on DV tape, one option for viewing it is to connect your camcorder to a television and play the tape. You could also make duplicates of the tape by connecting your camcorder to another camcorder or to a special DV deck.

Of course, not many people have DV cassette players in their homes, and so the more obvious solution for sharing your video with others is to transfer the movie from your camcorder to an analog video recorder—probably a VCR that plays VHS tapes.

In most cases, you can simply connect a special analog cable to your camcorder. That cable should have analog-out composite connectors that can plug into a VCR. Some camcorders come with a special cable that has a small mini-plug on one side (the side you connect to the camcorder) and three RCA-style plugs (yellow, white, and red) on the other side. Other camcorders provide a cable that has the three RCA-style connectors on both ends. The yellow connector is for video; the white (left) and red (right) connectors are for audio. You'll find those same ports on nearly any VCR and on most televisions made in the past ten years or so.

NOTE *Some high-end camcorders offer another option—an S-video port. S-video offers better quality than that offered by RCA connectors, and so, if your camcorder and VCR both support S-video, connecting an S-video cable between the two is a good idea. You'll still use the white and red composite connectors for sound, but you can leave the yellow connector hanging. S-Video doesn't increase the quality of the original production, but it helps to reduce the slight image degradation that occurs every time you copy a DV production to analog tape.*

With your camcorder connected to the VCR, making the transfer is as easy as cuing the tape on your camcorder, hitting Record on the VCR, and then hitting Play on the camcorder. If everything has been hooked up correctly, the VCR will record the video and audio from the camcorder just as if it were recording a television signal. Watch the movie all the way through. Once it has been transferred, press Stop on both devices.

There, you've got an analog recording.

TIP *If you use Final Cut, you have another way to export directly to analog tape. This alternative method requires that your Mac be equipped with video- and audio-out ports. (On modern Macs, you'll need an expansion card. The last Mac model that included composite video-out and audio-out ports was the "beige" Power Macintosh G3 minitower.) If you connect the out ports to a VCR, you should be able to use the Print to Video command within Final Cut to transfer your video to the analog deck using pretty much the same instructions previously outlined in the section "Final Cut Print to Video."*

13

Creating DVDs

When the first Power Macintosh models arrived with SuperDrive—an optical storage drive that could write to CD-RW and DVD-R media alike—they were accompanied by a new piece of software from Apple Computer—iDVD.

What you can do in iDVD is take QuickTime movies (in particular, those that you created yourself in iMovie or Final Cut) and arrange them in a DVD movie-style interface. You can then burn a DVD that can be read and accessed by consumer-model DVD players. That is quite a step forward, because being able to burn DVDs makes distributing, viewing, mailing, and storing movies created on your Mac that much easier.

iDVD is a great little program. Using it, you can import and translate video clips so that they can be shown, via DVD, on a standard television. (The associated compression and formatting process is actually fairly complicated, but iDVD takes care of it all behind the scenes.)

Once you have imported your video, you can design the look of the iDVD menus and place clips (if you have more than one clip) in those menus. When you're happy with the formatting, you export your project and burn a DVD.

But burning DVD movies can't be done without the right internal drive— Apple now offers the SuperDrive on all of its Mac models (the iMac, eMac, Power Macintosh, PowerBook, and iBook), but only in certain configurations. Adding an external DVD-R drive will *not* work: iDVD is designed strictly for the SuperDrive. But, if you've got a compatible Mac model, you've probably already got iDVD on your Mac, and you're ready to start burning.

NOTE   *In this section we'll be using iDVD 3, which is the latest version out from Apple at the time of writing. If you don't yet have iDVD 3, you can get it as part of the iLife package from Apple at www.apple.com/idvd. If you don't want to pay for iDVD 3, you can still use iDVD 2—we'll note the differences as we go.*

Preparing a DVD-Compatible Movie

iMovie and iDVD work hand-in-hand. In fact, iMovie 3 has a panel within the application that grants direct access to iDVD, making the creation of DVDs a natural process within iMovie. Final Cut doesn't offer a panel, but by taking certain steps, you can make working with iDVD painless.

iDVD can really be used in two ways:

- You can import a bunch of different video clips into iDVD and use them to build the DVD that you're going to burn. That approach can be handy for DVDs that are really collages of your experiences, or your art, or something else that you want to share with others. (Even lessons and training movies might be handled in this way.)

- The other approach is to take one relatively long movie, and use iDVD to burn that movie to disc. iDVD can handle movies up to about 90 minutes, so that burning long projects is certainly possible. For very long projects, though, some preparation is ideal. In either iMovie or Final Cut, you'll probably want to create *chapter markers*. iDVD then uses those markers to determine where individual chapters begin and end. Viewers can use those chapters later to skip to certain parts of the movie immediately.

NOTE   *Although iDVD can handle projects up to 90 minutes, it's worth noting that projects over 60 minutes in length are compressed at a higher level, meaning that their image quality is somewhat lower than that in projects of 60 minutes or less. For absolutely the best quality, stick to a total of 60 minutes of footage (or less) for iDVD projects.*

Defining Chapters in iMovie

If you edited a video in iMovie, and you're now ready to move it over to iDVD so that you can edit and burn a DVD, your first destination is the iDVD panel in iMovie. There, you'll define chapters for your movie.

Here's how it works:

1. Under the Shelf (or the Audio or Titles or Effects—or whatever—tools are currently open on the right side of iMovie), locate and click the iDVD button. The iDVD interface opens.

2. Now you need to define chapters. You may want to begin at the very beginning: Place the playhead at the start of your movie, and click Add Chapter. When you do, you'll see the first frame of your clip appear in the iDVD Chapter Markers window. Notice that the name of the clip is selected. Begin typing a better name for the chapter (see Figure 13-3). That name will be important later in iDVD.

3. Continue to add chapters throughout your movie, giving each a meaningful name. When you're done, you may have a panel full of chapter markers—that's good. Chapters aren't required in DVD movies, but using them takes advantage of the DVD format and enables a viewer to return immediately to a particular scene or section within the movie.

4. As a final step, click Create iDVD Project. Your movie is instantly transported to iDVD 3. (If you don't have iDVD 3, you can still export your video as an iMovie project and later load it into iDVD 2. To export the video as a high-quality DV project, choose File | Export. Then, in the Export dialog box, choose To iDVD from the Export menu. See Chapter 14 for details on exporting as a high-quality QuickTime movie.)

13

FIGURE 13-3 Creating chapters in iMovie looks like this.

Once the movie is transported, your Mac immediately switches to the iDVD 3 window (iDVD may have to launch first) showing a list of movies you can use in your DVD project.

Defining Chapters in Final Cut

Again, Final Cut can work well with iDVD, but the approach is a bit more complex. You begin by creating chapter markers, and then you export the video. Here's how:

1. To create a chapter marker, place the playhead on the Timeline where a new chapter should start.

2. Choose Mark | Markers | Add. You should see the frame in the Canvas window with the word "Marker 1" if this is your first chapter marker (subsequent markers will have higher numbers).

3. Now you need to edit the marker to label it correctly. Select Mark | Markers | Edit.

TIP *You can create and edit a marker in one operation by positioning the playhead and pressing M twice.*

4. In the Edit Marker window, click Add Chapter Marker to change this regular marker specifically into a chapter marker that iDVD will recognize:

5. Give the marker a meaningful name, and click OK.

6. Repeat the process for each new chapter you want to create.

Once the chapters are created, you need to export the movie with those chapters intact. Here's how:

1. To export correctly, Choose File | Export | Final Cut Movie. In the Save dialog box, give the movie a name, and then use the Include menu to choose the portion you want to save.

2. While still in the Save dialog box, pull down the Markers menu, and choose DVD Studio Pro Markers. Click Save.

NOTE *The option says "DVD Studio Pro Markers," but they work for both iDVD and its professional big brother DVD Studio Pro. So, don't let the name fool you if you don't have the "Pro" version of these tools—this procedure works fine for Final Cut Express and iDVD.*

13

At that, your movie is exported with its chapter markers intact. (DVD Studio Pro is the professional-level DVD creation tool from Apple, but its chapter markers work just as well in iDVD.) Now, as you'll see next, you can import the exported movie into iDVD.

Importing a Video into iDVD

We've already mentioned that transferring your iMovie project into iDVD is a cakewalk: you can simply click the Create iDVD Project button in the iDVD panel. Of course, that procedure works only with iMovie 3 and iDVD 3. In other cases—with Final Cut, for instance—you'll need to import the video into iDVD before you can begin to work with it.

TIP *Actually, iDVD 3 can work some special magic with movies that you've stored in your personal Movies folder, with photos that you manage using iPhoto, and with songs that you work with in iTunes. In the iDVD 3 "drawer" (which you can open by clicking Customize), you can click the Movies, Photos, or Audio buttons to see the contents of those folders and to gain direct access to the media stored in them. Just drag-and-drop to add those items to your DVD project.*

iDVD can work with all types of imported video clips—although it's best if you're using uncompressed DV Stream–format movies (or uncompressed, 720×480 pixel QuickTime movies). That's because, to create a DVD movie disc, iDVD needs to compress those files again so that they're properly formatted and stored on the disc. If you feed in files that have already been compressed once, the image quality of your video will suffer.

If you exported movies from iMovie or Final Cut with chapter markers turned on, those markers will be recognized and automatically broken out as a sequence of scenes that can be individually accessed. (That's the default setting. You can alter it in iDVD | Preferences so that iDVD asks before automatically adding scene selection for each chapter. Switch off the Automatically Create option. Note that you *should not do this* for movies that are more than 60 minutes long; only the Automatically Create option will work.)

Here's how to bring movies into iDVD:

1. Launch iDVD, and create a new project.

2. Choose File | Import.

3. When you import a movie with chapter markers, a dialog box may open, asking you whether to create the marked scenes. Click OK if you want the movie to be added and the scene selections to be created from the chapter markers in the movie.

In Figure 13-4 you can see the Scene Selection button. When the DVD has been burned and is being played back in a DVD player, the viewer will be able to access those individual scenes from the links, jumping directly to the scene start and beginning to watch the video from there.

TIP   *You can import other files into iDVD, including other movie file formats and still image formats. (In fact, you can import entire folders full of still images.) Use the File | Import | Image command to select and import still images or even File | Import | Background Video to import your own video as the motion background in your DVD menu (for example).*

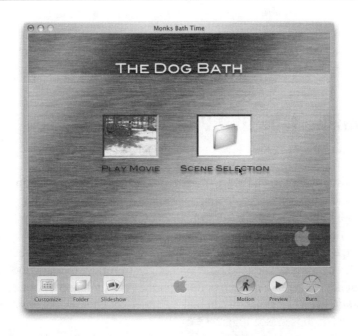

| FIGURE 13-4 | Here, a movie has been imported into iDVD, and a scene selection folder that holds links corresponding to the chapter markers has been created. |

Note that while in Edit Mode, you can click Folder to create a new folder in your project:

Folders store other clips or photos that you drag in from the Movies or Photos panels in the Customize drawer. In a commercial DVD, that's where you'd store the outtakes, second-language clips, "making of" features, and so on. You've got that same freedom here by using the folder to hold additional clips or still photos.

Having trouble opening a folder you just created while in Edit mode? Simply hold down the COMMAND *key, and double-click the folder in question. It will open in the interface so that you can drag movies and photos and edit the titles on the menu page in the folder.*

How about deleting folders and added multimedia items? Click them once while in Edit mode, then press DELETE. You'll see them disappear in a cloud of animated smoke.

Customizing Your DVD Project

Now that your movie, video clips, or still images have been imported, you can add a custom appearance to your DVD interface if you want to.

Click Customize to open the Customize drawer if it isn't already open. Now you can access the themes that Apple makes available for your video: Click Themes at the top of the drawer. When you do, the drawer changes to show you the various themes from which you can choose (see Figure 13-5).

To change the theme of your DVD, simply select one of the preset themes that Apple makes available. The DVD menu changes to reflect the new look and feel.

You can dig deeper into custom options for the current theme by clicking Settings. In the Custom Settings panel, you can make a variety of choices that augment or alter the theme you've chosen (see Figure 13-6).

FIGURE 13-5   Using the Customize drawer, you can select various themes for the menu interface on your DVD.

13

FIGURE 13-6   Once you've chosen a theme, you can switch to the Custom Settings panel to alter the behavior of that theme.

Some of the options include:

- **Motion Duration**   If the background to the theme includes motion, you can use the Motion Duration slider to set the period of time for which the motion will continue after the menu has loaded.

- **Background**   You can use the drag-and-drop targets in the Background area to change the background image or the audio that plays (or both) when the menu appears. Note that you can also click the small speaker icon to mute the audio playback.

- **Title**   Use the controls in the Title area to change the appearance, font, and position of the title in the DVD menu.

- **Button**   Use the Button controls to change the appearance of the buttons that play the movie or switch to the Scene Selection screen. (Note that, by choosing Free Position, you can drag the button or selection text to a different position on the screen.)

You'll want to choose a theme for each menu page in your project, including your Scene Selection menu (if relevant) and any other folders that you created. To open a folder or the Scene Selection menu while in Edit mode, hold down the COMMAND key and double-click the appropriate folder name or icon.

Saving and Burning Your DVD Project

While you're working on the appearance of your DVD, you may be interested to know that the *encoding* process for your movies (those that you import and any that you drag in via the Movies panel or from elsewhere) is going on behind the scenes. Those movies must be translated from QuickTime to the MPEG-2 format, which is the standard compression scheme and file format for consumer DVD movies.

To check the progress of the encoding, you can click Status in the Customize drawer. The resulting report also shows you how much time and storage space the project will take up on the DVD and how much time and storage space remains (see Figure 13-7).

Because encoding happens behind the scenes, you don't have to wait for the encoding process to end before you put the burn process into motion again. Once you've made your interface design decisions, you can go ahead and tell iDVD that you're ready to burn the disc.

FIGURE 13-7   Status in the Customize drawer shows you the size and storage details.

Here's how to begin the burn process:

1. Make sure you've edited the DVD and are happy with how it works. It's a good idea to click the Preview button in the main iDVD interface so that you can test the menus and buttons.

2. When you're satisfied that everything works as you expect, click Burn. The button will animate and open:

3. Click the nuclear symbol again to confirm that you're ready to start the burn.

4. At this point, the tray for the DVD-R drive should open automatically. (If your machine comes equipped with a slot-loading SuperDrive, you'll see action only if a disc has to be ejected.) An onscreen prompt tells you to insert a blank DVD-R disc.

13

5. Place a fresh disc into the tray and close the drive. (Or, for a slot-loading SuperDrive, slide the fresh disc into the slot until the mechanism takes it up.)

If all else goes well, you'll see iDVD jump right into the burn process, letting you know, on a dialog sheet, what's going on. iDVD steps through a multistage process of encoding, preparing, burning, and verifying the disc, which can take quite a long time—even hours—so be prepared to do something else in the meantime. (It's ideal to avoid using the computer *and* attempting to sleep the computer, power it down, or connect/disconnect peripherals while the burn is taking place.)

When all is said and done, iDVD will report its success (hopefully) and eject the completed DVD. You can now take it to a commercial DVD player or play it back using the DVD Player application on your Mac to see if it works correctly.

Where to Find It

Web site	Address	What's there
Apple Computer	www.apple.com/idvd	iLife (includes iDVD)

Chapter 14

Sharing QuickTime Movies

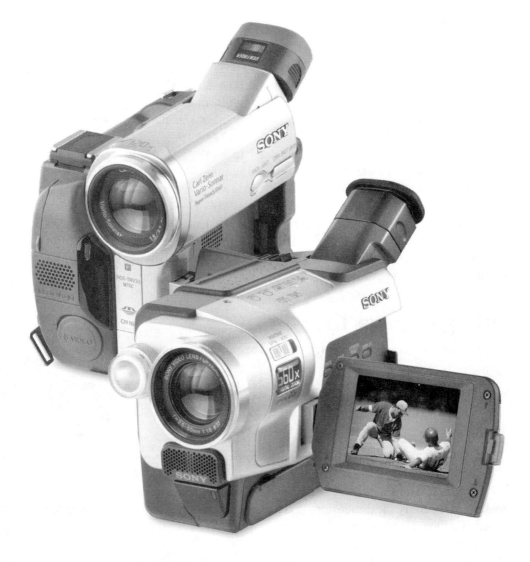

How To...

- Export to QuickTime

- Use advanced export settings

- Set up QuickTime and HTML pages

- Set up QuickTime movie streaming

- Burn movies to data CDs

- Create video CDs

On the Macintosh, QuickTime is king in terms of both the technology that creates and edits digital movies and the file format in which digital movies play back. If you're sending an edited movie to another Mac user, for instance, you'll definitely use QuickTime.

But QuickTime is also a popular playback technology for PC users. Some PC-based video editing software packages provide an option to save your movies in the QuickTime format—and, if not, the movies can always be translated to QuickTime.

In fact, QuickTime is the foundation of the MPEG-4 file format, a standard that's growing in popularity for video playback, particularly over the Internet. So, although formats such as Real Media and Windows Media are certainly popular for Internet playback, QuickTime is also a good choice—especially if you're trying to reach a cross-platform audience.

Exporting to QuickTime

You've probably decided to create a QuickTime movie for one of three reasons:

- You want to make a movie that can be stored and played back from a CD or hard disk.

- You want to deliver a movie file over the Internet.

- You want to stream a movie over the Internet.

The ultimate destination for your movie determines some of the choices that you make—particularly the dimensions and quality of the playback—when saving your video as a QuickTime movie.

Here's a slightly expanded look at those three approaches:

- **Disk-Based Movie**   A movie that you plan to store on magnetic media such as your hard disk—or, perhaps, burn to optical media such as a CD or DVD for computer-based playback—can be relatively large in terms of file size. Because you have the luxury of storage space, you can opt to create a higher-quality QuickTime movie. The better the quality and the larger the dimensions (in pixels) of the movie, the more storage space it will take up.

- **Internet Deliverable**   We'll call a movie that you plan to send by e-mail, display on a web site, or otherwise distribute over the Internet an *Internet deliverable* file. In this case, you need to trade the quality of playback against a reasonable file size. That trade-off often requires that you export a movie with very small dimensions (240×180 pixels or smaller, say) and very heavy compression. The resulting movie will not be as large and as smooth as a high-quality disk-based one, but it will be able to be more easily transported across the Internet.

- **Streaming Movie**   A streaming movie falls somewhere between the two choices already mentioned. With *streaming*, the data that makes up the movie flows steadily across the Internet from a server computer to a client computer so that it can be played back on the client computer "just in time." The viewer can be watching the movie before it has completely downloaded. (That's something you may have done if you enjoy watching movie trailers online, for instance. Visit www.quicktime.com for some official examples from Apple Inc.) In the case of streaming, you may still have to cut down on the dimensions and quality of the video. But streaming technology is constantly being improved and, with the combination of better streaming technology and expansion of broadband Internet access, streaming movies have reached the point at which their quality can actually be better than that of an Internet deliverable.

NOTE   *The MPEG-4 format—mentioned previously because it's based, in part, on QuickTime—was designed specifically for high-quality Internet streaming (although it can also be used for other types of movie storage and playback). As such formats and their compression technology improve, the quality of streaming video will increase dramatically.*

14

Performing a Basic Export in iMovie

If you are a beginner, simply knowing the movie format you're interested in creating can be enough to get you through a movie export in iMovie. The QuickTime export options, for instance, are fairly easy to follow:

1. To quickly export from iMovie, choose File | Export. That opens the iMovie: Export dialog box. As you can see in Figure 14-1, exporting for one of the reasons just discussed is simply a matter of choosing a preset option from the Formats menu in the dialog box.

2. Choose **CD-ROM** if you want to play a high-quality movie from your hard disk or create a QuickTime file good for burning to (and playing back from) a data CD or DVD. Choose **Email** or **Web** for settings that create Internet-deliverable movies. (The movie created by the Email option plays in a small window and is fairly low quality, but the movie file is relatively small. For instance, a 5-minute movie exported using the Email setting takes up about 9MB of disk space—not easy to send by e-mail, but very small for such a long digital movie.) Finally, you can choose **Web Streaming** if you'd like a file that's appropriate for placing on a web server that supports QuickTime streaming protocols. (One such place is the .Mac HomePage service, which we discuss a bit later in "QuickTime Movie Streaming.")

FIGURE 14-1 In the iMovie Export dialog box, you can select various preset QuickTime export scenarios from the Formats menu.

3. Once you've made your selection, click Export. A dialog box opens, asking you to give the movie a name.

4. Type a name for your movie, and click Save.

Now, sit back and wait—your iMovie project will be exported to QuickTime, which can take a little while. While that's happening, a small Exporting Movie box shows the progress of the operation; if you can't stand the wait, you can click Stop to halt the export.

Otherwise, go grab a good book or a cup of coffee—it's best to leave your Mac alone while the export takes place. (Not that you have to. Particularly in the case of Mac OS X, you can switch to other applications and keep computing, although that might slow down the export process and your other applications may seem a bit lazy. Also, you increase the chances of an error occurring it the export.)

Performing a Basic Export in Final Cut

A basic export in Final Cut isn't quite as automatic as in iMovie, but you can manage to produce movies of different sizes without digging too deep into the export preferences.

1. To begin the export, choose File | Export | QuickTime. The Save dialog box opens:

QuickTime is already selected in the Format menu; you can move on to the Use menu, where you can choose from a number of different target settings. Notice that the options in Final Cut don't focus on the physical destination of your movie (CD-ROM, Web, etc.); instead, they focus completely on various Internet connection types (Modem, DSL/Cable, LAN, and so on).

Actually, Final Cut assumes—in these presets, at least—that your QuickTime movie is destined for the Internet. Further examination reveals that, in fact, the assumption is that the movie will be a streaming movie, because the default setting in Final Cut is to switch on hinting, which is the key setting for streaming movies.

So, which option do you pick?

2. If your goal is to create an Internet-bound product, then choose one of the lower **Modem** settings for a movie that's appropriate for e-mail distribution or for web users who have only a dial-up connection. If you plan a movie that's more appropriate for a hard disk, choose the **Default Settings** option. If you're actually serving the movie from a web site, then choose one of the in-between options (high-end **Modem** or one of the **DSL** options) depending on the audience you're targeting. (That is, do they have high-speed connections? Then choose a higher-speed option.) For the fastest network-based connections, choose **LAN**.

3. When you've made your selection, the next step is to give the movie a name and to choose a storage location (this is a standard Save dialog box). Click Save.

A dialog box opens to show you the progress of the export. When the export is done, you're returned to Final Cut, your exported movie having been saved in the location you specified.

Exporting from PC Applications

We won't get too specific here, but many PC-based nonlinear editing applications can export their projects as QuickTime movies.

Adobe Premiere for Windows, for instance, has some sophisticated QuickTime options. To begin, choose File | Export Timeline | Movie. In the Export Movie dialog box, choose QuickTime from the File Type menu, and then click Next to move through some of the movie dimension and codec decisions. (Some of these decisions are discussed in the next section.) When you've made all the necessary settings choices, you can click OK to begin the export process.

Using Advanced Export Options

You've seen how your editing program can make your QuickTime export decisions relatively painless by offering preset options for certain types of video applications. But what if the presets don't quite do everything you're hoping for? In that case, you may want to dig into the more advanced options.

Opening Advanced Options

Interestingly, when you dig into advanced export options, you'll find that they tend to be extremely similar from application to application. That's because the QuickTime options are based on the QuickTime technology itself and are not closely controlled by the exporting application. In other words, when you choose an "Options" or "Advanced Options" button in your application, that application may then go directly to the QuickTime technology layer and say, in effect, "You handle this." The result is a standard dialog box for QuickTime settings (see Figure 14-2).

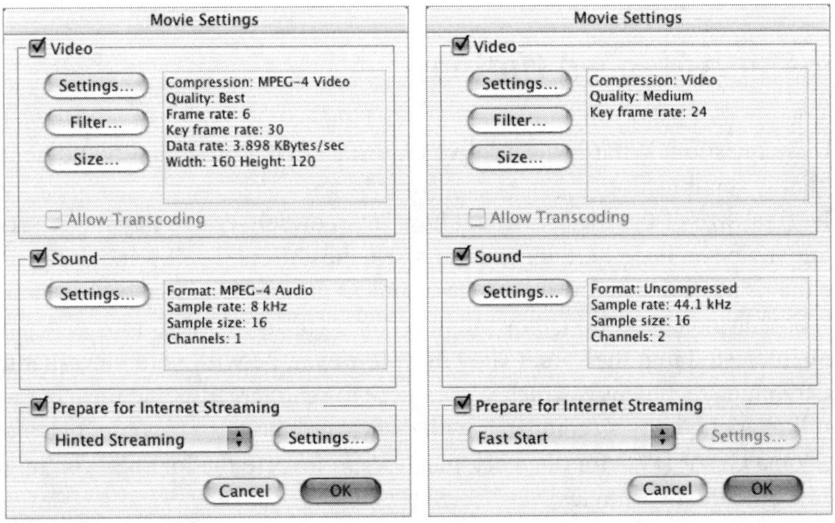

FIGURE 14-2   On the left is the Movie Settings dialog box in Final Cut; on the right is the dialog box in iMovie. Note that, aside from their default settings, they're identical.

14

In Final Cut, you get to the QuickTime Movie Settings dialog box by clicking Options in the Save dialog box (shown earlier in the section "Basic Export in Final Cut"). When you click Options, you'll see the Movie Settings dialog box (shown on the left-hand side in Figure 14-2).

In iMovie, it takes an additional step to get to the Movie Settings dialog box. Select File | Export to open the iMovie: Export dialog box. In the Export menu, choose Expert Settings, and then click Export. That opens the Save Exported File As dialog box, which looks exactly like the Save dialog box in Final Cut:

Save exported file as...
Save As: Monks Bath Time.mov
Where: Documents
Export: Movie to QuickTime Movie   Options
Use: Default Settings
Cancel   Save

In the Save Exported File As dialog box, click Options. The Movie Settings dialog box—the exact one shown on the right-hand side in Figure 14-2—now opens.

Choosing Advanced Options

How you go about choosing advanced QuickTime export options boils down to a very basic question: What is the relative importance of a high-quality movie versus a file that is small in size?

The final size of the file will affect how Internet-deliverable the movie seems to your target viewer. For entertainment purposes, most users won't want to download a movie that is more than a few megabytes—unless they have a broadband connection. With a broadband connection, they might go for a 10MB to 50MB movie, depending on how interested in it they are. (They may, however, be willing to view that movie using streaming technology, which you can use to send larger movie files, but which may still restrict quality as compared with disk-based movies.) If you're placing the movies on a CD or DVD for playback that doesn't involve the Internet, you might opt for higher-quality movies.

To make a video file smaller, you have to reduce the resolution or increase the compression (or both). Doing so results in a lower-quality image—sometimes a *much* lower quality image than that found in the original DV files. But, a lower-quality movie is the necessary trade-off if you want the download to take a reasonable amount of time. Other tradeoffs include the number of frames per second and the number of keyframes. Finally, your chosen *codec* (the algorithmic methodology used to compress and decompress the video) will affect quality and file size. New codecs that work to compress movies into smaller file sizes while delivering high-quality playback are being developed all the time.

So, with that discussion out of the way, the question becomes this: What settings do you choose when you're in expert mode?

In Mac applications, the Movie Settings dialog box has three basic sections: Video, Sound, and Internet settings. (PC applications that provide for QuickTime export may present these options in a slightly different way, but they should make most of them available.)

We'll start with the Video section:

Choosing the Video Settings

In the Movie Settings dialog box, click Settings in the Video section. That opens a dialog box called Compression Settings:

The unlabeled menu at the top of this dialog box is where you to select the codec that will be used to compress the video portion of your QuickTime movie. Choosing the codec is an important decision, and one that can get rather complex quickly.

We'll simplify your choice by tossing out some options that you might want to explore on your own. Here are our recommendations:

- **Video**   For disk-based movies, the codec most often used is the Video codec. This codec doesn't compress movies as much as some others do, but it allows for smooth playback from larger files.

- **H.261**   For very small (in file size *and* in dimensions) e-mail-type movies, H.261 can be a good choice. Often, it's the codec used for video conferencing, for instance. It can make a very small movie look good and compress well.

- **Sorensen**   For a medium-sized web-based movie—particularly one that will be delivered instead of streamed—the Sorensen codec does a good job. In fact, movies compressed with the Sorensen codec tend to "double" well (double both the vertical and horizontal dimensions of the movie as it plays back), so that you can increase the size of the movie when playing it back and get good results.

- **MPEG-4 Video**   For Internet streaming, MPEG-4 Video is the best choice— provided your audience is likely to have a fairly recent version of QuickTime on their computers. If not, Sorensen is a good fallback for streaming.

So, based on that advice, you can now make a selection at the top of the Compression Settings dialog box.

Next, depending on the codec you chose, you'll see a quality slider and perhaps some other settings, such as color depth. Make your choices depending, again, on the quality/file-size trade-off that you're aiming for.

Now, in the Motion portion of the dialog box, you've got some other choices to make that could affect both file size and quality. Here's a look:

- **Frames Per Second**   Television in North America runs at about 30 frames per second, and film at about 24 frames per second. Smooth QuickTime video has a lower-end limit of about 15 frames per second. For movie files that need to be small in size, you can drop the frames per second even lower—as low as 5–10 fps—to save storage space at the expense of quality.

- **Keyframe Every __ Frames**   A keyframe is a fully drawn frame of video that's used as a baseline for other frames in your QuickTime movie. The in-between frames simply store the *differences* in the picture that occur between keyframes. Choosing the number of keyframes is a bit of an art form. In general you're safe with a keyframe every second or two seconds (at 15 fps, that'd be a keyframe every 30 frames). If you space them out more than that, your video will appear very jerky. With too many keyframes (setting them to every 5 frames, for instance) your movie file will grow in size.

■ **Limit Data Rate To __ Kbytes/sec.** This choice is especially useful for streaming video, in which you may want to design a stream for a certain amount of bandwidth. For instance, a movie being streamed for 56 Kbps modems should be set to about 30 Kbps in the Compression Settings dialog box; for faster connections, a data rate of 100–200 Kbps or so should work. For the highest quality, you might try a 500 Kbps data rate. (And, of course, you can opt not to limit the data rate if you don't want to, particularly for movies that won't be streaming over the Internet.)

Click the OK button to head back to the Movie Settings dialog box (in Mac applications).

Choosing the Sound Settings

If your movie has sound, you can click Settings in the Sound section of the Movie Settings dialog box to change the sound compression scheme and certain other associated choices.

For disk-based playback, you might choose to use no compression, leaving the settings at high quality: 44.100 kHz, 16-bit, and Stereo. For Internet-based movies, you might opt for some compression. For deliverable movies, QDesign Music 2 is a good music compressor and Qualcomm PureVoice is a good compressor for spoken dialog. MPEG-4 Audio is the right choice if you've used MPEG-4 Video for your streaming QuickTime movie.

Again, click OK to return from the Sound Settings dialog box.

Choosing the Internet Settings

The Internet settings are the simplest.

At the bottom of the Movie Settings dialog box, deselect the check box next to Prepare For Internet Streaming if you'd like to turn streaming *off*—without that check mark, the movie will be saved as a typical QuickTime movie. However, there's little reason to do that, because the Fast Start setting can work well for Internet-based and disk-based movies.

But for movies that will be streamed, you should select both the Prepare For Internet Streaming check box and choose the Hinted Streaming option. (We'll look at these choices a little more closely in "QuickTime Movie Streaming.")

14

You're "Go" for Export

With all your settings choices made, click the OK button. In Mac applications, you'll be returned to the Save dialog box, complete with Most Recent Settings in the Use menu. Now you can save the movie and the QuickTime file will be created as ordered.

QuickTime on the Internet

Once your QuickTime movie has been created, you have a few different options for distributing it to friends. One is to store the movie on removable media of some sort. If you have a CD burner and you'd like to explore those options, see the section "QuickTime on Disc" later in this chapter.

Over the Internet, you've again got a few choices. First, you can work with an Internet deliverable—one that's small enough to send to someone else. If your movie file is sufficiently small, you can simply attach it to an e-mail message and send it directly to your recipients. (Many Internet service providers restrict the size of e-mail attachments, and so "sufficiently small" may mean less than a megabyte or two, depending on your recipient's service provider.) Delivery still takes a while (nearly any QuickTime movie is going to be at least a megabyte or more in size), but that method may be your best option for directly sharing your QuickTime movie with someone else.

NOTE *You may also find it handy to use other types of sharing services to transfer QuickTime files—for instance, you could use Apple iChat or a similar service to transfer the movie. Likewise, if you have Mac OS X, you might find it convenient to switch on Apple File Services or the built-in FTP server and allow a friend or colleague to download your QuickTime movie that way.*

Another option is to embed your QuickTime movie in a hypertext mark-up language (HTML) document—that way, in browsers that support QuickTime, the movie will play directly in the web browser window.

Finally, you can stream your movie over the Internet. In this case, the movie is generally played back within the QuickTime Player application.

We'll look at the latter two options next.

QuickTime and HTML

If you'd like to place your QuickTime movie on the Web and make it available to a standard web server, you've got two choices: you can link to it or your can embed it in the page.

When you set up a QuickTime movie as a link, your visitor can simply download the movie—or, in some web browsers, the movie will appear in a new window and play. To create a link, use the following HTML code:

```
<a href="http://www.yoursite.com/movie_file.mov">Click for the
movie</a>
```

You begin with the HTML anchor tag <a href=""> and, inside the quotes, you place the URL to the QuickTime movie file that you've stored online. (You'll want to have saved your QuickTime movie with a .mov filename extension so that it can be recognized by all types of computers.) The text between the opening tag for the anchor element and the closing tag (</a>) is the text that will be clickable in the browser window.

In this example, a small window pops up to display the movie when a viewer clicks the link:

Your other option is to *embed* the QuickTime movie in your web page. What embedding does is to give the browser a command that tells it to load the QuickTime movie and display it within the web page itself instead of showing a link to click.

14

You use the EMBED element, which is a bit more complex than a link, but not too much more so.

Here is what you add:

```
<embed src="movie_file.mov" width="240" height="180"></embed>
```

You don't technically have to include the width and height of the movie, but it can be handy to do so, because then the page loads a little more quickly. With code like that shown above in the HTML document, the browser window looks like this:

NOTE   *Unfortunately, the EMBED element isn't really standard HTML: it's something that Netscape created a long time ago as a Netscape-specific tag. Many browsers copied it, and it tends still to work. Where it doesn't work, however, is in the latest versions of Microsoft Internet Explorer for Windows, as well as some browsers that adhere only to official standards. In that case, you need to use the OBJECT element, which is a little outside the scope of this chapter. See the tutorial page from Apple on the matter at www.apple.com/quicktime/tools_tips/tutorials/activex.html to get the best code for all browser platforms. The EMBED element also has levels of complexity and other attributes that can be used with it—see www.apple.com/quicktime/authoring/embed.html for details.*

QuickTime Movie Streaming

To stream a movie to your viewer, you have to do two things. First, you have to save the movie so that it's prepared for streaming, as we discussed earlier in "Choosing Advanced Options."

What you're doing when you prepare a movie for streaming is saving it as a *hinted movie.* A hinted movie is one that has little directives or "hints" stored in the movie file itself. Those hints help the movie player application to know how the file is being sent and how it can be pieced back together. The more specific the hinting is, the smoother the playback will be (all else being equal).

In the Movie Settings dialog box, you can see, in most cases, just a single option for Hinted Streaming in the Prepare for Internet Streaming area. However, you can click Settings to dig a bit further:

When you do, you'll see the Hint Exporter Settings, where you can really get serious about your hints—however, doing so is a little outside the scope of this book. If you haven't determined your exact needs (and they vary based on purpose and your particular file format) then you can at least consider one option: Optimize Hints for Server.

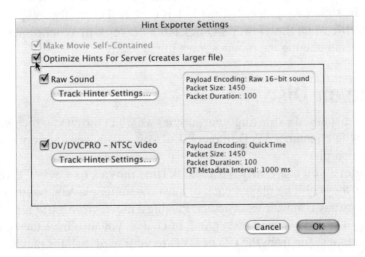

If you'll be placing your movie specifically on a server computer that's running QuickTime Streaming Server, then switching the Optimize Hints option on will make it possible for twice as many people to access the QuickTime stream at once. The drawback is that it makes the movie file about twice as large.

With a hinted movie exported, your next step is to upload the file to a server that's designed for streaming. This is a special server—not just a web server, but one that's specifically designed to serve up streaming QuickTime movies. Apple has information about QuickTime Streaming Server at www.apple.com/quicktime/ products/qtss on its web site. If you don't have access to an Internet server so that you can install QuickTime Streaming Server, then you might opt to find an Internet service provider (ISP) that offers QuickTime Streaming Server as an option. (Many of the ISPs that make a point of serving Mac customers will offer QuickTime Streaming Server as an option.)

To make your streaming QuickTime movie available to viewers, you have to upload the file to the location recommended by your ISP. (In many cases, this location will be different from the one in which your main HTML files reside.) Then, you have to create an HTML link that points to the file.

For instance, you might end up with a link that looks like this:

```
<a href="rtsp://www.yoursite.com/movies/movie_file.mov">Click to
view the movie stream</a>
```

Note that the link uses the rtsp (real-time streaming protocol) protocol instead of the http protocol. What the link does is launch the movie in QuickTime Player, and begin the streaming process. If the link is designed correctly and points to the appropriate file, then the viewer's QuickTime Player will synchronize with the server and begin playing the movie almost immediately.

QuickTime on Disc

Chapter 13 discussed exporting your movies as DVD movies, which can be played back in consumer DVD players. But you also have other options for distributing on disc.

For starters, you can easily burn QuickTime movies to a data CD or DVD. In that case, they can't be played back in most consumer players, but they can be played back in any compatible computer. Playing a movie from a CD is pretty much like playing it from your hard disk. (And, of course, you also have the option of copying the movie file from the CD or DVD to your hard disk for playback.)

Your other option is to create a VideoCD, which is a unique sort of hybrid. Many CD-RW burners can't create DVD movies using tools such as iMovie, but they can create VideoCDs. In many cases VideoCDs can be played back in consumer DVD players, and they can definitely be played back on computers that have VideoCD player software. The major difference is that the quality of a VideoCD is much lower than that of a DVD—in fact, image quality on a VideoCD is very close to VHS tape quality. Still, VideoCD is a handy way to distribute and play movies without having to go through the steps of creating a DVD.

Burning Data CDs

In Mac OS 9 or Mac OS X, burning a data CD full of QuickTime movies couldn't be simpler. If your CD-RW burner is built into your Mac or if it's an external model that's compatible with Disc Burner technology from Apple, all you really have to do is this:

1. Insert a blank CD-R, CD-RW, DVD-R, or DVD-RW disc into the burner tray or slot. When the Mac recognizes the disc, it will ask if you want to prepare the disc for burning:

2. Keep Open Finder selected, type a name for the disc, and click OK. The disc now appears on the desktop in the Finder.

3. Next, simply drag your QuickTime movies to the disc icon as you would with any files in the Finder. (If you want the movies to be accessible across computer platforms, it's a good idea to name them using the .mov filename extension.)

4. When you're done, select the disc's icon in the Finder and choose File | Burn Disc. Alternatively, drag the disc from the desktop to the Trash. In either case, a dialog box opens, asking if you want to burn the disc.

14

5. Click Burn, then sit back and wait for the burn process to finish.

When the burn is complete, the disc pops out of the drive, and you'll find your QuickTime movies on disc and ready to roll. (Again, it's a good idea not to use your computer while the burn is taking place.)

TIP You have other options for burning CDs and DVDs, including Roxio Toast Titanium (www.roxio.com) and CharisMac Discribe (www.charismac.com), two third-party utilities that can be used for more sophisticated control over disc burning. We'll actually look at those products in the next section because both are also capable of creating VideoCDs.

Burning VideoCDs

A VideoCD is a CD that use the same basic technology as DVD movies do, but lower-quality movie images are written to a CD-R disc instead of a DVD-R disc. Creating VideoCDs doesn't require a SuperDrive, just a CD-RW drive, which many more Mac models come with. VideoCDs can be played back in many commercial DVDs players and on most CD-ROM equipped multimedia computers. They tend not to hold as much video as a DVD does, and the image quality is lower, but they're a handy alternative for many situations.

Creating a VideoCD requires third-party software. Probably the most popular product for use on the Mac (and perhaps for PCs as well) is Roxio Toast Titanium, which is a full-fledged CD and DVD burning tool that you can use to manage burns of audio and data CDs for many different platforms. One of the many talents of Toast is its ability to create a VideoCD.

To burn a VideoCD, you have to export your movie at the highest quality level possible—a QuickTime movie with no compression at 720×480 pixels (standard DV quality) is ideal. That's because Toast will be doing some translation and compression: to work on a VideoCD, the movie must be encoded as an MPEG-1 file, which is then burned to the CD in the special VideoCD format.

In practice, creating a VideoCD with iMovie is incredibly easy to do, because Toast Titanium actually adds a command to the Save Exported File As dialog box within iMovie. Instead of choosing Movie to QuickTime Movie in the Export menu, you can choose Movie to Toast VideoCD as shown in Figure 14-3.

If you're working with existing QuickTime movies or with movies that you exported from Final Cut or another program, you can simply launch Toast, locate the VideoCD screen (under Other), and then drag a QuickTime movie to the VideoCD screen (see Figure 14-4). When you do, you'll be asked which format should be used

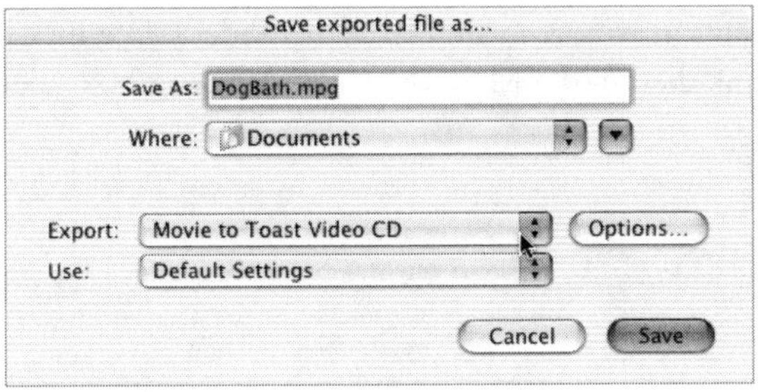

FIGURE 14-3   The easy way to create a VideoCD is to export using the settings that Toast adds for iMovie.

for the VideoCD, how you want the image to fit on the screen, and which "mode" should be used for the VideoCD encoding—Normal, Faster, or Better. When you click OK to accept your choices for those options, you'll then be asked to save the file that Toast is going to create when it encodes the QuickTime movie into the MPEG-1 format. Click Save, and the encoding process begins.

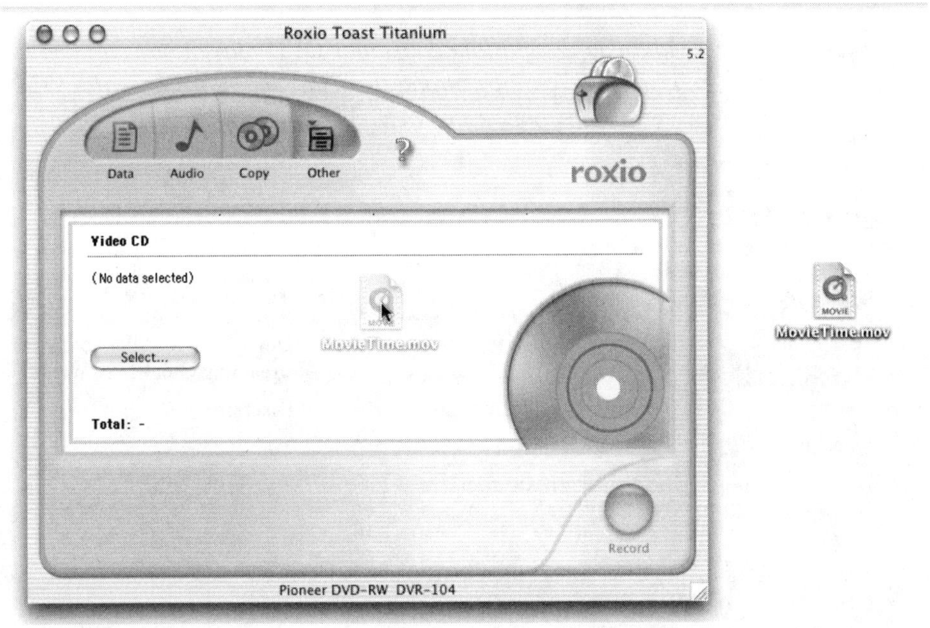

FIGURE 14-4   Dragging a QuickTime movie to VideoCD sets the encoding process into action.

Once the movie has been encoded, you'll be returned to the Toast interface, where the Record button is now available in the VideoCD window. Click Record. If you placed a blank disc in the Mac, the Record dialog box opens.

Choose one of the supported speeds (the non-italic ones) based on the rated write speed of your drive, and click Write Disc. If you're not sure which speed to choose, Toast has a Speed Check mode you can use to see if a particular speed will work. Also, if your CD burner is relatively old or slow, you might want to switch on Buffer Underrun Prevention to compensate; you can also choose Simulation Mode to test before burning to disc.

The burn process should then begin. Again, you'll see a progress bar, this time in the VideoCD window. When the burn is done, if all goes well, you'll have a VideoCD.

TIP   *If you have a VideoCD-compatible consumer DVD player, you can test it in that player. If not, you can download the shareware program MacVCD Player from www.mireth.com on the Web.*

Where to Find It

Web Site	Address	What's There
Apple Computer	www.quicktime.com	QuickTime installer and streaming QuickTime movies
CharisMac	www.charismac.com	Discribe
Mireth Technology	www.mireth.com	MacVCD
Roxio	www.roxio.com	Toast Titanium

Part IV

Appendixes

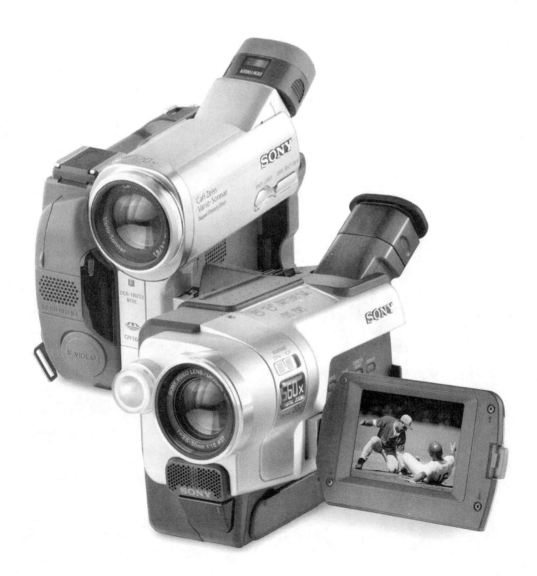

Appendix A

Digital Video Glossary

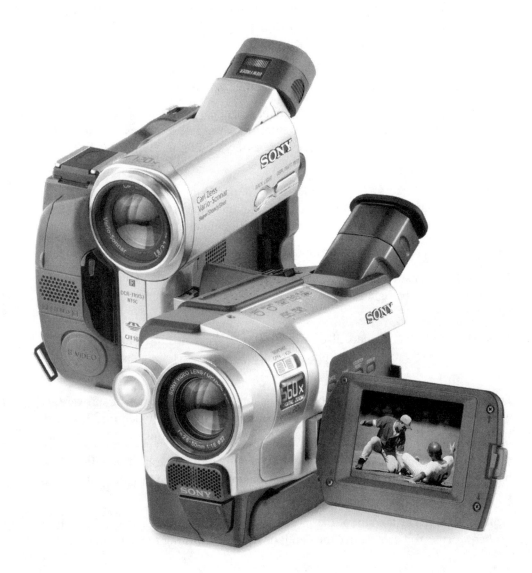

Analog video   Video captured by an older camcorder that uses a format like VHS, S-VHS, 8mm, or Hi8. These formats are all relatively low in overall video resolution and degrade with each copy made from the original source tape.

Animatic   A version of your movie that uses storyboard frames, in place of the actual video footage, to simulate the approximate flow, content, and run time of your finished movie.

Aperture   The size of the opening that lets light through the lens. The bigger the aperture setting—expressed in terms of "f/stop," as in f/2, f/5.6, or f/22, for instance—the smaller the aperture opening.

Backlight   A light reflected off the background onto the subject from behind to add a sense of depth between the subject and the background.

Bit rate   A measure of the overall quality of an audio or video file. A high bit rate means considerable data is stored in the file. A low bit rate indicates a low-quality file. MP3 files, for instance, can use a wide variety of bit rates, with 128, 160, and 196 Kbps being typical.

Bluescreen   A backdrop in your video that's replaced in postproduction with another video layer. For example, you can film your subject holding a blue screen (a uniquely colored board), which you can later edit to contain a second video.

Capture   To transfer the video from tape to your computer's hard disk.

CCD   A light-sensitive chip that acts somewhat like film. The Charge Coupled Device measures the light in the scene and converts it to a digital image that's stored on tape.

Clip   A short piece of video, also called a scene. When creating a movie, you string together several clips that play in sequential order to tell the "story" of your movie.

Codec   An abbreviation for compression/decompression, this piece of software enables a multimedia player to properly interpret and display a video file. The AVI format uses a variety of different Codecs for various applications.

Cut   To appear suddenly onscreen without any other kind of transition effect. The cut is the most basic kind of transition for changing scenes and dropping titles onto the screen.

Depth of field   The amount of the scene in front and behind the subject that stays in sharp focus. You can control the depth of field by adjusting the amount of zoom and aperture setting of the camera. Use depth of field to isolate the subject from the foreground and background or to keep the entire scene in focus.

Digital video   Video that conforms to the relatively new standards of miniDV or Digital8. These formats record video and audio like computer data and, thus, aren't subject to generational loss like analog video.

Digital zoom   A rather low-quality way of enlarging the image you record using an electronic shortcut. The digital zoom enlarges the pixels in the middle of the CCD, producing a noisy, grainy, and relatively unattractive image.

Dissolve   A video transition in which one video clip fades into the next.

Fade   A video transition in which the scene "fades" from black or white into another scene.

Fill light   A light reflected off another surface onto the subject. The reflector softens the effect of light on the subject.

Focal length   The distance from the lens to the point behind the lens at which the rays of light focus and create an image. Typically, the longer the focal length of the lens, the higher its magnification.

Foley effects   Special sound effects you can add to your video to suggest creaking doors, gunshots, car engines, and so forth.

Generational loss   The drop in video resolution that results when you make a copy of an analog videotape. The original videotape is called first generation. A copy of that is second generation, and so on.

Image stabilization   A camcorder's attempt to reduce the apparent jitter or shakiness in a scene, especially when you're using the zoom. This feature works best when the camcorder is equipped with optical image stabilization as opposed to digital image stabilization.

A

Key light   The main light in a scene, which provides the principal light on your subject.

Lossless   Any file-compression scheme that uses a nondestructive compression scheme and so does not degrade sound or video quality.

Lossy   A compression scheme for audio or video that makes the file smaller by discarding some unimportant data. Lossy formats like JPEG and MP3 try to eliminate information in subtle ways, so you aren't aware of the change.

Lux   A camcorder rating that indicates how low the light can be before the camera can no longer record an image. Lux values are not standard, but typically a 2-lux camera can record an image in candlelight.

MP3   A popular format for sound files. The MP3 compresses the sound file, so it takes up less room on the hard disk, and so it takes less time to upload or download to and from web pages.

Noise   The random errors generated by your camcorder when filming in low-light situations. A camcorder's CCDs are designed to work with a certain minimum level of light. Videotaping with less light results in "phantom" pixels in the video that appear as noise.

Optical zoom   A high-quality way of enlarging the scene you record using the camera's optics.

Produce   To render a video production on your PC in its final form, storing it on your hard drive. The produced video becomes the high-quality master from which you can make any number of copies that will be every bit as good as the first copy.

Resolution   The number of pixels used to display an image. Digital video cameras capture images at a resolution of 720×480 (720 pixels in a line by 480 lines).

Script   Text that identifies what everyone is going to say in the scene you're filming. The script can help you identify any weaknesses in the storyboard and can also flesh out the video you're about to film.

Storyboard   A series of cartoon-like panels you can use to describe, scene by scene, what happens in your movie. The storyboard can be drawn by hand or elaborately produced on a computer.

Streaming video   Video that plays onscreen even as it's being downloaded from the Internet to the viewer's PC. If the video file contains audio sounds, note that the audio portion of the clip streams right along with the video.

Talking head   A film segment that shows only the head and shoulders of a person who is talking. This tight focus is often used in interview situations where the background isn't as important as the talking subject.

Track   To follow a moving subject with the camera lens.

Transition   A graphical segue that signals the end of one scene and the start of the next. This can be as simple as a fade-out or as complex as seeing one clip fly offscreen as another clip enters the picture.

WAV   An older, but still popular, format for sound files. All video editors work with this lossless format.

White balance   A camcorder setting that tells the camera how to balance its colors to properly depict a scene. Because different light sources, such as daylight, fluorescent light, and candlelight, all generate different colors, they cause the colors in your scene to shift unless you compensate.

Wipe   A video transition in which the new video physically moves into the frame while displacing the old video.

A

Appendix B

Videography Quick Tips

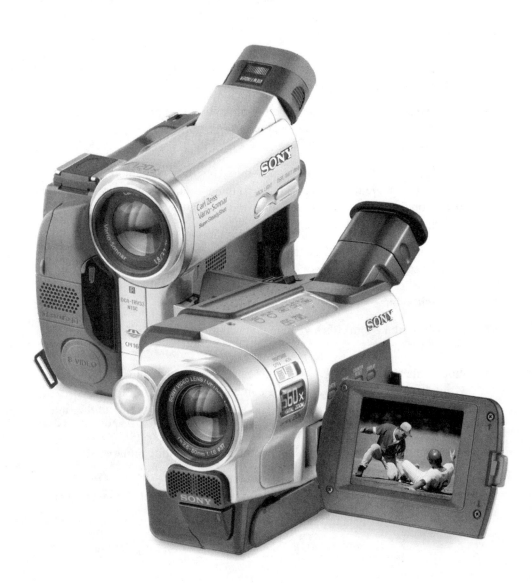

The differences between low-quality amateur videos and good-looking, "prosumer" home video isn't just a matter of how much you spend on your gear. You can get excellent results with fairly inexpensive hardware and downright awful results with top-tier gear. If you don't believe us, check out a movie like *Driven*, which is little better than most high school videography projects—and that's even before Stallone starts talking!

Bottom line: it comes down to one basic adage: "garbage in, garbage out." Here's a collection of handy, common-sense tips you should apply to your next video project:

- Shoot simply and steadily. Keep the camera as steady as possible. Don't do a lot of zooming, panning, or handheld movement.

- Use the Rule of Thirds. To achieve the most visually appealing shots, imagine a tic-tac-toe board covering your viewfinder, and then position your subject in one of the intersections where the lines cross.

- Get a tripod and use it as often as possible. Having your camcorder on a tripod is the single most effective way to make footage look more professional. If you move around a lot and have a few hundred dollars you wouldn't miss, consider a SteadiCam Jr.

- Don't zoom excessively. Use the zoom on your camcorder to change the focal length of your shot *between* important events, not *during* them. Fight the urge to zoom in and out for emphasis. As photographers like to say: zoom with your feet by moving closer to the subject.

- Turn off digital zoom. It's a visual effect that's rarely useful and almost always distracting.

- Shoot wide when walking. Back your camcorder away from any telephoto setting if you'll be walking with the camcorder because the slightest movement while in telephoto results in an exaggerated "bump" in the final footage.

- Remember to check the white balance in all new lighting situations.

- Think about the position of the sun or your light source. It's best to maneuver so the sun is over one of your shoulders, but not if your subjects are squinting into it.

■ Keep quiet. If you're using on-camera audio, think about the noise you're making when you talk or breathe deeply. And avoid fiddling with the camera. You'll hear it later when you review the tape. Many camcorder mics even capture the hum of the zoom motor.

■ Keep a fully charged spare battery on hand—two or three of them, ideally. Nothing ruins a shoot like a camera with no power.

■ Don't forget to shoot "B roll" footage you can use to mix in with the main event.

B

Index

INTERNATIONAL CONTACT INFORMATION

AUSTRALIA
McGraw-Hill Book Company
Australia Pty. Ltd.
TEL +61-2-9900-1800
FAX +61-2-9878-8881
http://www.mcgraw-hill.com.au
books-it_sydney@mcgraw-hill.com

CANADA
McGraw-Hill Ryerson Ltd.
TEL +905-430-5000
FAX +905-430-5020
http://www.mcgraw-hill.ca

**GREECE, MIDDLE EAST, & AFRICA
(Excluding South Africa)**
McGraw-Hill Hellas
TEL +30-210-6560-990
TEL +30-210-6560-993
TEL +30-210-6560-994
FAX +30-210-6545-525

MEXICO (Also serving Latin America)
McGraw-Hill Interamericana Editores
S.A. de C.V.
TEL +525-1500-5108
FAX +525-117-1589
http://www.mcgraw-hill.com.mx
carlos_ruiz@mcgraw-hill.com

SINGAPORE (Serving Asia)
McGraw-Hill Book Company
TEL +65-6863-1580
FAX +65-6862-3354
http://www.mcgraw-hill.com.sg
mghasia@mcgraw-hill.com

SOUTH AFRICA
McGraw-Hill South Africa
TEL +27-11-622-7512
FAX +27-11-622-9045
robyn_swanepoel@mcgraw-hill.com

SPAIN
McGraw-Hill/
Interamericana de España, S.A.U.
TEL +34-91-180-3000
FAX +34-91-372-8513
http://www.mcgraw-hill.es
professional@mcgraw-hill.es

**UNITED KINGDOM, NORTHERN,
EASTERN, & CENTRAL EUROPE**
McGraw-Hill Education Europe
TEL +44-1-628-502500
FAX +44-1-628-770224
http://www.mcgraw-hill.co.uk
emea_queries@mcgraw-hill.com

ALL OTHER INQUIRIES Contact:
McGraw-Hill/Osborne
TEL +1-510-420-7700
FAX +1-510-420-7703
http://www.osborne.com
omg_international@mcgraw-hill.com

Sound Off!

Visit us at **www.osborne.com/bookregistration** and let us know what you thought of this book. While you're online you'll have the opportunity to register for newsletters and special offers from McGraw-Hill/Osborne.

We want to hear from you!

Sneak Peek

Visit us today at **www.betabooks.com** and see what's coming from McGraw-Hill/Osborne tomorrow!

Based on the successful software paradigm, Bet@Books™ allows computing professionals to view partial and sometimes complete text versions of selected titles online. Bet@Books™ viewing is free, invites comments and feedback, and allows you to "test drive" books in progress on the subjects that interest you the most.

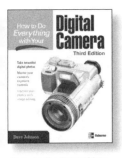
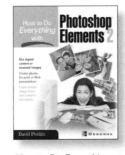
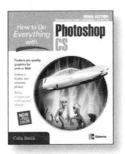
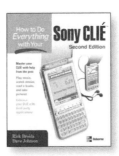

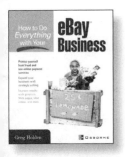